Between the Ottomans
and the Entente

Between the Ottomans and the Entente

The First World War in the Syrian and Lebanese Diaspora, 1908–1925

STACY D. FAHRENTHOLD

OXFORD
UNIVERSITY PRESS

OXFORD
UNIVERSITY PRESS

Oxford University Press is a department of the University of Oxford. It furthers the University's objective of excellence in research, scholarship, and education by publishing worldwide. Oxford is a registered trade mark of Oxford University Press in the UK and certain other countries.

Published in the United States of America by Oxford University Press 198 Madison Avenue, New York, NY 10016, United States of America.

Library of Congress Cataloging-in-Publication Data
Names: Fahrenthold, Stacy D., author.
Title: Between the Ottomans and the Entente : the first World War in the Syrian and Lebanese diaspora, 1908–1925 / Stacy D. Fahrenthold.
Description: New York, NY, United States of America : Oxford University Press, 2019. | Includes bibliographical references and index.
Identifiers: LCCN 2018039929 (print) | LCCN 2018046277 (ebook) | ISBN 9780190872144 (Updf) | ISBN 9780190872151 (Epub) | ISBN 9780190872137 (hardcover :alk. paper) | ISBN 9780197565728 (paperback :alk. paper)
Subjects: LCSH: Syrians—Foreign countries. | Syria—Emigration and immigration. | Lebanese—Foreign countries. | Lebanon—Emigration and immigration. | World War, 1914–1918—Refugees.
Classification: LCC DS94.7 (ebook) | LCC DS94.7 .F34 2019 (print) | DDC 940.3089/9275691—dc23
LC record available at https://lccn.loc.gov/2018039929

Portions of Chapter 3 appear in Stacy D. Fahrenthold, "Former Ottomans in the ranks: pro-Entente military recruitment among Syrians in the Americas, 1916–1918," *Journal of Global History* 11, no. 1 (2016), 88–112.

For Martha

CONTENTS

ACKNOWLEDGMENTS

Access to a quality public education saved my life and is the primary social mobility driver for American young people. The research presented in this book was made possible by countless contributions, large and small, by public institutions and the people who make them work. I owe so many people my heartfelt thanks, but in this moment of cruel financial austerity it feels appropriate to begin by demonstrating how deeply my research is indebted to the investments public institutions make in young scholars and their ideas. Thank you to Phoenix High School, an alternative school in the Gwinnett County public system in Georgia, for providing second-chancers a shot at a first-rate education. Thank you to Sherry Fowler for pushing your students to go to college and for offering your time, your ear, and sometimes your home to young people who would otherwise go without. Georgia State University gave me room to write, to struggle, and sometimes to fail, and Georgia's HOPE Scholarship and federal Pell grants made my education possible. Public funding for graduate education—language training, travel grants, and tuition waivers—helped my research on Syrian migration find its footing. Now, as a professor, I work to help my students find a toehold in an environment marked by mounting hostility to the public institutions they depend on. Whatever contribution this book makes to the literature on Middle Eastern migrations is extra, so long as it exemplifies the educational generosity I have enjoyed all these years.

And many people have been so generous with me. As a graduate student at Northeastern University, I was privileged to be among excellent scholars, gracious colleagues, and some of the best people I have ever met. Ilham Khuri-Makdisi is as brilliant an advisor as she is a scholar, mentor, and friend. Thank you to Akram Fouad Khater, Laura Frader, and Isa Blumi for providing me abundant, meaningful guidance for this project, first as a dissertation project and then, as a book manuscript. The history department's globally minded scholars made Northeastern a wonderful place to be and to work. I am especially grateful for Katherine Luongo, Anthony Penna, Christina Gilmartin, and Philip Thai. In Boston, I was privileged to prepare for comprehensives with Philip S. Khoury's help, a debt I may never be able to repay. Thank you to Shakir Mustafa, Samira Risheh, and Aref Arnous for your time and friendship, and for the intensive work and patience you exercised as I struggled to improve my Arabic. My graduate cohort was also an enormous source of strength: hundreds of cups of coffee were spent working on drafts with Ross Newton, Rachel Moloshok, and Victoria Hallinan. They each taught me how to write and, more importantly, when to stop writing. Rachel Gillett, Sana Tannoury Karam, Akin Sefer, and Burleigh Hendrickson each influenced how I think about networks in social history. Tara Dixon, James Bradford, Ethan Hawkley, and Malcolm Purinton challenged what I thought I knew about commodities and circuits of exchange. And Feruza Aripova, Regina Katzyulina, and Elizabeth Lehr generously assisted me with these chapters.

At Williams College, I was given valuable time to revise with the benefit of comments and insights by Sara Dubow, Jessica Chapman, Eiko Siniawer, Carmen Whalen, Scott Wong, and Magnus Bernhardsson. Julia Kowalski, Saadia Yacoob, Zaid Adhami, and Doug Kiel made my time in the Berkshires especially enjoyable, and I will never forget our pedagogical conversations. Thank you all. At University of California, Berkeley, my gratitude goes to Emily Gottreich, Lydia Kiesling, Christine Philliou, and Amber Zambelli for welcoming me as a visiting scholar at the Center for Middle Eastern Studies. At California State University Fresno, Lori Clune, Ethan Kytle, and Blain Roberts helped me navigate some critical stages of the publication process; additional thanks to Michelle Denbeste and Frederik Vermote for your continuing friendship and support. At California State University Stanislaus, my thanks go to Brandon Wolfe-Hunnicutt, who has been an engaging interlocutor in this project's final stages.

Mahjar studies is more than a research field; it is also a community, thanks to a culture of free and open collaboration among scholars working across Middle Eastern, Latin American, North American, and global scales of study. I jokingly call the group the mahjar mafia, but contrary to the name's connotations, I have found scholars in this subfield to be exceptionally generous with one another. Additional thanks to Akram Khater for his tireless work organizing biennial paper workshops at the Khayrallah Center for Lebanese Diaspora Studies at North Carolina State University. At those workshops and many others, I was repeatedly astounded by the brilliance of a company of scholars who inhabit this particular migration subfield. To Işıl Acehan, Charlotte Karem Albrecht, Andrew Arsan, Isa Blumi, Jennifer Dueck, Ted Falk, Sarah Gualtieri, Sally Howell, Steven Hyland, John Tofik Karam, Simon Jackson, Christine Lindner, Neda Maghbouleh, Amy Malek, Jacob Norris, Camila Pastor, Graham Pitts, Laura Robson, Vladimir Hamid-Troyansky, and Benjamin Thomas White, thank you for all our conversations over the years. To each of you (and anyone I left out), I look forward to the next ones. Among the mahjar mafia, I am especially grateful for close friends who critique my drafts and who daily remind me of who I want to be as a scholar: Reem Bailony, Lily Balloffet, Lauren Banko, and Devi Mays. I was fortunate to have Uğur Pece and Omar Duwaji help me locate some of the portraits contained within. Sandrine Mansour and Armen Manuk-Khaloyan also provided crucial archival support. Thank you all.

Interactions with the amazing scholars studying the First World War in the Middle East also enriched my professional development. These scholars pushed me out of my migration comfort zone to consider the multiple ways in which the Ottoman Empire and its French Mandatory successor treated the Syrian mahjar as an offshore frontier province. Special thanks go to Mustafa Aksakal and Elizabeth Thompson for including me in their 2014 NEH summer seminar on World War I in the Middle East at Georgetown University. Thanks, too, to friends and collaborators from that World War I boot camp, especially Annia Ciezadlo, Priya Dixit, Mari Firkatian, Aimee Genell, Dominique Reill, Chris Rominger, Melanie S. Tanielian, and İpek Yosmaoğlu. Among Ottomanists, I would like to thank Lale Can, David Gutman, Janet Klein, Chris Lowe, Elyse Semerdjian, and Sherry Vatter for their insights and feedback on various papers. I am grateful to have had readers within the Syrian Studies Association who were kind in their assessment of this work when it was at the dissertation stage, including Charles Wilkins, Laura Ruiz de Elvira Carrascal, Hasan Kayalı, Stephennie Mulder, Lorenzo Trombetta, and Tina Zintl. Finally, there are always scholars with whom we collaborate without ever meeting. My thanks to Abdul-Karim Rafeq for supporting this project when it was an ill-fated 2011–2012 trip to Damascus, and to William Gervase Clarence-Smith for inspired correspondence at critical turns.

My time at the Lebanese Emigration Research Center (LERC) at the Notre Dame University in Lebanon was exceptionally fruitful because of the hard work that Guita Hourani, Liliane Haddad, Elie Nabhan, and Eugen Sensenig put into that archive. LERC recaptures global Lebanese histories into an unparalleled collection of digitally accessible materials, which makes it a fantastic place to visit, but it was Guita, Elie, Liliane, and Eugen who also made it feel like home. My deepest thanks go to Riad Khuniesser and the staff at the Jafet Library at the American University of Beirut; to Ibrahim Assi at the Center des Archives Nationals in Beirut; to Sami Salameh at the Maronite Patriarchate in Bkerke; to Matthew Stiffler, Kirsten Terry, and Elyssa Bisoski at the Arab American National Museum in Dearborn, Michigan; and to Daniel Necas, Donna Gabaccia, and Haven Hawley for their assistance with collections at the Immigration History Research Center archives in Minneapolis, Minnesota. I have been privileged to sound out and refine these ideas at several workshops. I am especially grateful for constructive audiences at the Khayrallah Center for Lebanese Diaspora Studies at North Carolina State University (2012, 2015, and 2017); the Mashriq in the Age of Late Imperialism workshop at Princeton University (2013); the Lines of Identity workshop at University of Manitoba (2015); and the Western Ottomanists' Workshop at the University of California Berkeley (2016).

The work presented here has also been made possible by numerous grants, fellowships, and awards, including the National Endowment for the Humanities Summer Seminar grant; the Mellon Postdoctoral Fellowship at Williams College; the American Council of Learned Societies/Mellon Dissertation Completion Fellowship; the Syrian Studies Association dissertation award; the Immigration History Research Center Grant-in-Aid; and travel grants from CSU Stanislaus College of the Arts, Humanities, and Social Sciences; CSU Fresno College of Social Sciences; the University of California, Berkeley Center for Middle Eastern Studies; and the Khayrallah Center for Lebanese Diaspora Studies at North Carolina State University.

Thank you to my grandparents, Martha and David Burton, for always being at the ready with a kind word and a cup of black coffee; to Mara for long walks in the woods; and to my husband, David Schultz, who daily reminds me to step out of my work for a good meal, a good show, and a good sunrise or sunset. My thanks are due, finally, to my editor at Oxford University Press, Susan Ferber, whose incredible and efficient labor has made the publication process so streamlined and enjoyable. I have also benefitted mightily from impressive and thorough interventions by two anonymous reviewers, who constructively helped me ready this work for publication. Thank you. Any errors that remain within are, of course, entirely my own.

A NOTE ON TRANSLITERATION

Arabic and Ottoman Turkish words are transliterated according to the simplified system employed by the *International Journal of Middle East Studies*. Although Arabic diacritics have been omitted, ʿayns and hamzas have been retained. Ottoman Turkish diacritics have been retained.

ABBREVIATIONS, DRAMATIS PERSONAE, AND KEY TERMS

Organizations

AL   Hizb al-Ittihad al-Lubnani (Alliance Libanaise). Established in Cairo in 1909. Branches in Argentina, Brazil, Chile, Mexico, Cuba, and the United States. Originally affiliated with the Ottoman Decentralization Party, but promoted Lebanese independence during the war. Endorsed a French Mandate for Greater Lebanon in 1919, a controversial decision that led the party's president, Iskandar 'Ammun, to resign and its Latin American chapters to splinter into a rival party, Hizb al-Tahalluf al-Lubnani.

CCS   Comité Central Syrien (al-Lajna al-Suriyya al-Markaziyya). Established in Paris in 1916 by Shukri Ghanim and Georges Samné. Subsidized by the French Foreign Ministry as an advocacy network for Syrian émigrés. Organized war relief, humanitarian aid, and military recruitment across the mahjar, including a 1917 diasporic tour by CCS partisans Qaysar Lakah and Jamil Mardam Bey. A primary instrument of Franco-Syrian soft diplomacy during the war, but eclipsed by the French Foreign Ministry's commitment to a Greater Lebanese state in 1919. Official organ: *Correspondance d'Orient*.

CUP   Committee of Union and Progress (Ittihat ve Terakki Cemiyeti). Ruling party of the Ottoman Empire following the 1908 Young Turk Revolution.

FDNP   Free Democratic Nationalist Party (Hizb al-Dimuqrati al-Watani al-Hurr). Established in Buenos Aires in 1919 by Khalil Sa'adih. Hosted the 1919 General Syrian Congress in Buenos Aires. After 1920, its headquarters transferred to São Paulo. Anticolonial, pro-independence, and Syrian unionist. Official organ: *al-Majalla* (Buenos Aires), *al-Jarida* (São Paulo).

HY   Homsi Youth (Homs al-Fatat). Arab nationalist club established in São Paulo in 1915 by Jurj Atlas. Recruited Homsi men for pro-Entente military service. Official organ: *al-Zahrawi*.

LLP   Lebanon League of Progress (Jam'iyyat al-Nahda al-Lubnaniyya). Established in New York City in 1911 by Na'um Mukarzil. Chapters in the United States, Canada, Mexico, Cuba, Chile, Argentina, and Brazil. Aligned with the Beirut Reform Society before 1914. Also aligned with the Cairo Alliance Libanaise, but was more forthrightly Francophile during the war. Processed military recruitment paperwork and French passports for Syrians abroad. Supported the French Mandate for Greater Lebanon. Official organs: *al-Huda* (New York) and *Abu al-Hawl* (São Paulo).

ODP   Ottoman Decentralization Party (Hizb al-Lamarkaziyya al-Idariyya al'Uthmani). Established in Cairo in 1913. A loose coalition of societies seeking administrative reform in the Ottoman Arab provinces. Arabist organizations from Beirut, Jaffa, Damascus, and Basra (among others) organized under the ODP, as did the mahjari branches of Alliance Libanaise, al-Fatat, the United Syria Society, and the Lebanon League of Progress. One of the hosts of Paris 1913 Arab Congress.

NSNL   New Syria National League (Jam'iyyat Suriya al-Jadida al-Wataniyya). Established in New York City and Boston in 1918. Chairman Jurj Ilyas Khayrallah. Executive members included Najeeb Saleeby, Faris Malouf, Fuad Shatara, Philip K. Hitti, and Abraham Mitrie Rihbany. Promoted independence for greater Syria and, in 1919, a United States Mandate in cooperation with the Arab nationalist movement. Aligned with Cairo's Syrian Moderate Party and Buenos Aires' Free Democratic Nationalist Party. Disbanded after 1920, but reemerged in Michigan in 1925 as the New Syria Party.

SAC   Syrian American Club (al-Muntada al-Suri al-Amriki). Established in New York City and Boston in 1917. Assisted Syrian immigrants with the US naturalization petitions as well as US Army enlistment. Closely affiliated with the United Syria Society and the Comité Central Syrien during the war, and with the New Syria National League after 1918. Associated serials: *al-Nasr* (New York), *Fatat Boston* (Boston).

SLLL   Syria-Mount Lebanon League of Liberation (Lajna al-Tahrir Suriya wa-Lubnan). Established in New York City in 1917 by Ayyub Tabet,

Amin al-Rihani, N. T. Tadross, Khalil Gibran, Ilya Abu Madi, Shukri al-Bakhash, and Najib Diyab. Affiliated with the Comité Central Syrien through 1919. Associated serials: *al-Fatat, Mirat al-Gharb.*

SLPS   Syrian Lebanese Patriotic Society (Sociedade Patriótica Síria Libanesa). Established in São Paulo in 1917 by Naʿimi Jafet. Affiliated with the Comité Central Syrien until early 1919, and with the New Syria National League.

SOUS   Syrian Ottoman Union Society (Jamʿiyyat al-Ittihad al-Suri al-ʿUthmani). Established in New York in 1908, a semi-official advocacy club aligned with the Committee of Union and Progress party and the Ottoman Empire's consulate. After a series of disputes with the Ottoman consulate, it separated from the CUP hierarchy and changed its name to the United Syria Society (Jamʿiyyat al-Ittihad al-Suri) in late 1908. Also called the Syrian Union or Syrian American Association in English. Also aligned with the Syrian American Club and, during the war, with the Comité Central Syrien. Official organ: *al-Kawn.*

SPC   Syrian Protestant College. Established in 1865 in Beirut; in 1920 its name changed to the American University of Beirut.

UMS   Jamʿiyyat al-Ittihad al-Maruni (United Maronite Society). Established in New York City in 1921 by local clergy and Naʿum Mukarzil as a lay organization for Maronite political action. Acted as an early Chamber of Commerce linking Lebanese émigré commercial interests to historic Mount Lebanon.

Dramatis Personae

Emir Amin Arslan: b. Shwayfat (1868); d. Buenos Aires (1934). First and last Ottoman Consul General of Argentina (1910–1915). Partisan of the Syrian Union Society during the war. Critic of the French Mandate after 1920, author of *La revolución siria contra el mandato francés* (1926).

Jurj and Salwa Atlas: married in Homs and moved to São Paulo in 1914. Together they founded *al-Karma* (a literary serial), a girls' school, and a young men's fraternity, *Homs al-Fatat*. A pro-Hasmimite Arab nationalist, Jurj founded *al-Zahrawi* newspaper in 1916 and recruited Homsi men from Brazil for pro-Entente military service. Jurj Atlas established the São Paulo Homs Club (al-Nadi al-Homsi) in 1920.

Shukri al-Bakhash: b. Zahle (1889), d. Zahle. Partisan of the São Paulo Lebanon League of Progress in 1914, but by 1917 had moved to New York City. Editor of New York City's *al-Fatat* newspaper (1917–1919), enlisted in the US Army and served the War Department as a translator, propagandist, and recruiter. Executive committee of the Syria Mount Lebanon League of Liberation. Returned to Lebanon after 1920.

Mundji Bey: Ottoman charge d'affaires of New York City. Member of the CUP, and deposed Hamidian Ambassador Mehmed 'Ali Bey Abed in Washington, D.C. following the 1908 Young Turk Revolution. Served as interim ambassador before returning to New York. Sponsored the establishment of Syrian Ottoman Union Society of New York. Reassigned to London in 1909.

Najib Diyab: b. Roumieh, Mount Lebanon (1870); d. Brooklyn, New York (1936). Moved to New York in 1894, where he wrote for *Kawkab Amrika* before founding his own *Mirat al-Gharb* in 1899. Executive committee of Syrian Ottoman Union Society of New York (1908). Speaker at the First Arab Congress in Paris (1913). Executive committee of the Syria Mount Lebanon League of Liberation 1917–1919. Arab nationalist and critic of the French Mandate.

Shukri Ghanim: b. Beirut (1861); d. Paris (1929). Vice President on the First Arab Congress (1913). Founder/editor of *La Correspondance d'Orient* (1908), among others. Established the Comité Central Syrien with Georges Samné in 1916, and recruited Syrian men from the mahjar for the French Legion d'Orient through CCS. After 1918, supported a French Mandate for Greater Syria, a plan undermined by French sponsorship of an separate Greater Lebanon (*Grand Liban*).

Albert Hatem: b. Mount Lebanon 1894; d. 1981. Nephew of Na'um Hatem, *al-Huda* correspondent and Lebanon League of Progress partisan. Enlisted in the US Army in 1917, served as a recruiter. Promoted to sergeant and served as color guard at victory celebrations in early 1919. Discharged in May 1919.

Na'imi Jafet: b. Shwayr, Mount Lebanon (1860), d. São Paulo (1923). Built one of Brazil's largest cotton textile factories at Ypiranga in 1907. Established Brazil's Syrian Chamber of Commerce and the Syrian Lebanese Patriotic Society in 1917. Founder of the Hospital Sírio-Libanês of São Paulo in 1921.

Jurj Ilyas Khayrallah: chairman of the New Syria National League of New York (1919). Advocated for a United States Mandate over Greater Syria in 1919 and a treaty of friendship between America and the Arab nationalist movement. Corresponded with Faris Nimr on these topics.

Bishop Shukrallah al-Khuri: Maronite bishop sent to America to conduct an administrative census of Maronite emigrants in the Americas. Installed in Our Lady of Lebanon in Brooklyn, al-Khuri collected population data and information about Maronite clergy, ritual, and practice in 1921–1922. Some of his data was included in the Lebanese Census of 1921 but also laid the foundation for the Maronite Church's reorganization in the mahjar after the war.

Shukri al-Khuri: Founder/editor of São Paulo's *Abu al-Hawl/ Espinghe* (1906). Established the São Paulo Lebanon League of Progress (1912), which declared war on the Ottoman Empire (against the wishes of the party's New York headquarters) in 1914. Lebanist and Pro-French Mandate after 1918.

Jurj Ibrahim Maʿtuq (George Abraham Matook): b. Boston, Massachusetts (1896); d. Berwyn, Illinois (1957). Drafted in 1917 and deployed to France with the 101st Engineer Corps, where he worked as an interpreter. Sponsored Syrian leatherworkers enlisting in the US army, and corresponded with the Syrian American Club of Boston and Wadiʿ Shakir while deployed. Worked in industrial laundry after he was decommissioned in 1919.

Naʿum Mukarzil: b. Freike, Mount Lebanon (1864); d. Paris (1932). Established *al-Huda* newspaper in 1898; by 1905, it was the largest Arabic language daily in the United States. In New York City, founded the Lebanon League of Progress (1911) and attended the First Arab Congress (1913). Recruited for the French Legion d'Orient and US Army during the war. Promoted a French Mandate for Greater Lebanon (*Grand Liban*) after 1918. Partisan of the United Maronite Society of New York.

Rev. Abraham Mitrie Rihbany: b. Shwayr, Mount Lebanon (1869); d. Stamford, Connecticut (1944). Presbyterian minister educated at the Syrian Protestant College in Beirut before emigrating to New York City in 1897. Briefly edited *Kawkab Amrika* before taking on work as an advocate, social worker, and theologian. Raised humanitarian relief during the war, and wrote in favor of US trusteeship over Greater Syria. In 1919, appointed the New Syria National League's delegate to the Paris Peace Conference but was denied entry to its proceedings. Aligned with Hashimite Arab nationalism and anti-Zionism, critical of the French Mandate.

Dr. Khalil Saʿadih: b. Shwayr, Mount Lebanon (1857); d. São Paulo (1934). Graduated from Syrian Protestant College (1883); after emigrating to Egypt, moved to Buenos Aires (1914) and São Paulo (1919). Established serials *al-Majalla* (Buenos Aires), *al-Jarida* (São Paulo), and *al-Rabita* (São Paulo), among others. Member of the Syrian Masonic Society, and founder of the Free Democratic Nationalist Party in Argentina (1919). Pro-independence and host of the 1919 General Syrian Congress of Buenos Aires.

Najib Sawaya: editor of *al-Kawn* newspaper in New York City (1907–1909). Executive committee of the Syrian Ottoman Union Society.

Wadiʿ Ilyas Shakir: b. 1895; d. Boston, Massachusetts (1955). President of the Syrian American Club of Boston and aligned with the New Syria National League in 1919. Assisted Syrian immigrants with naturalization petitions and migrant advocacy within the city. Married Hannah Sabbagh Shakir and maintained accounting books for Sabbagh Brothers cloth wholesaling.

Gabriel Ilyas Ward: b. Tripoli (c. 1869). Naturalized US citizen by virtue of his military service in the Philippines in 1898. Ward enlisted in the Canadian Expeditionary Forces in 1915, fought in France in 1916, and was wounded in a gas attack. He spent 1917–1918 in London working with the British military police, occasionally corresponding with *al-Huda* newspaper in New York. After he was decommissioned in 1919, he returned to New York, became a police officer, and published his memoirs, *Kitab al-Jundi al-Suri fi-Thalath Hurub* in 1919.

Key Terms

mahjar
: lands of emigration; refers to the physical space of the Arab diasporas.

Mashriq
: the eastern Mediterranean; refers to the Arab Levant, historic greater Syria including Palestine (*bilad al-sham*).

mutasarrifate
: Ottoman administrative subdivision of Mount Lebanon. Created by the 1861 Règlement Organique, the mutasarrifate structure guaranteed a degree of administrative autonomy for Mount Lebanon backed by European diplomatic pressure. After 1908 the Committee of Union and Progress government sought to reform and centralize its structures, ultimately abolishing it in 1914.

nahda
: renaissance; refers to the late nineteenth-century Arabic literary revival usually credited to Syrian and Lebanese writers in Egypt writing in the private press. Also associated with Arabic prose, poetry, and social critique (especially of liberal, secular, or radical leanings) in the Arab mahjar in the Americas c. 1900–1920s.

sauf conduit
: safe conduct passports; ad hoc travel documents granted to foreign nationals, refugees, displaced persons, or prisoners of war to facilitate cross-border travel or to grant diplomatic protection to migrants of uncertain nationality status.

Between the Ottomans
and the Entente

Introduction

Between the Ottomans and the Entente

The trouble in the Syrian colony of Buenos Aires began on April 12, 1915, outside the Ottoman Empire's consulate on Avenida Corrientes. On that day, the city's Ottoman General Consul, a Syrian emir named Amin Arslan, met a crowd of one thousand Syrian migrants on the steps of his office. Although an Ottoman official working for the Committee of Union and Progress (hereafter CUP) government, Arslan was an outspoken opponent of Istanbul's alliance with Germany, a strategic maneuver that had brought the empire into the First World War in October 1914. Arslan spent the months since the declaration of war speaking out against his government's alliance with Berlin. Arslan's popularity among the Syrians of Argentina soared, but the city's German consulate resented his disloyal behavior and reported Arslan to his superiors in the Ottoman Foreign Ministry. Istanbul was already uneasy with Amin Arslan: the consul's open friendship with French diplomats in Argentina, seen as a major boon for the Empire a decade earlier, was no longer seen as such in 1914. The ruling Ottoman triumvirate—Enver, Talaat, and Cemal Pashas—began to see the Argentinian emir as a liability. They also saw the Syrian mahjar (lands of emigration, often translated as diaspora) as a dangerous place, its half million emigrants full of potential for sedition, collusion with the Empire's enemies, and recruitment to the Arabist opposition mounting against Unionist rule.

In April 1915, the embattled Ottoman consul received a letter from the Germans, invoking the Berlin-Istanbul alliance and ordering Arslan to stop defaming Germany. The letter demanded that Arslan cease all contact with the French consulate and refrain from public statements about the war in the Argentinian press. Finding it absurd that he should take orders from Germany, Arslan marched up the steps outside of the Ottoman Consulate building on that April day. Meeting a crowd of Syrians, Lebanese, Palestinians, and other Ottoman nationals from the Argentine colony, Arslan read Germany's threatening letter aloud, tipping off a day of Arabist protest against the Unionist government and its involvement in the First World War.[1] Arslan then read a letter he penned in response to the German consul general in Buenos Aires:

> Señor Consul General, I have the pleasure of acknowledging your letter . . . I think it goes without saying how surprising this letter was, as its contents conflict with all established diplomatic protocol, and it has not come to my earnest attention that my Ottoman Empire forms a mere part of your German Imperium. And I keep hope, nevertheless, for the honor and dignity of my poor country, dragged unwillingly into the abyss of this war by you, a savage foreign power.[2]

Lamenting that "the interests of the [Syrian] community are now in the hands of foreigners,"[3] Amin Arslan reaffirmed his loyalty "to my august sovereign, the Sultan . . . and my only superior, the Grand Vizier (Talaat Pasha)."[4] He announced that he had written Talaat Pasha to demand that Istanbul either renounce its alliance with Germany or terminate him from Ottoman diplomatic service.

Fire him they did. Receiving more complaints from the Germans, Talaat Pasha relieved Arslan of his post via telegram on May 19, 1915 and ordered the closure of the empire's Buenos Aires consulate.[5] Arslan was instructed to deliver the contents of his office's archives to the German consulate and to return immediately to Istanbul.[6] Seeing this course of events as further proof the Unionists had become German puppets, Arslan closed the consulate but refused to surrender its papers. "These documents provide legal protection and justice [for Syrians] in this country," he explained to *La Prensa* newspaper. "No foreigner has the right to take and oversee the files of Ottomans [living in Argentina], nor to determine the interests of my countrymen, who . . . have an interest in defending what is rightfully theirs."[7] If the Germans came for the records, he threatened he would submit them to Argentina's supreme court for protection. Istanbul responded by convicting the impudent emir of treason in absentia. He would never be allowed to return to the Ottoman domain.[8]

South American newspapers noticed the Syrian protests against the Ottoman Empire's entry into the First World War, especially in Brazil and Argentina, where hundreds of thousands of Syrian migrants already lived. Both countries were then formally neutral in the war but were allied with the Triple Entente. The Syrian protests against their own sovereign grabbed public attention, fed a wider anti-German sentiment, and turned Arslan into a local champion. The Argentinian press called Germany's takeover of Ottoman affairs an "act of piracy."[9] Brazilian papers congratulated "the Consul of the Turkish colony [*colonia*

turca] for so energetically opposing the pretentions of a foreign monarchic regime."[10] But the Latin American public remained unaware of Arslan's reasons
for refusing to surrender his consulate's archives, papers that documented the
citizenship claims, migration status, political activities, and intelligence files for
an estimated 110,000 Syrians in Argentina. Arslan was convinced the records
would be used to levy criminal charges against Syrian emigrants, or even those
who had returned to the Ottoman empire.[11]

Arslan's fears were well warranted. Only weeks before, Syria's governor-
general, Cemal Pasha, ordered Ottoman troops to seize records from Beirut's
abandoned French Consulate, using them to indict and convict dozens of
Arabists, reformers, and Syrian elites of treason.[12] The gallows went up in Syria,
and over forty men were hanged en masse in Damascus and Beirut between
August 1915 and May 1916.[13] Their crimes originated with their ties to foreign powers and connections to Arabist émigré associations. Only those who
fled the empire escaped this fate; like Arslan, they could only be convicted in
absentia.[14]

The Ottomans had not always seen the mahjar as dangerous. For a time, this
diaspora represented an overseas frontier, a source of economic development,
its emigrants a useful population to be groomed and reclaimed through diplomacy. The new Ottoman consulates had themselves been a manifestation of that
mission. But under the shifting politics of the First World War and Cemal Pasha's
repression of Arabism at home, the state's view of the mahjar shifted: it became
a site for sedition, opposition to CUP rule, and collusion with the empire's
enemies. This book recounts that transition. It is about the empire's momentary embrace of Ottoman migrants and the emergence of a political society organized across the mahjar's major colonies in Brazil, Argentina, and the United
States. It is about the breakdown of Ottoman control over migrant activism in
the war's early months, the result of an ill-fated alliance with Berlin and a crack-
down on civil society. It is about the various means that Syrian and Lebanese
migrants abroad had at their disposal to protest and rebel against the Ottoman
state, and the readiness of the Entente powers to ally with these émigré activists.
Ultimately, this book explores how this diaspora's uneasy entanglement with the
forces of European imperialism shaped the political fate of its Middle Eastern
homeland.

Writing the Mahjar Back into Syrian History

Until now, the story of the First World War in the Syrian mahjar had fallen into
a historical ellipsis, a curious silence produced by a rift in available archives and
the distinct preoccupations of two separate historiographies: migration history,

on the one hand, and Ottoman histories of the war, on the other. A recent flowering of writing on the war has demonstrated the Ottoman Empire's centrality to the conflict, which experienced it not as four years of devastation but as over a decade of revolution, disintegration, and reassertion from the Young Turks of 1908 through Turkish independence in 1923. Employing Ottoman state records from Istanbul, Jerusalem, and elsewhere, Ottomanist scholars argue that the war reshaped the modern Middle East, not only by tearing down the Ottoman state and inviting European colonialism into the region but through intimate, lived experiences of occupation, conscription, famine, and genocide. Although this historiography has effectively narrated the war from an Ottoman perspective, its focus on metropolitan centers, the seats of government, and the imperial state itself means that the half million Ottoman subjects who lived beyond the imperial domain continue to be hidden from this retelling. Much of this elision, moreover, is a consequence of the empire's wartime efforts to forcefully disengage with the diasporas during the crisis.[15]

In recovering the Ottoman experience of the war, questions about the relationship of peoples to territorial spaces predominate: mobilization, displacement, and conscription, on one hand, and ecological disasters, famine, and epidemic, on the other.[16] This book similarly examines state-society relations, but by taking the perspective of Ottoman Arabs outside the empire during the conflict as opposed to those suddenly displaced by it, this work also questions the territoriality of the war itself. Although it is conceptually hazardous to draw sharp distinctions between them, this book is about migrants rather than about refugees.[17] But migration has the capacity to transform how states function even if it is not directly compelled by conflict or systemic displacement. States manage wartime migration in a number of ways. In addition to the production of refugees, this work analyzes the regulation/restriction of travelers, the extraterritorial assertion of state sovereignty over diasporas, the politics of migrant naturalization and denationalization, and the inclusion (or exclusion) of migrants from nationality protections and, by extension, from the most basic infrastructural elements of the state.

Ottomanist historiography has also successfully made the wartime imperial state an object of analysis.[18] But pursuing the war as social experience lived, survived, and endured by Ottoman subjects as individuals also requires the integration of informal archives. Migrant activists conducted intelligence for the Entente, produced anti-Ottoman propaganda, managed smuggling networks, and recruited for armies at war with Istanbul. These activities were clandestine by definition. To the extent that Ottoman officialdom captured this at all, state records documenting activities in the Syrian mahjar were contradictory and incomplete because the activists involved evaded the attentions of the state where possible. Thus, this study also utilizes private papers, diaries, personal correspondence, and club records from the Syrian mahjar as well as the daily reporting of the Arabic periodical press.

Syrian migrants inhabit the margins of Ottomanist historiography by virtue of its territorial focus and framing, but an entirely different kind of bookending occurs in migration histories of Syria and Lebanon. In mahjar studies, the First World War falls between two core periods: the late Ottoman mahjar before 1914, and the diaspora's relationship to the French Mandate after 1920. Histories of the mahjar before 1914 describe a soft Ottoman frontier zone, a site for the nahda (renaissance) as evidenced by the vibrant print cultures of Cairo, New York City, São Paulo, and elsewhere. Their guiding questions have been shaped by the concerns of a rising Arab middle class at the turn of the twentieth century, the population best represented in these periodicals.[19] By contrast, scholars working on the interwar mahjar draw upon the papers of the French Mandate, the League of Nations, or the Permanent Mandates Commission and consequently have focused principally on the role the diaspora played in sustaining, repatriating to, or protesting against the French administration in Syria and Lebanon. Working through Syrian petitions to the League of Nations or the French High Commissioner's office in Beirut, these scholars uncover new facets of mahjari politics and their links to colonialism: were the emigrants colonial middlemen, for instance?[20] Were they developmentalists working with France to build a new Lebanon?[21] Were they a policy challenge for French administrators managing other colonies in the French Empire? Was the mahjar a site for political contest, revolt, or anticolonial revolution?[22]

Scholarship on the interwar mahjar makes clear that this diaspora presented a specific blend of opportunities and obstacles for the French Mandate, but the origins of these dense transnational entanglements remain murky in histories focused primarily on French imperialism and its discontents. Drawing on new bodies of archival materials and on personal documents written by and between Syrian activists during the First World War, this study links the prewar Ottoman mahjar to the postwar French Mandate. It examines politics and activism among Syrians abroad from the 1908 Young Turk Revolution through the French Mandate's first five years (1920–1925), with a particular focus on the wartime work of Syrian, Lebanese, and Arab nationalists who believed that collaborating with the Entente powers would lead to their homeland's liberation from Ottoman suzerainty and, eventually, to independence. It uncovers some brand-new means of Syrian collaboration and questions the roots of the mahjar's entanglements with foreign powers. Ultimately, it complicates persistent images of the Syrian diaspora as complicit with (or complacent about) foreign colonialism in the Middle East.

Pursuing Migrants Across Archival Regimes

Writing the history of the wartime Syrian mahjar requires careful recognition of the ways that war simultaneously compels and impedes migration across borders. The First World War followed on the heels of several decades of unprecedented international labor migration, the "first wave globalization" of the late nineteenth century (1880–1914).[23] The deepening structures of global capitalism compelled new proletarians to move around the world, facilitated by new modes of transportation—steamships and railroads—that carried workers farther afield than ever before. The trans-Atlantic corridor carried millions of Mediterranean workers to meet the needs of rapidly expanding agricultural and industrial sectors of the post-abolition Americas. So, too, came Ottoman Arabs from Syria, Mount Lebanon, and Palestine, mostly (but by no means exclusively) Christian, of peasant and working-class stock. The lion's share of the half million Syrians who emigrated between 1880 and 1914 concentrated in the three largest settler societies in the Atlantic world: Brazil (107,000), Argentina (110,000), and the United States (100,000), with smaller communities in Canada, Mexico, Chile, Ecuador, Cuba, Haiti, and elsewhere.[24]

As these migrants moved, they left a paper trail of passports, entry papers, legal declarations, quarantine and arrest records, as well as personal correspondence, diaries, memoirs, and printed materials such as serial newspapers, dime novels, political broadsides, and poetry. Departing migrants were processed first at the port in Beirut, where anxious Ottoman authorities frequently discussed Syrian emigration as a problem but infrequently attempted to police it.[25] After stops in Egypt or at port cities in Mediterranean Europe, those Syrians who made it "beyond the seas" typically arrived in New York City, Buenos Aires, or Rio de Janeiro, although others soon appeared in Havana, Port Au Prince, or the land border between Mexico and the United States. Confronting immigration officials, the new arrivals were subject to routine questions but also non-routine investigation, detainment, and quarantine. Whether admitted or rejected upon arrival, each interaction generated a documentary footprint, but only some of them can be captured through the formal archives of any single receiving state. Histories of the Syrian mahjar have thus been refracted through the disciplinary approaches of Middle Eastern, Latin American, and American ethnic studies. Through this rich empirical work, historians can now follow Syrian migrants across multiple archival regimes and, where necessary, across disciplines. This book sets out to accomplish that by placing Syrian migrants at the fore, reconstructing their routes, the social geographies of mahjari communities that were interconnected, and the transnational scope of mahjari activism by using documents from four continents.

The pursuit of migrants means activists and their networks are examined at both microhistorical and transnational levels. Although migrant politics and particularly the politics of diasporic nationalism emerge from this study, the study does not analyze nationalism as an ideology or project targeting a carefully delineated homeland. During the period under investigation, Syrian activists had yet to coherently work out the ideological stuff of nationalism: irredentist historical narratives; claims to nationhood on ethnic, linguistic, confessional lines; or even the borders that a post-Ottoman Syria would take.[26] An abundance of such ideas floated around in the mahjar, in the press, and among activists organizing in political committees in the eastern Mediterranean, but these ideologies proved to be flexible and transformed readily when confronted the pragmatic demands of wartime activism. If any moment hardened their projects into firmer nationalist programs, it was after the armistice with the 1919 Paris Peace Conference and its demand that petitioners be uniformly representative of their community's national aspirations.[27]

Rather than analyzing protonationalist ideas or representations in the mahjar, it is more fruitful to target wartime migrant politics, not through sentiments but through action. Syrianists, Lebanists, and Arabists competed, engaged in sabotage, and routinely called each other traitors (often while secretly collaborating in war work), but there was a remarkable degree of consensus among them regarding the means and ends of their work. All of the activists discussed here came to believe that Syria must be liberated from Ottoman rule, that migrants abroad were obligated to work toward that goal, and that the best means of accomplishing this was through cooperating with the Entente Powers.[28] Some of these activists left Syria as late as 1913. Others had lived abroad for decades, and more were born in the mahjar, had never been Ottoman nationals, and had never been to Syria. Such distinctions mattered little, because these activists believed they were constructing a post-Ottoman community composed not only of Syrians (or Lebanese, Palestinians, or Arab nationalists) living in the homeland but also spanning the entire diaspora. Mahjari activists carried these assumptions with them as they engaged in transnational political work, recruited for the army, petitioned foreign leaders, sought repatriation to the homeland, and registered with the census. The assumption that the diaspora was responsible for liberating its homeland is reflected in the shape and scope of the mahjar's press but also in its ethnic associations, political clubs, and fraternities—organizations whose records form the core of this research.

At the center of this diaspora's politics sat the production and circulation of specific sorts of papers: periodicals, propaganda, passports, and petitions. Borrowing from the nahda-era periodicals of Cairo and Alexandria of the late nineteenth century, Arabic print culture boomed in the Americas after 1900.

Syrian newspapers printed in New York City, São Paulo, and Buenos Aires gained unprecedented popularity during this period; in New York alone, nearly a dozen Arabic language periodicals operated simultaneously by 1914.[29] Trading stories with journalists in the Middle East via telegram, mahjari editors established a functional press syndicate by 1908. Together with mail-order subscriptions, the invention of an Arabic wax linotype machine in 1910 made newsprint cheap to produce and easy to disseminate. Wider classes of Syrian men (and women) typed their thoughts for a global Syrian audience.[30]

The CUP's lifting of censorship restrictions further encouraged these trends, allowing a generation of mahjari public intellectuals and editors to connect with audiences in the Ottoman Empire. The CUP's subsequent attempts to curtail press freedoms after 1909 did little to shut down these printing houses, only angering Syrian émigrés already critical of Ottoman policies. Cemal Pasha's closure of private printing houses in Damascus and Beirut, moreover, left only their diasporic counterparts in operation. Even though the CUP banned the importation of "foreign" periodicals written by émigrés abroad in 1915, most of the empire's censorship policies missed their mark.[31] The mahjar newspapers continued production, were comparatively free to criticize the CUP, and were the uncontested voice of Arabic-language journalism as the war went on. In this venue, emergent and competing nationalist associations found the vocabulary to protest Ottoman policies and organize Syrian migrants across continents. Arabist, Syrianist, and Lebanist propaganda appear in the pages of these serials, but more significantly, so do the quotidian reports of these activist networks: meeting minutes, funds raised, transcribed stump speeches, and angry letters to the editor. Contrary to Andersonian visions of vernacular printing as a space for "national imaginings," these newspapers figured as spaces for semiotic conflict at a moment of imperial disintegration. The newspapermen believed they were printing the nation into existence; theirs was a battle for the nation and for subscribers simultaneously.

At the other end of the documentary spectrum are papers that individual migrants carried on their person: passports, travel passes, and other forms registrations that marked an individual's relationship to the state. Issues of national belonging had little everyday relevance for Arab migrants in the Americas before 1914, but the war's geopolitical pressures prompted empires and nation-states to make new claims on their labor, their loyalties, and especially their mobility. Wartime travel regimes were designed to restrict Ottoman movements: passport laws, travel bans, diplomatic disputes, and criminal charges each confronted Ottoman Syrians during the conflict.[32] The migrants who could manage it petitioned for legal exemptions to these restrictions; those who could not get exemptions traveled clandestinely. This work thus builds on records of such transactions, especially passports, naturalization records, and criminal prosecutions of clandestine migrants, but it does so with the significant caveat that regulatory documents tell incomplete stories. While brushes with the law were significant, they were infrequent and avoided where possible.

Capturing the lives and travels of Syrian migrant activists beyond the prying eyes of the state requires a flexible approach to the archives, drawing primarily on indigenous writings between migrants and complemented by state records. Where possible, this work places individuals at the center of the action, pursuing them across the regimes they traversed. Most of their wartime work occurred in clandestine spaces only partly accessible to Ottoman, US, or Latin American authorities but within well-trod networks linking the Syrian colonies of the Americas to one another. The remarkable degree of political coherence the mahjar achieved was a result of the war and the activism it inspired, but the mahjar's interconnectedness persisted into the French Mandate period, thus presenting governance problems for France as the emigrants made new citizenship claims on their homeland after 1920.

Mahjar Matters

Producing papers, collecting them, stamping them, and directing their travel across oceans consumed the attentions of an entire generation of Syrians abroad. Activists believed that to make their community, papers must be delivered into the hands of the proper readers: serials to the cafés, broadsides to the draft-worthy, petitions to the powerful, and visas to the needy. Dozens of mahjari newspapers vied for control of the narrative and, with it, the aspirations of a global Syrian reading public. The nationalist politics these periodicals promoted were themselves fluid, shifting, and in competition with one another, but they rested on a common understanding that paper and its production were powerful. It was through powerful papers that the mahjar mattered to an emerging post-Ottoman Middle East, for on these pages the politics of Syrians abroad came home.

Several historical circumstances coalesced to empower Arab migrants in the Americas to participate in homeland politics: a 1908 invitation by the Ottoman state; the collapse of Syrian civil society after 1914; the willingness of the Entente powers to work with émigré activists against Istanbul in 1917; and a process of emigrant minoritization impacting the repatriation rights, citizenship claims, and post-Ottoman nationalities of Syrians and Lebanese in diaspora after 1919. Mahjari politics depended on the same migrant institutions that had facilitated the out-migration of so many Arab workers abroad. Chapter 1 recounts the global history of Syrian emigration, focusing on the emergence of Arab ethnic associations and the periodical press in the mahjar, the twin pillars of an émigré social field by the 1890s. Initially invested in bringing the literatures, arts, and cultural politics of the nahda to the Americas, these organizations provided a new social infrastructure that the Ottoman empire "rediscovered" following the Young Turk Revolution of 1908.

Following the revolution in July 1908, the new Ottoman government under the CUP party courted the empire's diasporas. Hoping to tap into Syrian associational life and the social capital of the Syrian press, the CUP constructed new consulates in Arab communities around the Atlantic. From the consulate, the Ottomans subsidized pro-CUP migrant clubs, supported remittance economies, and attempted to reclaim the empire's emigrants abroad. Chapter 2 illustrates how early Syrian optimism about the Young Turk movement strengthened linkages between Syrian clubs across the Americas but this politics soon melted into disillusionment with the Unionists and, eventually, with Ottoman rule altogether. Syrians organizing with the Syrian Ottoman Union Society, for instance, freely interpreted CUP calls for liberty (hürriyet) in ways beyond the intentions of the party's underwriters. Istanbul hoped to stoke these organizations into a politics of reclamation, but the Syrian clubs disagreed with their consular partners over the extraterritorial rights and privileges of migrants. New CUP policies curtailing the free press, free expression, and free association further frustrated emigrants who, using the press as a platform, organized new networks of decentralists, reformers, and Arabists beyond Ottoman jurisdiction.

The beginning of the First World War and the disintegration of Syrian and Mount Lebanese civil society under Cemal Pasha emboldened Arab activists living abroad. Raising humanitarian relief was an early act of resistance, usually conducted alongside other, more overt political acts. In war work, Syrian associations across the Americas cooperated with the Entente powers from the relative safety of diaspora. With the deepening crises of famine, epidemic, and political repression in Syria in 1916–1917, competing Arabist, Syrianist, and Lebanist parties in the mahjar called for the homeland's liberation from Ottoman rule and a restoration of the constitutionalist principles of 1908. Chapter 3 recovers a strand of this endeavor, documenting a clandestine network of Syrian military recruiters who assisted with the enlistment of some ten thousand Syrian migrants into the armies of the Entente. These recruiters moved men from the Syrian colonies of North and Latin America to enlistment centers in New York City, Boston, Le Havre, and Montreal, managing the traffic with unofficial state sanction but no formal oversight. They employed popular narratives about migrant patriotism and the responsibilities of the mahjar to save the homeland, but the flexibility of immigrant patriotisms belied US discourses about whether Ottoman nationals (and Syrians among them) could be considered American patriots, Syrian liberators, or Ottoman traitors.

Enlistment provided one powerfully symbolic means for emigrant cooperation with the Entente powers, but it was in the months following the 1918 armistice that emigrant politics "came home" to Syria. Syrian associations headquartered in the mahjar swiftly repurposed their networks to respond to the challenges of the Wilsonian moment: they negotiated post-Ottoman national borders with the victorious Entente, drew up new maps, circulated petitions in favor of national self-determination, and underwrote the first systems of travel passes, passports, and nationality laws that emerged in Syria and Lebanon after 1920. Chapter 4 follows the politics of one cell of migrant activists calling themselves the "new Syrians" in 1919. Organized under the New Syrian National League in New York City, Boston, Buenos Aires, and Cairo, the new Syrians lobbied for the United States of America to assume the mandate over a greater Syrian state, possibly in partnership with Hashemite Emir Faysal in Damascus. Building on American expansionist ideas about benevolent empire, the new Syrians argued that America would find in Syria a nation much like itself: a recently colonized land with a heterogeneous population requiring both federalist constitutional democracy and economic development to survive.

President Wilson's Fourteen Points electrified nationalist politics all over the world, but the new Syrians were different: they believed Syria should be developed within a US Mandate, with the mahjar's support through mass repatriation of migrants from the Americas. Because of their anti-French politics, the new Syrians were excluded from the negotiations taking place in Paris, allowing that conference (and the historiography arising from it) to produce a vision of the Syrian mahjar as supportive of French tutelage.

The Paris Peace Conference roiled in claims and counterclaims to former Ottoman territories, carving proposed borders for a post-Ottoman world of nation-states. In the mahjar, meanwhile, the Syrian and Lebanese associations employed American racial, religious, and ethnic markers to iterate new nationalities in diaspora. Chapter 5 documents the emergence of "Syrian" national origins as a juridical category during the war, and examines how exercising the right to travel, to repatriate, or access citizenship depended on the negotiation of a post-Ottoman identity. In 1918, the United States of America imposed a cross-border travel ban on Ottoman subjects within its territories. Maintained through Paris negotiations in 1919, the ban impacted a quarter million Ottoman subjects domiciled in US territories, many of whom were simultaneously eager to return to former Ottoman lands to settle household affairs after the war. These restive migrants—Syrians, Armenians, Turks, and Kurds—sought foreign passports where possible but paid smugglers for fake ones when necessary.

The enlistment loopholes granted Syrian migrants during the war also gave activists a precedent for special exemptions from the travel ban, an exemption not given other Ottoman subjects. Starting in 1918, Syrian and Lebanese migrants could travel across borders freely if they first registered as temporary French colonials. Given a French *sauf conduit* (safe conduct) passport, Syrians could exit through US ports and proceed to Syria, Mount Lebanon, or Palestine. As a document usually reserved for refugees, displaced persons, or prisoners of war, the employment of *sauf conduits* for Syrian and Lebanese repatriation depended on prevailing legal categories concerning "Syrian" national origins. Chapter 5 examines the *sauf conduit* process through the lens of smugglers who exploited it. Using US Bureau of Investigation cases concerning smugglers who assisted ineligible Ottoman Kurds and Turks out of the United States by passing them off as Syrian Arabs, this chapter argues that the *sauf conduit* was a means by which France claimed Syrian migrants as its colonial population months before it was awarded mandate over Syria and Lebanon.

French attempts to claim the mahjar for her Mandate persisted through the 1920s. After being awarded the Mandate in 1920, France partitioned the territory, created the new state of Greater Lebanon, and instituted a series of policies designed to domesticate the Lebanese diaspora. Chapter 6 examines the role that Lebanon's first census, conducted in 1921, played in Mandate colonial policy. The Mandate enumerated Lebanese within the new territory but also counted 130,000 Lebanese emigrants in the Americas. The census allowed the French to embrace some emigrants and further facilitate migrant repatriation to Lebanon, in a moment when the Mandate specifically sought to bolster a constructed Christian majority for Lebanon. But though the Mandate used the census to embrace some emigrants, it also severed nationality ties with others. In sum, the Mandate governed the diaspora to ensure political compliance from emigrants, who were variously cast as transnational citizens or troublesome subject populations.

In some ways, Mandate policies toward the Syrian and Lebanese diaspora mirrored those of their late Ottoman predecessors. For both polities, the mahjar and its activists provided opportunities to refract state power across an overseas frontier; for both, the emigrants were a population to be juridically reclaimed and perhaps even relocated for the good of the state. France's goal to impose and harden territorial borders across a new post-Ottoman geography, however, represented a significant departure. In an international order premised on the forced fixing of identifies into the "cartographic mold of nation-states," the Mandate ultimately partitioned the mahjar from the Mashriq, instituting policies to preempt the return of Syrians with presumed anticolonial politics.[33] This book's conclusion examines French attempts to deprive select emigrants of passports and nationality during the Great Syrian Revolt of 1925–1927. The denationalization of Syrians abroad amounted to a diasporic partition, revealing French desires to cut the very ties with the mahjar they had nurtured a decade earlier.

The pages that follow recover a social history of the Syrian and Lebanese diaspora at a crucial historical moment: the fall of the Ottoman empire, the region's subdivision within new national borders, and the emergence of the imperial European Mandates. In their core function, borders create new territories, and in doing so seek to contain nations, discipline and define societies, and regulate cross-border mobility. As shall be seen, borders also manufacture histories, contriving a territorial determinism that this work critiques. Contrary to popular ideas about border-making as a process driven wholly by states (whether we think of borders as expressions of "natural" sovereignties or assertions of invented ones), Syrian and Lebanese activists in the mahjar played an enormous role in defining the post-Ottoman politics of their homeland. From revolution in 1908 to revolt in 1925, contests over nationalist politics, national borders, nationality laws, and citizenship norms in Syria and Lebanon happened somewhere beyond the seas (*wara' al-bihar*), in the political headwaters running between the Ottoman empire and the Entente. For a time, emigrants abroad navigated these currents in order to stake political claims on their places of origins. The mahjar mattered, not only because of the historical endurance of the Syrian colonies in the Americas, but also because its politics frequently returned home.

1

Mashriq and Mahjar

A Global History of Syrian Migration to the Americas

Arriving in Cairo in 1897, Naʿum Mukarzil was unaware that he was only on the first leg of a journey that would define the shape and scope of the Syrian mahjar of the Americas. Born in the village of Freike, in Mount Lebanon, Mukarzil had graduated from Beirut's French Jesuit Université Saint-Joseph.[1] He came to Cairo seeking work with another Jesuit school but instead found himself drawn to the city's Syrian press: Yaʿcub Sarruf and Faris Nimr's *al-Muqattam* and *al-Muqtataf*, together with Jurji Zaydan's *al-Hilal*, fostered a new intellectual culture within the Syrian émigré communities in Cairo, Alexandria, and beyond.[2] Mukarzil wrote ad hoc contributions to these papers before boarding a steamship bound for the United States, where he founded his own publication, *al-Huda*, in 1898.[3] By 1905, Mukarzil's paper had become the largest Arabic-language title produced in the Western hemisphere, one of dozens of Syrian, Lebanese, and Palestinian newspapers produced in the mahjar.[4]

Mukarzil's journalistic success may have been exceptional, but his route and his settlement in the Syrian colony in New York City by way of Cairo was quite commonplace. Between the 1880s and 1914, an estimated half million Syrian Ottoman subjects departed the empire, most of them bound for the Americas.[5] The combined pressures of global capitalism, Syria's economic peripheralization, and the draw of the New World's post-abolition settler states pulled Syrian migrants abroad. Their numbers were massive: by 1914, an estimated 20 percent of Ottoman Syrians lived not in the empire but beyond it; in Mount Lebanon, this figure climbed to one-third of the population.[6] Arriving at the Atlantic ports in Brazil, Argentina, and the United States, Syrian migrants quickly established ethnic colonies (al-jaliyyat in Arabic) on the Atlantic seaboard, usually in proximity to other pockets of Mediterranean migration and settlement.[7] Whether Manhattan's "little Syria," São Paulo's Rua 25 de Marzo, Avenida Corrientes in Buenos Aires, or elsewhere, the Syrian colonies of the Americas were connected to one another. Syrians traveled readily to these "mother colonies" and, from there, into the reaches of the mahjar's inland peripheries.[8] Migrants in this diaspora built and maintained a transnational circulation of goods and workers, newspapers, ideas, and remittances among Arab communities across North and South America, as well as between the mahjar and its Ottoman homeland. By the late 1890s, this Atlantic system generated its own economic gravity, centered on industries in textiles, lace, and petty commerce ("peddling"), that fed ongoing migration of Ottoman Arabs into the mahjar.

Mukarzil's contribution to this diasporic social formation would be through its vibrant print culture. *al-Huda* and dozens of Arabic language titles like it served as a vital source for politics, news, and employment information, reporting on economic conditions and providing a sense of social connection with a Syrian world that encompassed mahjar and Mashriq simultaneously. Printing houses and their attached social institutions—reading rooms, mutual aid societies, fraternal associations, and cafés—played a generative role in the Syrian politics and culture before the First World War. Borrowed from Egypt's Syrian neighborhoods and grafted upon the foreign soils of the Arab Atlantic, these institutions offered diasporic men a social space to assert a late Ottoman politics of dissent and critique that transformed into nationalist politics after 1914. This chapter contextualizes the settlement patterns of the American mahjar, documenting the emergence of its institutions and print culture before the 1908 Revolution.

The Arab Atlantic

Syrian migrants constituted one of many groups of migrants participating in the circuit that linked the eastern Mediterranean littoral to its Atlantic counterpart. The late nineteenth century was a time of intensifying labor migration across the globe.[9] The expansion of steamship passenger transport in the century's third quarter, combined with the economic dislocations of post-abolition capitalism, inspired waves of trans-Atlantic labor migration by peasant classes in the Mediterranean.[10] Syrians from the Ottoman Empire joined Italians, Greeks, and various eastern Europeans in passage; often, they shared the same third-class quarters, settled in the same cities, and pursued the same trades as their Italian counterparts.[11] The Syrians were also joined by other groups of Ottoman subjects: Anatolian Turks, Armenians and Kurds from Cilicia, and Sephardic Jews from Palestine and the Balkans. Whether merchants, laborers, weavers, peddlers, or proletarians, all of these groups participated in a system made possible by steamship technology and the abolition of slavery in the Atlantic world.

Working abroad allowed Syrians to turn the Mediterranean's economic peripheralization to their advantage.[12] In Ottoman Syria and the mutasarrifate of Mount Lebanon, the structural explanations for emigration are well understood: the disintegration of peasant economies before the demands of European capitalism, the appearance of migration "industries" feeding labor migrants into a trans-Atlantic pipeline, land hunger in the Levant, and Mount Lebanon's silk crash. These all collided with broader patterns of intense urbanization and the proletarianization—and mobility—of Arab labor.[13] Beyond these structural factors, the decision to move was made at the level of the family and was influenced by access to networks of capital, information, and trust.[14] Once established in villages in Mount Lebanon or Syria, migration agents made a tidy profit connecting workers with steamship companies, lenders, and employment agencies before departure and with social welfare clubs, boarding houses, or factory foremen upon arrival in the Americas.[15] Beginning in the 1860s, Syrians traveled out of Beirut and through various Mediterranean ports, commonly Alexandria, Marseilles, and Barcelona.[16] The emigration reached massive proportions by the mid-1880s, and by the end of that decade, Syrians departed the Ottoman Empire at per capita rates comparable to the Italians and Greeks with whom they traveled.[17]

Though spurred by economic circumstances particular to the late nineteenth century, Syrian labor emigration was also the culmination of structural processes already a century old. The first destination for Syrian migrants was Egypt, where colonies of Syrian Christian elites had emerged as early as the 1750s, working as merchants or in the professions. The Syrian émigrés in Egypt came from the wealthiest households in Aleppo and Damascus.[18] Settling in enclaves of Cairo and Alexandria set them apart from native Egyptians; from there, they worked as foreign merchants and, after 1882, on behalf of Egypt's British colonial administration.

The elite character of the Cairene Syrian colony throws a sharp contrast between them and the massive labor migration of Syrians, Mount Lebanese, and Palestinians to the Americas in the 1880s; the Syrian mahjar had its own professional class, but most migrants came from middling peasant stock, from skilled textile work, or from unskilled agricultural labor. But Cairo's Syrian community nevertheless played an important role in facilitating Syrian labor migration. Cairene Syrians, for example, ran some of the shipping companies that brought both Egyptian goods and migrant bodies across the Atlantic. Others published newspapers that became a significant source for information about the Americas for Syrians headed there. Some of Cairo's Syrian journalists even relocated across the Atlantic, circulating among the Syrian colonies on professional business. Farah Antun, for instance, successfully transferred his Cairo periodical, al-Jama'a, to New York City in 1899, establishing a series of publications there before returning to Egypt in 1909.[19] Antun's identification of the American mahjar as a new print cultural frontier was prescient; by 1900, many of the men writing for Syrian papers from the United States, Brazil, and Argentina had spent significant time in Cairo. The liberal literary revival that emerged in the mahjar was imported primarily from Cairo's contributions to the nahda; it came in the mail along with copies of *al-Muqtataf, al-Muqattam,* and *al-Hilal.*[20]

On a more practical level, Egypt served as a major waypoint for Syrian travelers who later established themselves further abroad. Bankers, lawyers, journalists, and other educated Syrians tarried in Egypt for weeks, months, or years on the route to the Americas. They were helped along this route by American missionaries and alumni networks joining Beirut and Damascus to Cairo, particularly of the Syrian Protestant College (renamed the American University of Beirut in 1920).[21] Bringing their commercial ventures, capital, and their politics with them, these men transformed into a mahjari political elite. But even as Syrian migration to the Americas surpassed that to Egypt and drew on a different class and geographical strata, Cairo remained the mahjar's historical mother colony and continually conditioned political culture in the Syrian Atlantic.[22]

Of course, new technologies also connected Atlantic and Mediterranean migration circuits to one another. The advent of steamship passenger transport put trans-Atlantic travel within the means of many Syrians, but tickets were still expensive enough that households opted to selectively send sons abroad.[23] Middling but upwardly mobile, the first emigrants were of a generation of rising expectations frustrated by contracting economic opportunities at home.[24] Mount Lebanon's 1870s silk crash did not destroy the Syrian family economy so much as encourage its diversification. Men emigrated (typically considering this emigration to be temporary) and women performed wage labor at home; even as Syrian women and entire families began to move abroad, this pattern persisted.[25] The system depended on both male and female contributions to function.[26] Young women brought capital, offsetting the risks of men's commercial endeavors that, if all went well, enhanced the family's financial standing.[27] Tales of fantastic wealth from abroad continually fed the system, and once in the Americas, Syrians depended on a budding system of credit and employment agents to find quick work in petty retail or in textiles (silk and cotton) and dry goods (coffee, sewing notions, groceries, etc.).[28] This selective emigration strategy was part of a global pattern that emerged in Italy, China, Japan, and throughout Europe. These migrations were immense in their scale: 50 to 55 million Europeans, 20 percent of the continent's entire population, participated in the trans-Atlantic circuit in the late nineteenth century.[29] Between 1870 and 1914, 14 million Italians emigrated, 39 percent of Italy's population. In this light, the departure of between 18 and 25 percent of Syria's total population was typical of global trends.[30]

Emigration from Syria and Mount Lebanon accelerated at a steady clip from the 1890s until the start of the First World War in 1914.[31] The Ottoman state made infrequent attempts to slow the pace of emigration, focusing mostly on departures through Beirut's port via rudimentary passport control. Most Syrians carried with them an internal passport document called the *mürûr tezkeresi*, which entitled them to travel within the imperial domain but not beyond its limits.[32] Ottoman lawmakers complained that Syrians and Mount Lebanese had begun using the *mürûr tezkeresi* to travel abroad or even to expatriate from the Ottoman Empire. Such attempts reveal an emerging desire among officials to regulate the departure of migrants abroad and to maintain an extraterritorial authority over them. Even so, the empire made only limited attempts to stymie emigration, and even these dissipated after 1900 as incoming cash remittances from the mahjar formed a new pillar of the Syrian economy.[33] In a diaspora a half million strong by World War I, 50.7 percent of Syrians lived in one of the three largest settler societies of the Atlantic: the United States, Brazil, or Argentina. Emigration was halted by an Entente naval blockade during the war, but it quickly resumed after 1920.[34] Despite attempts by both the French Mandate in Syria and Lebanon and the receiving countries of the Americas, the Lebanese diaspora swelled to over 688,000 by 1926.[35] Although these estimates do not account for clandestine migration or permanent repatriation to the Middle East, there is a clear pattern of Syrian migration favoring one of three major epicenters: New York City, Buenos Aires, and São Paulo. These cities became loci for mahjari economic activities and, later, for nationalist politics.

Syrian banks formed in the Americas, linking the mahjar's colonies to one another and to the Ottoman Empire. The cash reserves found there fueled investment in Syrian textile factories built in both North and Latin America, as well as in Syrian shipping lines that linked them to the larger Atlantic economy.[36] The Syrian practice of sending cash home in the pockets of returning relatives rather than through formal banking channels makes tracing the depth of the mahjari economy impossible, but even rudimentary data illustrates that Mount Lebanon's economy became increasingly dependent on remittances. In 1900, Mount Lebanon received 200,000 British pounds in remittances from the Americas; by 1910, this number appreciated to 800,000, reflecting the growing numbers of emigrants and their commercial success.[37] By 1917, remittances constituted Mount Lebanon's single largest economic resource, comprising 220 million Ottoman piasters per annum compared to the silk trade's 60 million, agriculture's 30 million, and industry's 10 million piasters.[38] In peacetime, these remittances enhanced the buying power of the Arab middle class. In times of want and catastrophe, they provided an essential economic lifeline.

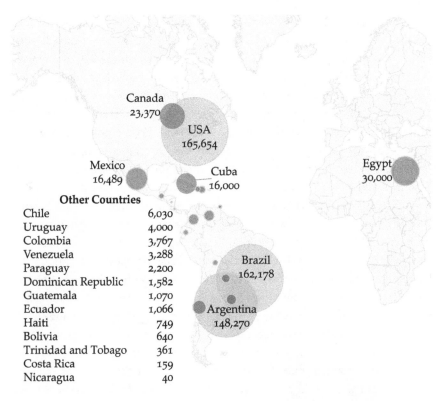

Canada
23,370

USA
165,654

Mexico
16,489

Cuba
16,000

Egypt
30,000

Other Countries

Chile	6,030
Uruguay	4,000
Colombia	3,767
Venezuela	3,288
Paraguay	2,200
Dominican Republic	1,582
Guatemala	1,070
Ecuador	1,066
Haiti	749
Bolivia	640
Trinidad and Tobago	361
Costa Rica	159
Nicaragua	40

Brazil
162,178

Argentina
148,270

Figure 1.1. Syrian and Lebanese settlement patterns in the Americas and Egypt, according to 1926 French Mandate estimates. Kohei Hashimoto, "Lebanese Population Movement 1920–1939, Towards a Study," in *Lebanese in the World: A Century of Emigration*, eds. Albert Hourani and Nadim Shehadi (London: I.B. Tauris, 1992), 105.

Peddling is remembered as the mahjar's most identifiable economic activity: recalled as a romantic entrepreneur carrying his or her *kasheh* (the peddler's suitcase) into private homes or across continents, oral histories capture the nostalgia that has come to define the history of this work in America.[39] Despite its outsized reputation, however, peddling was never the dominant means of employment. Syrians engaged in a variety of trades, including dry goods retail, boarding houses, shipping, and processing of raw cotton and coffee; proletarian wage labor was most common of all. Arab migrants worked in machining, automobiles, or other heavy industries such as leather, textiles, and garment making. Cloth—both cotton and silk—offered an especially unique opportunity. At the turn of the twentieth century, the Ottoman Empire experienced a boom in cloth production. As they enriched themselves at home, Syrian elites started looking into the mahjar for investment opportunities; all-Syrian textile firms emerged in Atlantic cities in North and South America.

Previous experience with weaving technology and the availability of textile work played a major role in who emigrated from Syria and on the economic opportunities Syrians discovered once abroad. Before 1900, the typical
Syrian sojourner was a young man, unwed or recently married, traveling with
male relatives working as weavers, cutters, or clothiers. Women came to comprise 35 percent of all Syrian migrants by 1900; they, too, worked in textiles.[40]
Although many Syrians worked in large American firms among other immigrant groups, the all-Syrian factories became an increasingly popular option.
The Abdallah Barsa factory in Brooklyn, New York, for instance, employed
both men and women and promoted ethnic solidarity as part of its brand. The
Barsa factory was also spatially sex-segregated; although men and women both
worked there, the factory's two floors were divided into separated spheres of distinct types of labor. On the first floor, Syrian men ran sales of broadcloth and
wholesale garments; in the back, men weaved and cut raw cloth. Upstairs, on the
second floor, Syrian women sewed garments, laces, and lingerie, including the
"Oriental kimonos" that made New York's Syrian quarter famous in the 1920s.[41]
As it was in Mount Lebanon, the preservation of gendered spheres of wage work
assuaged patriarchal anxieties accompanying women's work in this industry.[42]

In Brazil, factory work was not only common, but an entire class of Syrian
industrialists emerged, built factories, and contracted thousands of migrant
workers from weaving houses in the Ottoman Empire for relocation abroad.
The largest numbers of Syrians came in the decade before the First World War,
concentrating in the Syrian colony on Rua 25 de Marzo in São Paulo as well
as in Rio de Janeiro, where the Ottoman Empire established its consulate.[43]
Syrians were drawn to Brazil by the cotton industry, especially after 1907, when
Naʿimi and Antunius Jafet opened their Ypiranga Cotton Factory just outside
São Paulo.[44] The Jafet brothers came to Brazil from Mount Lebanon in 1903,
looking to expand on a commercial network that already linked Mount Lebanon
to Egypt and a garment-making venture in New York City. In Brazil, the Jafets
discovered a favorable convergence of available Syrian workers, diasporic financial institutions, and liberal Brazilian trade policies that favored foreign investment in manufacturing. Naʿimi Jafet constructed the Ypiranga factory to be large
enough to operate 1,000 mechanized looms and employ more than two thousand men.[45] Like Brooklyn's Barsa brothers, the Jafets maintained an all-Syrian
workforce; when they ran out of local Arab workers to run the looms, they
contracted weavers from Hama, Aleppo, and Homs, offering them easy credit
to facilitate the trans-Atlantic move.[46] By 1914, the Jafet ventures sponsored so
many new migrants from the Syrian city of Homs that São Paulo's Syrian quarter
was the single largest Homsi settlement outside the Ottoman Empire. By 1920,
Brazil hosted the largest documented community of Syrians and Lebanese outside of the Middle East.[47]

Figure 1.2a and 1.2b Textile work at the ʿAbdallah Barsa factory in New York City, 1920. The Syrian and Lebanese textile factories of the mahjar maintained a gendered division of labor: men worked in weaving, cutting, and sales, while women completed piecework and laces. Sallum Mukarzil, *Tarikh al-Tijara al-Suriyya fi-l-Muhajara al-Amrikiyya* (New York: al-Matbaʿa al-Suriyya al-Amrikiyya, 1921), 50. James Ansara Papers, IHRC208, Immigration History Research Center Archives, University of Minnesota.

Brazil's Syrian textile industry quickly became a major source of income not only for migrants but also for their families back home. Although the First World War temporarily stymied worker remittances from abroad, by the early 1920s Syrian textile workers in São Paulo sent an average of 2,000 to 4,000 francs home annually, at a time when "a one-way ticket from Syria to South America cost only 250 francs."[48] Cotton made Na'imi Jafet fantastically wealthy, and he established himself not only as a businessman but also as a philanthropist, educator, public intellectual, and in 1913, as the head of the first all-Syrian Chamber of Commerce in Brazil.

Historians describe economic motivations and the chance at enhanced social mobility as the driving factors behind Syrian emigration. But these motivations alone did not determine who would migrate, to where, or for whom emigration was a good investment. Political and social capital played a strong role, as did access to the confessional, village, and kinship networks within which migrants operated. Christians from western Syria and Mount Lebanon were most likely to emigrate, particularly from the Maronite, Greek Orthodox, Melkite, and Protestant sects. Druze, Sunnis, and Shi'is also found their way to the mahjar, but this diaspora's demographic weight was heavily tilted toward Arab Christians until 1948.

Discerning precise figures about the mahjar's confessional makeup, however, is fraught. The politicization of Lebanon's 1921 and 1932 censuses, the US census's uneven accounting of Syrian immigrants, and a general lack of empirical data elsewhere makes even preliminary guesses about the mahjar's confessional makeup difficult. The statistic that is often repeated is that in 1920, the Arab American community was 90 to 95 percent Christian, but this figure relies on Lebanese and US census data that have been shown to bolster Christian

Figure 1.3. Jafet Factory in Ypiranga, Brazil, established in 1907. Antunius Jafet, *Na'imi Jafet: Hayatuhu, Amaluhu, wa-Atharuhu* (São Paulo: Antunius Jafet s.p., 1934), 51.

immigrant numbers while underreporting Muslim ones.[49] Other studies rely on an Arab American survey of population conducted by historian Philip K. Hitti in 1924, whose work also built up from census data to conclude the Syrian diaspora was overwhelmingly Christian.[50]

These census data are inaccurate for several reasons. In the United States, Syrian Muslims were often classified as Turks (as Ottoman nationals) or in many cases temporarily retained "Turkish" nationality after the 1918 armistice and even the 1920 foundation of the French Mandate in Syria and Lebanon. Lebanon's 1921 census was also fundamentally flawed. Conducted by the French High Commissioner of Beirut, the census enumerated Lebanese emigrants alongside residents for the purposes of drawing new administrative districts for the new state of Greater Lebanon.[51] The men responsible for counting the emigrants—almost all of them Lebanese clerics—were under intense pressure to represent the diaspora as almost entirely Christian. Meanwhile, Sunni leaders at home and abroad boycotted the census, thus leaving its results deeply flawed.

Historians of the mahjar have thus developed a healthy skepticism about population estimates describing this diaspora as 95 percent Christian, but more precise figures have not been reached.[52] Neither US, nor Argentine, nor Brazilian immigration agents considered "Syrians" as distinct from "Turks" before the turn of the century; anyone holding Ottoman documents originated from "Turkey in Asia."[53] Even when the United States began to categorize Syrians as a distinctive Ottoman nationality in 1897, what made this group distinct from the rest in the eyes of the authorities was their Christian religion, not their geographic place of origin.[54] Although Brazilian and Argentine immigration agencies also eventually recognized Syrians as a group, the distinctions were applied unevenly and on the basis of confessional allegiances, making the term virtually meaningless to historians seeking to precisely map the mahjar's confessional makeup.[55] That said, Christians certainly constituted the simple majority of migrants living in the Syrian mahjar before 1914.

In addition to the economic factors that drove them there, the proliferation of foreign educational institutions in Syria and missionary networks linking Syria to points abroad opened the gates of emigration for a generation of men enrolled in these schools.[56] Two Syrian Protestant College graduates, Dr. Khalil Sa'adih and Na'imi Jafet, demonstrate how access to missionary networks facilitated emigration and bolstered the emergence of a Syrian professional class in diaspora. Khalil Sa'adih traveled through the Syrian colonies in Cairo, Buenos Aires, and São Paulo between 1892 and 1925, facilitated by former classmates.[57] Before Na'imi Jafet arrived in São Paulo to become one of the mahjar's most important textile moguls, he accompanied his brother, Antunius, and a small group of co-villagers in a passage from Beirut to Alexandria and then to Naples, Italy. Three weeks later, his group boarded a steamship headed for Spain, stopping in

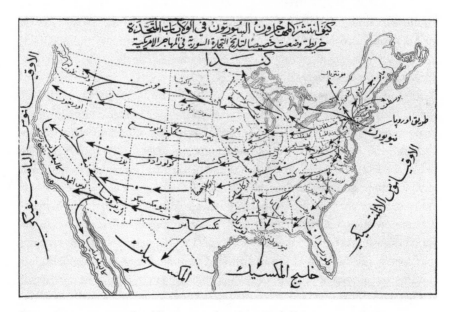

Figure 1.4. 1921 map of peddling routes from New York City. Mukarzil, *Tarikh al-Tijara al-Suriyya*, 144. James Ansara Papers, IHRC208, Immigration History Research Center Archives, University of Minnesota.

Barcelona, and on to Rio de Janeiro. He arrived in Brazil in 1903 and made haste for São Paulo, where he would build his cotton empire.[58]

Migrants of humbler origins would arrive at the Syrian colonies in the Americas and reconnect with relatives or with employers visiting the ethnic enclave to hire laborers. Syrian employment agents frequented New York City's "little Syria" neighborhood from the textile factories of Massachusetts, from Michigan's automotive plants, and from pack-peddling businesses in Ohio, Pennsylvania, or the Midwest.[59] Networks of employment nearly always began at the ports of entry but drew migrants toward the interior. However, the Syrian neighborhoods in New York City, São Paulo, and Buenos Aires remained critical nodes in this emerging system. Step-by-step, most Syrian migrants in the Americas set foot in one of these three communities.[60]

Mother Colonies

Although Syrian migrants appeared virtually everywhere in the Americas between 1900 and 1926, no destination came close to the demographic weight of the Argentine, Brazilian, and US collectivities. Why these three countries in particular? The same economic convergence that fed mass migration from the

Mediterranean also changed the economic foundations of the Atlantic basin. In North and South America, this convergence produced rapid, exponential expansion in industrial agriculture that fed a booming export-driven economy. Nowhere in the Americas were the labor demands more intense than the United States, Brazil, and Argentina following the abolition of slavery. As recently postcolonial entities that were territorially large and underpopulated, pacifying the frontier and developing new lands under their domains was a key preoccupation. The institution of African slavery served as the foundation for an agrarian economy in the Atlantic world before 1853, but its abolition in Argentina (1853), the United States (1865), and Brazil (1888) led these countries' governments to turn to foreign immigration as a means of domesticating new lands, increasing cultivation, building infrastructure (especially railroads), and developing their agricultural and industrial labor forces.

Importing foreign labor to settle and develop interior frontiers facilitated agrarian development, but Atlantic settler societies also deployed immigrants and foreign workers to the frontiers as a means of securing new sovereignty over them. By every measure, the system produced exponential economic growth. Between 1870 and 1914, the United States doubled its population and its acreage under cultivation, tripled its imports, quadrupled its exports, built a coast-to-coast rail, and increased its foreign investments by a factor of five.[61] Although tempered slightly by an 1889 military coup and the birth of the Republic, Brazil's railroad industry grew thirty-fold, and its agricultural exports (particularly coffee) grew steadily enough to support a doubling in population.[62] With the hemisphere's most permissive immigration regime, Argentina saw its population and level of foreign investments quadruple between 1870 and 1914, its exports increase seventeen times, and its imports multiply seventy-two fold.[63]

This economic growth directly depended on the ability to attract, settle, and employ migrant workers from the trans-Atlantic circuit. As a result, all three states equated the immigration of workers with national prosperity and progress, leading each to develop liberal immigration policies designed to attract migrants through incentive programs and state subsidies. In the United States, the Immigration Act of 1864 endorsed government sponsorship of labor migrants. It established a federal Immigration Commission charged with verifying the employment contracts of would-be migrants prior to arrival, offering loans to support travelers, and facilitating transportation to American shores. It channeled all trans-Atlantic immigration through New York City and gave the Commissioner powers to create incentives to encourage both temporary and permanent immigration. The 1864 Act provided the basis for all US immigration policy until the more restrictive Immigration Act of 1882.[64]

Brazil also subsidized new immigrants through much of the nineteenth century, targeting European immigrants in particular. After declaring its independence from Portugal in 1822, Brazil emerged under Don Pedro I, who advocated well-managed, state-sponsored immigration as the path to economic development and self-sufficiency.[65] This began with a series of state-sponsored German agricultural settlements in the provincial towns surrounding Rio de Janeiro and São Paulo in the late 1820s. The project continued through the 1850s and established Brazil's coffee industry.[66] Brazil's imperial government selectively resettled migrants from Europe in the interior and saw in colonization a means of domesticating new lands, expanding cultivation, and shoring up Brazil's sovereignty in its hinterlands.

To be sure, resettlement strategies were a standard means of securing frontier zones that were employed by empires around the world in the nineteenth century, including in the Middle East. In the same moment, for instance, the Ottoman Empire resettled Circassian, Arab, and Kurdish nomads in its southern provinces within carefully provisioned agricultural settlements. In Egypt, Muhammad 'Ali constructed a massive, state-owned cotton industry that depended on the forced resettlement and corvée of local labor.[67] But in Brazil, Dom Pedro I's incentive programs drew not only the German, Italian, Spanish, and Portuguese immigrants his policies actively solicited, but also unintended Mediterranean groups: Sephardic Jews, Syrians, Lebanese, and Turks, who made their first appearance in the 1880s.[68]

In Argentina, the 1853 Constitution codified an open philosophy linking the free immigration of foreign workers to national prosperity. In articles 20 through 25, it endorsed the immigration of any national group that could demonstrably contribute to Argentinian society. The document emphasized the promotion of European immigration but awarded all foreign residents the same legal and civil rights (including property rights) that Argentinian citizens enjoyed. Any foreign arrival could apply for naturalization after only two years of residence, making Argentina's the most liberal citizenship regime of the time.[69]

The immigration regimes of the United States, Brazil, and Argentina resembled one another, in part, because they were written in reference to one another. The three states actively competed for the most "desirable" immigrants, creating labor hierarchies and influencing the migrant flows between them.[70] For instance, when the United States placed new restrictions on ships coming from Mediterranean ports (citing health considerations, quarantining ships, or even sending them south of the equator) in the 1880s, greater numbers of Syrians, Italians, and other Mediterranean migrants arrived in Buenos Aires, where quarantine laws were more relaxed.[71] When Argentinian nativists caught wind of these changes, they initiated efforts to restrict the immigration of those potentially rejected by their northern neighbors.[72]

It was this Atlantic world in which Ottoman Syrians found themselves upon their arrival to "America," an expansive geography that comprised the entire Atlantic. In Brazil, Argentina, and the United States, mass immigration constituted a core part of economic policy; it was also central within these states' selectively multicultural national narratives.[73] As settler societies, there was purportedly space for all newcomers, as long as they fit the settler narrative and appeared to adhere to its racial and religious contours. Like other Mediterranean immigrants, the Syrians folded themselves into the expanding Atlantic economies they encountered. The development of certain types of migrant institutions in the Syrian colonies of New York City, São Paulo, and Buenos Aires was aided by a desire to protect and integrate new migrants, as well as by a need to present the colony's self-sufficiency, productivity, and contributions to the larger societies they inhabited.

As mentioned, Syrian migrants arriving in the Americas often filtered through one of three cities: São Paulo, Buenos Aires, or New York City. Each city hosted large Syrian colonies and seeded the earliest mahjari institutions: mutual aid societies, patriotic clubs, fraternal orders, reading rooms, and cafés. Over and above all of these institutions, however, sat the Syrian printing houses, for it was in the physical space of these buildings that Syrian clubs of various sorts met, organized, and recorded their conversations with the larger Syrian colony. The printing houses provided the setting for mahjari intellectual movements, Syrian book clubs, philanthropic and social gatherings, and political rabble-rousing.

Figure 1.5. New York City's *al-Huda* printing press, 1920. Mukarzil, *Tarikh al-Tijara al-Suriyya*, 142. James Ansara Papers, IHRC208, Immigration History Research Center Archives, University of Minnesota.

Like their counterparts in the Middle East, mahjari printing houses produced novels, poetry, translations of European literature, biographies, plays, and language primers in addition to serials.[74] Most of them maintained these materials in their own libraries, small spaces filled with shelves of pulp print books, newspapers from around the colony and across the diaspora, comfortable chairs, and the small cups of black coffee and backgammon boards that transformed these spaces into men's cafés after dark. During the day, newspaper editors pieced together the latest edition, but Syrians from the neighborhood also took advantage of the translation, notary, and legal services often available in the printing house. It was usually legal fees and quotidian documentary work like this that offset the cost of producing newspapers, especially amid the climate of intense competition that defined the mahjari newspaper industry.[75]

As it was in the eastern Mediterranean, reading was a communal activity in the mahjar, a social gathering where men could learn the day's news, recite or listen to *zajal* poetry, or argue with their neighbors over homeland politics.[76] In the late Ottoman context, belonging to a reading room signaled participating in an enlightened Syrian political culture organized around civic education and patriotism.[77] But when the war began in 1914, the printing houses also became the headquarters for competing nationalist associations, who printed their propaganda there.[78] Syrian political parties organized in these spaces and used the press to disseminate open letters, pamphlets, petitions, and calls to arms across not just the local Syrian colony but also throughout the mahjar. Texts appeared in Arabic, French, Portuguese, and Spanish for both Arab and foreign audiences.

Each periodical was organized around the politics of its masthead and, sometimes, around distinct confessional communities. The societies meeting in the printing house then followed suit. The development of this confessionally categorized newspaper press has led some scholars to describe it as an engine for sectarian fragmentation within Syrian migrant communities, even concluding that the mahjar lacked a coherent sense of community beyond religious confession.[79] Of course, intense political rivalries existed among Syrian émigré printers, producing significant tension and lending their periodicals their characteristic bombast, heat, and hyperbole. Public scuffles between editors who disliked one another provided grist for the rumor mill, tit-for-tat insults, occasional fisticuffs in the street, and even an arson or two. However, a divided community is still a community. Conflicts like these in the press were not manifestations of inherent sectarian tensions in the Syrian colonies. Rather, they are indicators of a developing political community struggling for control over the terms of its civic nationalism and the responsibilities of the mahjar toward its homeland.

As a rule, printing houses were uniformly male spaces, offering a space for homosocial leisure and the cultivation of a culture that largely excluded women.

Syrian women in the mahjar consistently critiqued the culture of the cafés and their fraternities, sometimes mocking them as sites for indolent nostalgia and bachelor's folly and other times criticizing the segregation of men's from women's spaces more broadly. Women were also largely excluded from writing for the mahjar press; 'Afifa Karam's pioneering work for *al-Huda* and *al-Alam al-Jadid* was an exception. Syrian women in the Americas worked at rates comparable to men and carried on a tradition of associational life that paralleled the fraternities, meeting in private homes rather than in public spaces of the printing houses.[80] The women's press, furthermore, was just as transnational as its masculine counterpart: Syrian women could pick up a copy of *Fatat al-Sharq* in Cairo, *Fatat Lubnan* in Beirut, or *al-Mar'a al-Suriyya* in New York City and read the same editorials by 'Afifa Karam, Labiba Hashim, and Salima Abu Rashed on issues such as women's right to work, the desirability of marriage, and the importance of philanthropic endeavors.[81] The women's press was a powerful tool for social critique, and Syrian women writers targeted not only standard mahjari ideas about renewal, progress, and social uplift but also pushed for concrete advancement in women's rights, legal status, and access to education and employment.[82] Their papers, however, were pressed in the very printing houses from which they were physically excluded.

Conclusion

Although the Ottoman Empire under Sultan Abdel Hamid II displayed little interest in emigration restriction, the Syrians of the mahjar remained Ottoman subjects, both in word and deed. Some Syrian migrants petitioned for legal naturalization in their countries of domicile, but the overwhelming majority of them saw little strategic value in renouncing their ties to the Ottoman Empire. In Argentina, for instance, Syrians were legally eligible for voluntary naturalization after two years of residence, but only a paltry 385 Syrians had petitioned for Argentinian citizenship before 1914.[83] Not only did Ottoman laws prohibit emigrants from renouncing their legal status as Ottoman subjects, but many Syrian emigrants believed they would ultimately return to the Ottoman Empire. That said, French Mandate officials in Buenos Aires complained in 1928 that they had been unable to convince Syrian migrants to either seek Mandate citizenship or naturalize as Argentinians, a decade after Ottoman rule in Syria had ceased. A full 90 percent of them preferred instead to hold onto the Ottoman *mürûr tezkeresi* even though the Empire it represented had collapsed.[84]

Similarly, that Ottoman migrants maintained their citizenship ties with their empire of origin was of little concern to the host societies they settled in before 1914. Although Arab migrants were sometimes confronted by popular nativism and racism in the mahjar, they were far less likely to encounter legal complications or discriminatory immigration regimes than were other Asian groups. That host societies struggled to categorize Middle Eastern immigrants within the racial schematics that defined post-1882 immigration law across the hemisphere worked in Syrians' favor. Establishing colonies at ports of entry, the Syrian clubs negotiated vigorously for their inclusion in the Atlantic world, often working across diasporic advocacy networks. Syrian migrants were ultimately impacted by immigration and naturalization restrictions after 1900, for instance, through racial prerequisite laws limiting access to citizenship in the United States. But even as these laws placed limits on Syrian access to naturalization, immigration laws in the United States and elsewhere were unconcerned about the immigrants' Ottoman nationality or ongoing fealty to the empire.

There came a moment, in 1908, when the Ottoman Empire rediscovered and started to reclaim their colonies in America. The Young Turk Revolution restored the empire to constitutional rule, and the ruling Committee of Union and Progress party reached out to the mahjar in new embrace. Ottoman migrants, Syrians among them, were suddenly cast as a crucial source of political support for Istanbul; their trans-Atlantic colonies represented a new overseas frontier from which political support, commercial partnership, and repatriates would return home to regenerate the empire. Their printing houses and attached political clubs, furthermore, could provide the Young Turks with the institutional means to refract Ottoman imperial sovereignty and power across extraterritorial space, putting the diasporas to work for the good of the empire. From 1908 until the First World War, the new Ottoman government looked for ways to draw Syrian migrants back into the fold. Ultimately, they got more than they bargained for.

The Mahjar of the Young Turks, 1908–1916

On August 26, 1908, Washington Street's "Little Syria" neighborhood in lower Manhattan was covered in festive paper streamers. The revolution in Istanbul had passed quickly: a palace coup shunted aside the Ottoman Sultan Abdel Hamid II, and the Young Turks restored the empire's 1876 constitution, bringing three decades of autocratic rule to a close. In the United States, the empire's diplomatic offices experienced a tumultuous shakeup, as Hamidian loyalists were dismissed from their posts and replaced by supporters of the Young Turk movement and its party, the Committee of Union and Progress (hereafter CUP). After several weeks of chaos, excitement, and bureaucratic uncertainty, New York's Syrian colony began the festivities around the first "Ottoman Constitution Day" ('id al-dustur al-'uthmani) fashionably late.

The city's Ottoman charge d'affaires, Mundji Bey, ascended the platform, addressing an assortment of American and Ottoman festivalgoers with a convocation to set the tone for a day of food, fundraising, and speeches.[1] Mundji Bey had just returned from the Ottoman Legation in Washington, D.C., where he evicted the empire's Hamidian ambassador on behalf of the revolution. In his speech, the consul set out the history of the Ottoman constitution: its establishment by the Young Ottomans in 1876, the fate of the first parliament and its conflict with Sultan Abdel Hamid II, and the red sultan's abrogation of the document two years later. The document's restoration was a renewal of Young Ottoman promises for universal citizenship and parliamentary representation; at the same time, the revolution articulated a commitment to state-led development. Mundji Bey argued that Syrian migrants in America formed a critical part of that project, stressing the role that Ottomans abroad would play in their empire's regeneration:

> Syria needs agricultural, industrial, and commercial development, and
> the emigrants in this locality have already established themselves [in

these trades]. They carry the torch of civilization, light, and liberty here in America, and they have received these each through hard work with its residents and will bring these gifts back [to the Empire] when they return to the homeland.[2]

The Ottoman consul argued that Syrian emigrants were uniquely positioned to bring liberty back to the empire and also to reintroduce Istanbul's new government to foreign powers in North and Latin America. But to succeed in bringing the Young Turk revolution to the mahjar, Mundi Bey proposed the formation of a new network of Syrian patriotic associations, clubs that would foster a culture of civic Ottomanism among Syrians and institutionalize a space for soft diplomacy. Closing his speech, he invited New York City's Syrian leaders—newspapermen and lawyers, bankers, philanthropists, and clergy—to reach out to the Ottoman consulate toward these goals.[3]

Syrians who attended the Ottoman Constitution Day festivities had reason to be hopeful about the Young Turks. Mobilizing around the banner of constitutionalism, liberty, and unionism, the CUP quickly restored rights of free expression and association, lifted press censorship, and promised parliamentary representation to all regardless of creed, class, or religion. Arab Ottomans welcomed the revolution; popular celebrations sprang forth in Damascus, Beirut, and Jerusalem, as well as across the mahjar. Arabic papers reported on Constitution Day events from New York to Cairo, from Havana to São Paulo, Buenos Aires to Santiago.[4] Ottoman flags hung from street lamps in Egypt.[5] In Buenos Aires, CUP placards appeared in shop windows, their proprietors closing early to clear the *avenida* for a parade honoring Ottoman unionists alongside Argentinian icons such as Bartholomew Mitre.[6] Onlookers in New York dined on kibbe and drew comparisons between this celebration and America's Independence Day, three weeks earlier.[7] Mundji Bey welcomed such comparisons, and his speeches suggest he intended them.[8]

At the heart of Mundji Bey's declaration was his goal to reclaim Syrian migrants for the empire, marking a dramatic shift in the Ottoman state's attitude toward the mahjar, a warming of relations paired with the desire to exert extraterritorial sovereignty over Ottoman subjects. There were several reasons that migrants were worth Mundji Bey's pursuit. Remittances, for instance, already constituted a major economic pillar, accounting for an estimated 800,000 British pounds annually in Mount Lebanon alone by 1910.[9] But pursuing Syrian migrants across the mahjar could also open venues for transhemispheric diplomacy. Between 1903 and 1912, the CUP built new consulates in Argentina, Brazil, and the United States, targeting communities with large Syrian populations and establishing pro-CUP Syrian clubs connected to each of them. The new Syrian clubs incentivized émigré investment in the homeland, promoted commercial links with foreign powers, and encouraged guest-work programs as well as permanent migrant repatriation. Taken together, these policies illustrate a desire to domesticate the diaspora while simultaneously refracting Ottoman imperial power into the Americas.

Syrian migrants themselves believed that their partnership with the CUP would enhance their rights as transnational citizens of the Ottoman Empire. Even as Syrian clubs worked with the Ottoman consulates, they interpreted CUP slogans in ways that far exceeded the intentions of their framers.[10] CUP overtures provided them with key opportunities to exercise a new substantive citizenship, asserting emigrant rights to travel, petition for redress, or enjoy diplomatic representation.[11] Rather than Ottomanizing the mahjar, the migrant clubs identified the empire's consulate as a site for renegotiating imperial policies and for protesting them when necessary.

Battle of the Consuls

The Ottoman Empire's July Revolution came to America by telegraph.[12] The message announcing the palace coup landed on the desks of the empire's chief diplomatic officers: Ambassador Mehmed 'Ali bey 'Abed at the empire's Legation in Washington, D.C. and Mundji Bey, charge d'affaires of New York and New England. The revolution cut the ties that once existed between the two men, tipping off a "battle of the consuls" that splashed across the headlines of the mahjar's Arabic press.[13] In New York City, Mundji Bey hastened to support the revolutionary CUP, breaking ranks with his superior officer in Washington, Ambassador 'Abed, a hardline Hamidian.[14] 'Abed was the son of Izzet Pasha, the sultan's second Chamberlain, who fled the empire in the chaos of the coup. Izzet Pasha narrowly escaped arrest in Geneva and then disappeared, setting off rumors that Ambassador 'Abed had smuggled his father to America, where the men hid $7.5 million in embezzled funds.[15] 'Abed responded to these rumors by locking down the D.C. Legation compound, refusing to speak with Istanbul, until the revolutionary government dismissed him three weeks later.

Istanbul sent Mundji Bey to Washington to temporarily replace 'Abed and take control of Ottoman affairs.[16] Arriving at the Legation in August 1908, he exchanged angry words with his deposed boss before meeting a press scrum outside. There was no attempt to save face; Mundji Bey told the press that 'Abed ignored several telegrams recalling him home. He argued 'Abed's termination was "the logical result of the downfall of the supporters of the old regime in Turkey" who were "the implacable enemies of the Young Turk Party." He also accused 'Abed of hiding his father, Izzet Pasha, in America: "maybe even in this legation here in Washington," he said, gesturing to the building behind him, "I do not know for sure; I suspect." An amused *Washington Post* reporter asked whether he had "caught a glimpse" of Izzet Pasha, perhaps by "looking under the beds (or) in the closets?" Mundji Bey smirked and concluded, "Gentlemen, I have ninety percent reason to believe" the disgraced Hamidian was hiding in America.[17]

Mundji Bey's public insults prompted 'Abed to excoriate the CUP, the July Revolution, and "that insurrectionist Mundji Bey" to the US Department of State and in the press. 'Abed received nothing but death threats in return.[18] He was assigned a police detail before departing for Europe, reportedly without paying the Legation's butcher, baker, or launderer.[19] Some reports claimed Mundji Bey was behind threats made on 'Abed's life. More likely the handwritten threats streaming in from Boston, New York, and Philadelphia came from overzealous Young Turks incited by the yellow press peddling descriptions of 'Abed as the corrupt hand-servant of a bloody autocrat.

'Abed's dismissal was part of a sweeping move to replace the empire's diplomats with CUP loyalists. Ottoman ambassadors from St. Petersburg, Berlin, Belgrade, and Sofia were all recalled and replaced with men the CUP believed would enhance the new government's standing abroad.[20] In Washington, Mundji Bey served as interim Ambassador until Hussein Kiazim Bey arrived to replace him.[21] He then returned to New York City to organize the Empire's expatriate communities and combat negative perceptions of the Ottomans. Mundji Bey targeted these goals through three programs: a 1908 general amnesty for political exiles, a public relations campaign to win US support for the Young Turks, and the establishment of pro-CUP migrant associations to generate a sense of obligation to the empire among Syrian migrants abroad.

The Ottoman Empire announced its amnesty for all Turkish, Syrian, and Armenian exiles accused of "political crimes" during the reign of Abdel Hamid II on July 31, 1908.[22] Mundji Bey saw the policy as a valuable opportunity to encourage migrant repatriation, especially of Armenians who had taken asylum in the United States following the violent pogroms in the 1890s. "Turkey is now as free as the United States," Mundji Bey explained in an interview with the *New York Times*, "the Constitution granted in my country . . . is like that of England and France. It grants amnesty to all her political refugees. Let those who work for the good of their country return. The Government needs them."[23] He identified 400,000 eligible Ottomans in the Americas—Syrians and Armenians, Turks and Albanians—who he hoped would consider returning.[24] In practice, the amnesty particularly targeted Armenians, but the city's Syrian papers applauded his assurances that "like the Syrians and the Kurds, the Armenians are among the Ottoman nationalities" and that they all had a place in a revitalized Ottoman Empire.[25]

A few Armenian leaders described having faith that "a very large number of them will take advantage of the opportunity to go home without fear of further persecution," but the mass repatriation of Armenians Mundji Bey hoped for never actually materialized.[26] That said, Mundji Bey's assurances that he would protect Armenians in his jurisdiction lent credence to other public statements that the CUP would "abolish the religious question" entirely and proclaim "hereafter the country will be ruled by her citizens. The Turk, the Armenian, the Greek, the Syrian, the Jew, the Kurd, the Circassian . . . there will be no more Turkey, but a regenerated Ottoman Empire."[27] Arab activists from Syria, Mount Lebanon, and Palestine took notice and saw the effort as proof they would also find room for themselves in Mundji Bey's project.

Mundji Bey's second goal was to gain American favor for Istanbul's new government, and he initiated a cautious public relations campaign that included correspondence with policymakers and cultural events showcasing the new Ottoman spirit in its migrant colonies. In a September 1908 letter to the *North American Review*, he underlined the role Ottoman migrants would play in revitalizing the empire. "Ottoman subjects," he began, "have been educated in the universities and colleges of this country. Some of them will, no doubt, become important factors in Ottoman politics, and they will always look back to the land where they took refuge and where they obtained their education."[28] He described his desire to repatriate Ottomans as a means of cultural diplomacy through borrowing:

> Thousands of Ottoman subjects who will return to their homes will carry with them American ideas and American ways of living. Will this not make a good bond between the two nations?[29]

The focus on American-educated migrants as vectors of enlightenment harkened back to the late nineteenth century. The idea that these migrants would serve as agents of sovereignty, however, was new. As representatives of their empire while abroad, emigrants who returned to the Ottoman Empire would usher in its "ent[rance] into the field of international politics" on equal footing with other European powers. In Mundji Bey's vision, second-generation Ottomans (those born or raised abroad) played a vital role. If they could be convinced to make the trip, "liberty-loving" Ottoman-American youth would join the "younger generation in Turkey" and "reformers in their fight for the final establishment of Ottoman freedom."[30]

It was in pursuit of possible repatriates that Mundji Bey announced his intention to found a network of Syrian patriotic associations across the Americas. The establishment of new Syrian clubs mirrored events within the empire: in Syria and Palestine, Syrian clubs sprang forth in alignment with CUP slogans.[31]

In France, a prominent Syrian CUP leader named Nakhle Mutran founded one such club in Paris, calling it the Syrian Ottoman Union Society (Jam'iyyat al-Ittihad al-Suri al-'Uthmani). Arriving via steam ship in August 1908, Mutran attended New York's Constitution Day festival with a public announcement: he was there to found a local chapter.

The Syrian Ottoman Union Society of New York

In New York, Nakhle Mutran discovered a Syrian colony that already boasted a vibrant associational life, with dozens of Syrian periodicals, ethnic clubs, and reading rooms serving the urban Syrian Quarter of Washington Street.[32] A Parisian guest of the Ottoman consulate, Mutran's role was to tap into mahjari political society through its clubs and print culture, harnessing its power for the CUP government at home. Requesting a meeting with the city's most prominent Syrian leaders, Mutran and Mundji Bey proposed a partnership between the Syrian clubs of New York and the Ottoman consulate. Under the umbrella of Mutran's organization, the Syrian Ottoman Union Society (hereafter SOUS), they would together enhance Syrian civil society.

Originally from Ba'albek, Nakhle Mutran was an outspoken critic of Sultan Abdel Hamid II after being forced to flee the empire in 1890, fearing assassination. After stints in Egypt and Latin America, he settled in Paris and joined the CUP there. Mutran's reputation as a Syrian liberal gave him credibility that Mundji Bey did not easily command among the Syrians in New York. The disgraced ambassador Mehmed Ali 'Abed, for instance, was a Syrian whose family was close to Mutran's; he fled the United States in fear for his life while some Syrian migrants vehemently opposed Mundji Bey, a Turk.[33] Mutran's involvement with Mundji Bey's outreach project convinced émigré leaders to hear the project out. Once they arrived at the consulate, Mutran explained that his loyalties were to the revolution and to an Ottomanism that eschewed ethnic and religious divisions. He set forth a plan for the formation of a network of Syrian associations with the support of the empire's diplomatic corps, which gifted him $20,000 in start-up funding.[34]

The SOUS was established in August 1908. Its executive board was made up primarily of printers and journalists, some of whom later became bitter rivals: Najib Diyab, Sa'id Shuqayr, As'ad Malki, As'ad al-Hamati, Na'um and Sallum Mukarzil, As'ad Melham, Nusri Bey Hatem, Ilyas Maqsud under the leadership of Najib al-Hani, Qaysar Sabbagh, and Najib Sawaya. Nakhle Mutran served as the society's president at large and as its point of contact with the Paris CUP. Chairman Mundji Bey provided a link to the Ottoman state.[35] As the CUP's institutional wing in the United States, the SOUS focused primarily on building its network, founding satellite chapters across Latin America and the Caribbean. By 1909, the organization also created a global Syrian press syndicate, powered primarily by Naʿum Mukarzil's *al-Huda* newspaper and its growing contacts with correspondents across the Americas and Europe, as well as Istanbul and Beirut.[36] Benefiting from the CUP's relaxation of press censorship laws, the organization went about promoting CUP goals in the mahjar. The press was "an engine for strengthening national unity," chairman Najib Sawaya recalled in *al-Kawn* newspaper, "and this is no less than the most important enlightened work that confronts us."[37] *al-Kawn* newspaper became the SOUS's unofficial organ, a bullhorn for writings by CUP officers around the mahjar and their partners at the empire's consulate.

That Syrian migrants in the Americas bore responsibilities toward their homeland was a dominant motif in the press after 1908, bolstered in part by the talkative newspapermen at the helm of *al-Kawn* and the SOUS. Syrians abroad had "experienced the benefits of personal freedom and liberty in America," argued Najib Sawaya, uniquely qualifying them to "bestow gifts of light upon their benighted fellow citizens" in Syria.[38] Sawaya was especially interested in reaching Syrian workers: "Despite that Syrians—wherever they may be—marry in the same manner, drink the same Syrian coffee, eat Syrian foods, work into the evening and are lord of their own house, the average Syrian worker [in Syria] values little in spaces like theaters or reading rooms."[39] They could not be found in spaces marked for Syria's intellectual elite; they could, however, be reached by repatriating Syrian American workers. Sawaya argued that returnee experience with American labor politics and civic democracy could be a boon for Syrians at home, "because, praise be to God, the Syrians these days have had their political capacities restored to them."[40] Inhabiting the shop floor alongside returning Syrian workers could help them fully realize these capacities. Sawaya left ambiguous exactly how this acculturation would occur. That Syrians would discover natural solidarities was simply assumed.

As patronizing as this rhetoric may have been, it resonated with Sawaya's emigrant readership; his editorials in *al-Kawn* drove some $275,000 in cash donations for Syria in 1908, aid that went toward medical relief and the construction of a national school for workers.[41] Fellow chairman Naʿum Mukarzil conducted similar campaigns aimed at Mount Lebanon, reporting his progress in his own paper, *al-Huda*, to a widening readership in Latin America. Mukarzil was an unmatched fundraiser in the Syrian community in New York, but he was also a controversial figure. His strident tone, Francophilism, and pro-clerical politics led him into conflict both within and beyond the city's Maronite community. In 1905, for instance, Mukarzil fired his colleague at *al-Huda* newspaper, Amin al-Rihani, for criticizing the Maronite Church in its pages.[42] Relatedly, Mukarzil engaged in public dispute with the city's Greek Orthodox bishop,

Raphael Hawaweeny, a fight that escalated into gunfire, reprisals, and assassination attempts made on both men's lives.[43] Mukarzil was instrumental in steering the SOUS toward legal advocacy for migrants, but his influence also produced the association's first dispute with the Ottoman government barely ten weeks after its establishment.

In October 1908, the government of Haiti passed new nativist legislation barring the entry of Syrian migrants through Port Au Prince, prompting Syrian advocates in the United States to protest.[44] Both Cuba and Haiti had established Syrian colonies, and Ottoman migrants settled in smaller numbers across the Caribbean. Because these communities lacked formal diplomatic representation, the Syrians of Haiti submitted a petition to New York's SOUS, asking the association to convince the Ottoman Consulate to confront Haiti about its discriminatory immigration laws.[45] Mukarzil broached the matter to Mundji Bey, reminding him that the protection of Ottoman travel rights was among the empire's duties to its extraterritorial subjects. Just weeks earlier, Mundji Bey had publicly endorsed the principle of free and unrestricted movement in encouraging mass repatriation to the Ottoman Empire. The Haiti petition, however, clearly challenged the consulate's position on protecting Syrian travelers: would Mundji Bey's mandate extend to Syrians seeking admittance into foreign lands or issuing challenges to foreign immigration laws?

The SOUS unanimously cosigned the petition from the Syrians of Haiti, presenting it to Mundji Bey and his superior in Washington, D.C., Ottoman Ambassador Hussein Kiazim Bey. Mundji Bey initially supported issuing a letter of protest to Port Au Prince, but as he attempted to hash out specific policy recommendations with the SOUS, he became uneasy about the prospect of confrontation.[46] One demand struck Mundji Bey as contradicting CUP goals: the demand that Haiti not only lift the ban on Syrian immigration, but that it also allow Syrians access to Haitian citizenship.[47] Clearly, Mundji Bey could not cosign this demand; not only was renouncement of Ottoman nationality illegal, but his consulate's mandate was to draw Ottoman migrants back into the empire, not assist them in severing ties with Istanbul.[48] Was the Syrian Ottoman Union Society an institution devoted to Ottomanizing Syrian migrants abroad, or was it a migrant advocacy network? It could no longer be both.

Immigration laws turned into an enduring issue, convincing Mundji Bey and the CUP that there were irreconcilable differences between the government and its diasporic partners. This suspicion was confirmed when the Union took up the issue of immigrant rights in US law; specifically, in advocating for Syrian rights to petition for US citizenship. Na'um and Sallum Mukarzil were then working with Syrian American lawyers through a series of court cases involving Syrian immigrants denied naturalization rights on the basis of racial prerequisites. In October 1908, the Mukarzils brought the matter before the SOUS, and the body voted to offer free legal advocacy to Syrian Americans seeking legal naturalization. The cases brought the union into the courtroom and culminated with *Dow v. United States* (1915), in which a US appellate court ruled that Syrians could obtain US citizenship on the basis that they were free white persons.[49]

The Dow ruling was a landmark win for migrant advocates, but it was also only one of dozens of cases that the Mukarzils, their legal team (organized ad hoc as the Syrian American Association), and the SOUS sponsored between 1908 and 1915.[50] The union's decision to invest resources in legal advocacy had an immediate chilling effect on its relationship with the Ottoman consulate. Mundji Bey's official views were not captured in the press, but it was in late 1908 that the Syrian Ottoman Union Society separated from the consulate and changed its name to the United Syria Society (Jam'iyyat al-Ittihad al-Suri).[51] In six months' time, Mundji Bey resigned his post in New York and requested reassignment. He was sent to London, where he remained until the start of the First World War.[52]

Though Mundji Bey's support for the SOUS had not gone as planned, the CUP government in Istanbul remained steadfast in its determination to make migrant diplomacy a priority. Between 1908 and 1912, the Ottoman Empire expanded its consular networks into new cities hosting Syrian communities, helping to normalize political relationships between the state and Ottoman subjects abroad and encourage economic development and remittance-based commerce within each migrant colony. In 1910, Istanbul completed construction of a new consulate in Buenos Aires, staffing it with consul general Emir Amin Arslan and local Syrian-Argentinian officials Wadi' and Alejandro Schámun.[53] Like Mundji Bey in New York, Amin Arslan depended on the press as his entry point into the Syrian colonies of Argentina. The Schámuns were journalists; Arslan granted their newspaper, *Assalam,* a government subsidy, and in return it functioned as an official voice for the Empire's South American diplomatic corps.[54]

The CUP's choice to send the Arslan to Argentina was strategic. From a Druze notable family in Shwayfat, Arslan began his career in Ottoman public service at the Syrian port of Latakiyya and entered diplomacy in the 1890s when he asked the empire's General Consul Ruhi al-Khalidi to be sent to Belgium, partly out of concern that his outspoken Ottomanist views would clash with Sultan Abdel Hamid II.[55] Having established himself in socialist circles, Arslan was reassigned to Argentina to establish a political dialogue with the Argentinian Republic in the name of economic development.[56] Arslan's mission, therefore, was to standardize Ottoman-Argentinian relations with the goal of plugging his government into Argentina's booming industrial agriculture through Syrian guest work programs.[57] Arslan also wished to ease trans-Atlantic shipping to the Ottoman Empire and to facilitate cross-mahjar trade favoring Syrian garment-making, textile, and cotton industries and the Syrian banks that bolstered them.

In addition to representing a Syrian migrant constituency that then numbered 100,000 and liaising with Istanbul, Arslan focused on regulating the migration of Syrian workers.[58] He embraced temporary Arab labor migration as a mutual economic benefit that would enrich Syria and Mount Lebanon, and he pursued bilateral migration management schemes with the Argentinian government.[59] In a moment of mounting nativism, he hoped to undermine racist stereotypes about venal "turco" peddlers living at the edges of urban society by instead channeling Arab workers into more respectable trades.[60]

Of course, nativists who argued that itinerant commerce contributed marginally to Argentina's economy ignored that peddling was itself big business. In Buenos Aires, Syrian small-scale commerce accounted for an impressive 65.7 million pesos annually in 1907, according to Alejandro Schámun.[61] But with thousands of new Syrian migrants arriving annually by 1910, Arslan's consulate pushed Arab labor into the agricultural sector through a system of guest work passes, subsidies, and partnerships with local employers.[62] The program failed, though, because Arslan made a significant miscalculation: Syrians had no interest in working the fields as landless tenants. For many of them, coming to the mahjar was about making one's fortune: they had left cousins, daughters, and wives engaged in industrial wage labor, which funded their ventures abroad but introduced significant pressure to quickly succeed.[63] Unhappy with the prospects of farm work, most Syrian men took their chances on new businesses, ranging from peddling and sales to groceries, boarding houses, haberdasheries, or other services within the Syrian colony. *Assalam* lamented in 1917 that farm work never attracted more than 11.4 percent of Argentina's Syrian population.[64] Easy access to credit in the city's Syrian lending houses further undermined Arslan's plans. Defeated, the consul settled for building relationships with European diplomats in Buenos Aires.[65] His rapport with foreign statesmen—especially French ones—distinguished him as a unique asset to the CUP in 1910. Four short years later, these same ties transformed him into an object of official suspicion.[66]

Another contact that Amin Arslan cultivated was Na'imi Jafet, whose family had by then permanently settled in Brazil. Jafet relied on sponsorship programs through the Ottoman consulates in Rio de Janeiro and Buenos Aires to draw skilled workers from the textile factories of Syria. In the meantime, together with his brothers, Antunius and Basilius, Na'imi Jafet gave generously to the Syrian charities across Latin America, making a name for himself as a public man in the meantime. Jafet also engaged the Syrians of São Paulo politically; an ardent Ottomanist, he wrote in the press and supported causes be believed would bring the Young Turks' vision of an engaged, cultured, and politically educated citizenry to the mahjar. Beginning in 1909, Jafet opened his São Paulo storehouse to host the festivities associated with Ottoman Constitution Day, including parades and speeches commemorating Ottomanist virtues. Syrian factories, cafés, and shops closed city-wide, and food vendors set up stalls along the Rua 25 de Marzo to feed society folk, misbehaving children, and Brazilian onlookers in the thousands.[67]

Like its counterparts in New York City and Buenos Aires, the São Paulo Constitution Day festival commemorated Ottoman history, extolled constitutional progress, and invoked the duties of extraterritorial citizenship. The festivals were celebratory, but they were not devoid of critique, particularly as the Empire stumbled into successive wars in Libya and the Balkans after 1911. Men like Naʿimi Jafet saw those crises as unwise or even self-imposed. As the CUP widened conscription powers and levied men from wider segments of Syrian and Mount Lebanese society, a ticket to "Amrika" and a job offer from the Jafet factory turned into a powerful way out. A self-described Ottoman patriot but a critic of the Balkan wars, Jafet continued offering contracts to Syrian men of military age, an act of civil disobedience that his elite status allowed him. Nevertheless, these tensions inflected the Constitution Day festival in São Paulo, because they turned into spaces where speakers openly questioned whether Istanbul was capable of delivering on the principles enshrined in the empire's charter.

So as Ottoman flags adorned the Syrian quarter in July 1912, Naʿimi Jafet took the platform to deliver a convocation laden with ambivalence about the liberal Ottomanist dream, mirroring a larger tonal shift in the Syrian mahjar and its press. Honoring tradition, Jafet narrated the history of the Ottoman constitution, a conflict between a Ottoman patriotism (*Otomanidade* in Portuguese, *Osmanlılık* in Ottoman Turkish) and Abdel Hamid II's absolutism that had yielded a worthy revolution. But four years into the Young Turk moment, Jafet raised serious doubts about whether the Revolution was succeeding. He believed, for instance, that the Young Turks could only save the Empire from disintegration and foreign interference through the maintenance of a flexible, polyglot, and secular (or at least a multiconfessional) vision of Ottoman citizenship. The Ottomanists of 1876 had perfected this philosophy, according to Jafet, but their descendants in the CUP depended too much on the solidarities of sect and race:

> Now, these nations [defined as Ottoman *millets*], diverse in religion, separated by language and yet lacking in patriotic sentiment; can these nations in four years, or any infinite number of years, reach harmony and create a union like those of the British, French, or the world's other advanced peoples? Is it possible for any nation or people to reconcile, to live in concordance with peoples completely distinct and divergent in language, religions, race, and traditions? Everything is possible under

the sun, because these divisions were caused by governments past. With the elimination of those causes for social disintegration comes the cessation of disunity. But now I ask you all: has this Constitution actually set down conditions that will make the divisions of the past disappear?[68]

Jafet identified common grievances that fed Syrian public discourse in 1912: the underrepresentation of Syrian Arabs in imperial administration, checks against Mount Lebanon's administrative autonomy, concerns about Syrian conscription into the army, and war in the Balkans.

But foremost among Jafet's concerns were the new restrictions imposed on constitutional liberties to free expression, association, and political activity in Syria. By 1912, the Ottoman government had eroded these liberties considerably and, with them, the support of Syrian liberals. Jafet described constitutional rule as an imminently fragile thing, demanding vigilance from citizens and the nurturance of a patriotism that could overcome pervasive ethnic, religious, and political divisions:

> The Constitution guarantees the unity and life of the nation. We struggle, then, for its conservation, to ensure a straight and true path for ourselves; a life of ease; a life of hope. The thick clouds we see forming in the Ottoman sky are made up of ignorance, remnants of the ancient regime of subsistence and submission. Let us disarticulate these clouds with breaths of knowledge and harmony.[69]

Even as Jafet warned his company about the dangers of division that threatened the constitutionalist idea, his criticism remained a thoroughly Ottomanist one. His message was reformist, not revolutionary, and he addressed the Syrians of São Paulo as an Ottoman community, with Ottoman origins and continuing political obligations to Istanbul.

In 1912, no one in the mahjar envisioned a Syrian future outside the framework of the Ottoman Empire. Although the politics of Arabism, decentralism, and reformist criticism of the CUP were mainstream among Syrian migrants, there is little evidence to support assertions about Arab separatism in this diaspora before the First World War.[70] Na'imi Jafet's 1912 address closed with a vision of an Ottoman Empire not on the brink of destruction, but on the cusp of renaissance: "Ottomans! Know that our love of country should be the pavilion under which we will gather and unite. Join me here, join me in patriotism, in Ottomanism (*otomanidade*); let us shout together: long live the Constitution! Long live the Ottoman nation (*viva a pátria otomana*)!"[71] July 24 continued to be Ottoman Constitution Day in São Paulo through the

First World War, after the Empire's demise, and into the early 1920s during Syria's occupation by France. The festival's meanings transformed into a day of nostalgia, national mourning, and finally into a day of demands for Syrian independence. Na'imi Jafet could not have dreamed it, but on July 24, 1914 São Paulo's *al-Fara'id* newspaper would sum up the day's celebrations saying, "today it is Constitution Day signifying liberty and brotherhood, but soon it will be Independence Day, celebrating autoemancipation ['id al-istiqlal, 'id al-in'itaq]."[72] Although the seeds were there for a Syrian mahjari opposition to Istanbul before 1914, that opposition turned on the logic that the CUP failed to live up to the spirit of 1908, particularly by curtailing the liberties of two institutions that brought the revolution to the mahjar: political associations and the press.

Laws of Association

The CUP's turn toward imperial unionism and away from Arab autonomy in Syria and Mount Lebanon after 1909 alienated Syrian liberals at home and abroad. Although the CUP "placed emphasis on individual rights and local autonomy" to unite disparate political groups in 1908, these ideas quickly "took a backseat to developmental issues and to the Young Turks' brand of cultural assimilationist plans and centralizing goals." The postrevolutionary Ottoman government envisioned the "state's role as the main instrument of change" and was pointedly illiberal in terms of means and methods.[73] Censorship laws abolished in 1908 were quickly reimposed, and in 1909, the CUP announced a new Law of Association that forbade the creation of societies touting specific ethnic identities. The law targeted Arabist and Armenian political activities in the empire, groups the CUP argued contradicted the state's goals. As they watched the spaces for political activism within the empire shrink, Syrian activists in the mahjar argued that the association law reneged on the core objective of the revolution: the construction of a universal Ottomanism large enough to allow full Arab participation and autonomy.

Other CUP policies threatened the administrative privileges of the mutasarrifate of Mount Lebanon, frustrating activists in Beirut as well as in the mahjar.[74] And the new conscription laws imposed on the Arab provinces raised complaints of opportunism or, more stridently, of "Turkification."[75] Taken collectively, these policies reveal a consistent logic of imperial centralization and the expansion of state powers, a logic that animated Mundji Bey's outreach to the diaspora. But for Syrian activists at home and abroad, this top-down centralism contradicted their liberal reading of the constitution's promises. The Arab decentralist movement emerged to oppose these unionist policies.

Organizing across Cairo, Beirut, and Damascus between 1909 and 1911, the decentralist movement came to the Syrian mahjar along the same networks the CUP had helped activate. Syrian elites established a full spectrum of associations critiquing unionist politics, including the Alliance Libanaise (Hizb al-Ittihad al-Lubnani) in 1909, the Ottoman Decentralization Party (Hizb al-Lamarkaziyya) in 1911, the Beirut Reform Society, the Literary Society, al-Fatat, and others.[76] Whether in Cairo, Beirut, or the American mahjar, the men who founded these parties were mutually disenchanted by the CUP's embrace of illiberal centralism. Each association established satellite chapters in the Americas, competing with one another in concert with the political fortunes of Ottoman factions at home.[77] This was a moment of extraordinary associational fecundity; it was also one of extraordinary turbulence.

In the wake of the consular controversies and whiteness cases of Syrian New York, the SOUS divested itself of its connection to Ottoman officialdom. Soon the club itself split in two: the United Syria Society (Jam'iyyat al-Ittihad al-Suri, also called the Syrian Union Society, the Syrian American Association, and the Syrian American Club in English), founded in 1908–1909, and the Lebanon League of Progress (Jam'iyyat al-Nahda al-Lubnaniyya but also known as the Mount Lebanon Club in English), emerging in 1911. Both clubs shared members and broadly endorsed the reformist outlook of Cairo's Ottoman Decentralization Party and, to a lesser extent, the Alliance Libanaise. These associations were not nationalist political parties; insofar as they subscribed to political ideologies, they differed from one another only in degrees.

Na'um Mukarzil's Lebanon League of Progress (hereafter LLP) began as an affiliate of the Alliance Libanaise in Cairo under Iskandar 'Ammun, but the New York club was also closely tied to Farid al-Khazin's Beirut Reform Society.[78] Mukarzil's newspaper, al-Huda, became its official organ in 1911.[79] The LLP's purpose was to lobby for the retention of Mount Lebanon's adminis-trative privileges in relation to the Ottoman government, as legislated by 1861's Règlement Organique.[80] The group's executive board was made up largely of journalists, men who traveled through Cairo and developed connections with Syrian publications there. What distinguished Mukarzil from his Egyptian collaborators, however, was his willingness to lobby foreign powers—especially France—to create leverage in negotiations with Istanbul.[81] This was one major reason the Ottoman government indicted him for treason in 1916.[82]

Though headquartered in New York City, the LLP operated in several places at once. Mukarzil depended on his professional contacts as a publisher to estab-lish chapters across four continents. In São Paulo, for instance, Shukri al-Khuri reprinted Mukarzil's editorials in his paper, Abu al-Hawl, and founded a Brazilian Lebanon League of Progress in 1912.[83] By 1914, al-Khuri and Mukarzil together founded twenty-nine active chapters across the United States, Canada, Mexico,

Cuba, Colombia, Brazil, Argentina, and Costa Rica.[84] Beyond the American mahjar, the LLP also had permanent representatives in Paris and Istanbul. *al-Huda*'s Istanbul correspondent, Ibrahim al-Najjar, spent most of his time between 1911 and 1913 on steamships shuttling between these cities, speaking with prominent Ottoman figures such as Yusuf Franco Pasha (*mutasarrif* of Beirut), Syrian émigré leaders such as Shukri Ghanim and Khairallah Khairallah, and French diplomats Raymond Poincarré and Jean Gout.[85] In 1912, al-Najjar founded a Paris chapter, providing the organization with a local presence when the First Arab Congress came to the city the following year.[86]

The First Arab Congress convened in Paris in June 1913, bringing together Arab reformers from Beirut and Damascus with migrant activists from Cairo and the Americas. *al-Fatat* and the Ottoman Decentralization Party hosted the three-day event, and delegates from the Beirut Reform Society, the United Syria Society, the Alliance Libanaise, and the Lebanon League of Progress all attended.[87] An Ottoman delegate also attended as empire's representative, recording the congress requests.[88] Several of the delegates had extensive ties to Syrian clubs abroad, but three men represented the mahjar formally: Najib Diyab (editor of New York's *Mirat al-Gharb*), Na'um Mukarzil (editor of *al-Huda*), and 'Abbas Bijani, a local member of Paris's *al-Fatat* who spoke on behalf of Syrians in Mexico.[89]

The congress's recorded proceedings underscore two significant themes. First, the emigrant delegates saw the mahjar's political fate as intrinsically tied to that of Ottoman Syria. Second, they described the United States as a cognate for Syria's situation, proposing a developmentalist vision for reforming Syria

Figure 2.1. Jam'iyyat al-Nahda al-Lubnaniyya delegates among others at the First Arab Congress in Paris in June 1913. Seated in the first row, from the right: Iskandar Bey 'Ammun; Na'um Mukarzil; Shukri Ghanim. Second row: Sallum Mukarzil (far right); Émile Eddé (fifth); Jamil Mardam Bey (sixth). Mukarzil, *al-Kitab al-Lubnani*, 12.

using America as a model. In his speech, for instance, Najib Diyab described the political liberties enjoyed by Syrian migrants in America, arguing that if they repatriated to Syria, they would bring the gifts of democracy, federalism, and constitutionalism with them:

> Syrian emigrants' most earnest hopes (for Syria) are the same as those of their brothers left behind [*ikhwanihum al-mutakhallifin*]. This is our moment as it is yours, as some of those emigrants—oh sons of Syria— fled their fled country clandestinely, escaping from tyranny.[90]

Diyab described the malady Syrians were facing as *ghurba*, the alienation felt by migrants in a strange land but which he argued also defined Syria's experience of a changing Ottoman regime that no longer reflected Arab political desires. Sharing a common sense of alienation, Syrians at home and abroad could together restore the Ottomanist vision of a civics-minded citizenship.

Selective repatriation to Syria was a crucial part of Diyab's plan. He argued before the congress that Syrian repatriates would play a role in the reforming Ottoman Syria:

> The emigrants have received the benefits of popular constitutional governments and the protection of individual rights. They have comprehended the meaning of civilization in Europe, in America, and they have seen with their own eyes the protection of personal rights. They can put these principles to the test in their dear homeland, arriving to where their forefathers' blood was spilled to enlighten the ignorant and engage their Arab Ottoman brothers in an intellectual revolution where the forces of ignorance and tyranny had once defeated them. . . .[91]

Diyab's references to the darkness of tyranny, intellectual revolution (*thawra fikriyya*), and the goal of enlightenment situates his speech firmly within the wellspring of the nahda.[92] But the link he drew between Syria and its emigrants, the obligations they had toward "brothers left behind," and the conclusion that repatriation would revitalize the homeland are all ideas that emerged in the Syrian colonies after 1908 and with the promises of Ottoman officials like Mundji Bey.

Najib Diyab and Na'um Mukarzil, it should be mentioned, absolutely detested one another. But even as rival printers with radically different visions of what an "awakened" Syria would look like, they popularized the idea that returning emigrants represented a force for enlightenment. Borrowing from the Americanization rhetoric then popular among social workers and exceptionalist ideas about the United States as beacon for the world, Diyab folded them into Arabist notions about renewal, reform, and exiles' sense of obligation.[93] Returnees became humanist missionaries, bringing their love of American constitutionalism and governmental know-how to develop the homeland, a new frontier. This potent complex of ideas recurs in pro-Entente propaganda written by Syrians after 1914.

Though the men congregated in Paris in 1913 had strong opinions about the need for intellectual revolution, none of them expressed separatist ideologies or nationalist objectives. Rather, attendees framed their appeals as reforms necessary to restore the Ottoman Empire's legitimacy in the Arab world, returning the polity from the brink of foreign intervention. Syrian activists wished to "remain in the Ottoman bosom by preserving its patriotism, a necessary precondition for protecting the rights of our brothers left behind," in Diyab's words.[94] The Congress resolved that "real reforms are necessary and obligatory to the Ottoman sultanate and must be swiftly undertaken."[95] Arab political disenchantment lay not in any nationalist pretentions, but in the "extreme centralization" being implemented by the CUP.[96]

Upon its adjournment, the Arab Congress sent Charles Debbas, Shukri Ghanim, ʿAbd al-Hamid al-Zahrawi, and Iskandar ʿAmmun to the Ottoman embassy in Paris to deliver the meeting's resolutions: Arabs must be guaranteed their political rights to participate in Ottoman administration at the local and imperial levels; the Arab provinces must be given a provincial authority and assured a degree of decentralized autonomy; and these reforms must be carried out swiftly.[97] The same week, another delegation met with French Foreign Minister Stephen Pichon, who assured them of France's "deep friendship with both the Ottoman state and with the Syrian people."[98]

The outbreak of war in Europe the following year, however, sharply stalled discussions with Syrian reformers. Instead, the Ottoman government considered the costs and benefits of a new alliance with Germany. Facing a scenario where armed neutrality proved an increasingly untenable position, Istanbul embraced a strategic alliance with Berlin, unilaterally abrogated its treaties with the British, French, and Russians, and entered the war in October 1914.[99] The sudden shift in the geopolitical winds mooted the Arab Congress's demands; not only were they built on treaties abrogated by Istanbul, but also the Unionist triumvirate in power increasingly saw Arabism as a political threat because of its ties to foreign powers. Ottoman general governor Cemal Pasha came to Syria in early 1915, and he saw Syria as "a semi-colonized part of the Empire that had to be cleansed of foreign influence and reintegrated into the body of the Ottoman state."[100] Cemal Pasha administered Syria to bend it toward provisioning for total war, applying an emergency law that expanded his executive authority. Crop requisitions; universal conscription; and closure of presses, schools, and civilian hospitals defined the Syrian experience of this war.[101] A locust plague in 1915 and an subsequent famine deepened this desperate experience, as did Cemal Pasha's campaign of repression against Syria's Arabist movement.[102] Activists who once formed the Ottoman reform movement found themselves targeted by government scrutiny, accusations of disloyalty, and charges of collusion.

A Mahjar at War

The empire's descent into war sent shockwaves into the mahjar. Cemal Pasha's hawkish policies fundamentally changed the relationship Syrian migrants had with the Ottoman Empire. The Entente imposed a naval blockade on the eastern Mediterranean, ending all passenger traffic and cutting the flow of new migration to the Americas.[103] Meanwhile, Ottoman censors closely examined the mail, adding to the anxieties emigrants felt when unable to reach their relatives.[104] Cemal Pasha also censored Syrian periodicals imported from abroad before banning them completely in 1916.[105] Syria's newspaper industry sputtered in an environment defined by press closures and extra-judicial harassment of journalists. Neither the fire that burned down *al-Nasir*'s printing house nor the beating of *al-Barq*'s editor in Beirut in 1915 were formally investigated.[106] Ottoman diplomats returning from Europe and their French counterparts leaving Beirut were the last civilians to legally cross enemy lines. Shortly after the French vacated their Beirut Consulate, Ottoman gendarmeries broke into the building and seized the documents housed inside. Cemal Pasha used them to charge dozens of Syrian reformers with treason.[107]

Despite the blockade, a trickle of Syrians still managed to emigrate, typically by way of Egypt, where they would either join the local Syrian community or depart for the Americas. Other travelers found themselves marooned in the mahjar as exiles, as tourists, or even as honeymooners. One Homsi printer found himself in precisely this circumstance with his new bride in 1914. Jurj Atlas and Salwa Salama Atlas ran a printing house in Homs with Salwa's brothers. They married in 1913 and traveled to Latin America in summer 1914 on honeymoon. When the war began and Allied ships blockaded Ottoman ports, Jurj and Salwa Atlas were stranded across the Atlantic. They resettled in São Paulo, where they opened a school for Syrian girls, established *al-Karma* newspaper, and participated in homeland relief efforts with Brazil's large Homsi community.[108] In 1915, Jurj Atlas founded *Homs al-Fatat*, an Arab nationalist club devoted to opposing Cemal Pasha's government from abroad.

Unlike the Arabist societies in the Middle East, some Syrian émigré activists promoted independence from the Ottoman Empire as early as 1914.[109] By the summer of 1916 these voices were a chorus endorsing armed resistance to the Unionists and, if necessary, collaboration with the Entente Powers. Cemal

Pasha's efforts to cut the ties that existed between Syria and its mahjar inspired this resentment, which deepened with his prosecution of the Arabist movement, the hangings of martyrs' square, and Syria's descent into humanitarian crisis.

The first Syrian migrant society to declare revolt against the Ottoman state was the São Paulo chapter of the LLP. In September 1914, Shukri al-Khuri produced a circular on his press at *Abu al-Hawl*. Alongside a call for open re-bellion against Istanbul, the broadside featured an image of al-Khuri and the São Paulo LLP's executive committee standing with the standard of Mount Lebanon's subgovernorate: a white flag bearing a green cedar. They urged Lebanese migrants across the mahjar to join them in supporting the Entente to overthrow the "Turkish yoke" (nir al-atrak). "Only with their victory," argued al-Khuri, "will we see the betterment of our homeland."[110]

Shukri al-Khuri's call to arms came weeks before the Ottomans went to war and two years before any other migrant club would make similar proclamations. It also contradicted the politics of the LLP's own central committee; in New York City, Mukarzil reiterated his relationship with the Alliance Libanaise, a group that was critical of the Ottoman state's centralist policy but still committed to reform, not revolt.[111]

The São Paulo pamphlet is remarkable for representing the perspective of what was then a separatist fringe. But it nevertheless demonstrates that a new hard line was emerging, and the CUP's alliance with Berlin and subse-quent entry into the war compounded the appeal of separatist ideas among Syrian migrants. In the meantime, the CUP sharply disengaged with emigrants abroad, reversing previous policies toward the mahjar and recalling the empire's diplomats across the neutral American powers. Beginning in 1914, Istanbul's stance toward the Syrian mahjar was suspicion bordering on hostility. In Buenos Aires, Ottoman consul Amin Arslan received instructions to send spies into the colony to learn more about Arabist activities in the region. If Arslan's statements to the American consul to Argentina are to be believed, his opposition to such measures led Talaat Pasha to treat his office as a threat, setting the stage for his standoff with Istanbul in April 1915.[112]

Like many Syrians in Buenos Aires, Amin Arslan saw the new war as a European affair, a tragic but entirely self-imposed conflict and the natural cre-scendo after a century of European imperialism. He saw no reason for his own empire to enter the fray, and he vocally opposed Istanbul's military alliance with Berlin, a choice that reduced his empire to unwilling puppets serving the "in-solent pretentions of a foreign monarchic regime."[113] Because the Unionists had subsumed themselves to foreign tutelage, Arslan believed, they abnegated their right to rule Syria and to serve its diasporic constituencies. In an Argentina where racist rhetoric against German immigrants became the new normal, the press gleefully reprinted Arslan's speeches describing the Germans as "Teutons,

Figure 2.2. Executive Committee of the Lebanon League of Progress in São Paulo, Brazil, 1914. From bottom right: Mansur al-Khuri; Shukri al-Bakhash (who later served in the U.S. Army as a propagandist and recruiter), Wadiʿ ʿAbboud; Yusif Latif; Antun Jabbara; Habib Khitar; Asʿad Bitar; Daud al-Khuri; ʿAbduh Furnis al-Mathini. Second row, from left: Wadiʿ Abu Samra; Naʿum Mina Farhat; Ghattas al-Tayar; Salim ʿAql; Ayyub al-Khuri. In the window: Shukri al-Khuri. Shukri al-Khuri, "Lubnan wa-l-Harb al-Haliyya," *al-Nahda al-Lubnaniyya* Pamphlet, 29 September 1914, 1.

a historically unlettered people" who used this war to flirt with their own "un-civilized ambitions."[114] Such undiplomatic language contributed to Talaat Pasha's decision to fire Arslan in 1915, but his firing ignited widespread resent-ment among the Syrians migrants, who rallied to Arslan, held vigils outside the empire's shuttered consulate, and marched with the deposed consul in numbers approaching one thousand.[115]

Confrontations like this convinced the Unionists that the Syrian mahjar was not the friendly frontier that Ottoman liberals had believed it was. The Buenos Aires consulate remained closed for the war's duration, and the Ottoman Empire also recalled its diplomats from Brazil and the United States by 1917. In neutral countries like Argentina, the German consulates handled Ottoman diplomatic affairs. In the United States, which became a belligerent in 1917, Istanbul left its diplomatic affairs in the hands of the neutral Spanish consulate, giving them instructions to neither process repatriation claims by Ottoman migrants nor allow Entente powers to naturalize or conscript them.[116]

Ignoring demands that he return to Istanbul, the deposed emir of Buenos Aires opened legal proceedings against the Ottoman Empire to tie the archives of his diplomatic office up in probate.[117] Arslan's claim that delivering the records to Ottoman hands would result in political prosecutions convinced the Argentinian government, especially after news broke that Cemal Pasha had hanged men named in documents seized from Beirut's French consulate.[118] Arslan's insolence also threatened his own legal standing, so the French granted him diplomatic protection. After 1915, Arslan collaborated with the Syrian Union (Jam'iyyat al-Ittihad al-Suri) of Buenos Aires, an organization founded that year by Dr. Khalil Sa'adih. Together, they recruited Syrian migrants for pro-Entente military service.[119] Because the Germans requisitioned his Arabic printing press, Arslan also founded a Spanish language serial called *La Nota*.[120]

The martyrs' square hangings in Beirut and Damascus were designed to shock Syrians into political quiescence, but these acts instead offended international observers and angered Syrians abroad. Cemal Pasha published his justification for the hangings in 1916, arguing that the condemned men had planned a revolt, conspired with the French, and developed powerful funding ties to the mahjar.[121] That the hanged were actually Ottomanist reformers working with associations with recent ties to the CUP is a tragic irony. By shredding the remaining loyalties that many Syrians felt toward the Ottomans, the hangings precipitated the very mahjari revolt that Cemal Pasha was trying to stop.[122] By sending the Arabist movement into the mahjar, furthermore, the Ottoman state rendered itself incapable of policing it. Ottoman press censorship effected the same change: Cemal Pasha successfully repressed Syrian newspapers at home, but mahjari periodicals published strident condemnations of his government, promoted revolt, and collaborated with foreign powers with impunity.

Syrian migrants resisted in many ways. Arab migrants in the Americas participated in vast humanitarian relief efforts alongside agencies such as the American Red Cross and the Near East Committee for Armenian and Syrian Relief, but this relief work also constituted part of a wider spectrum of resistance activities.[123] The Syrian committees made little distinction between humanitarian work and overtly political acts like translation of pro-Entente propaganda, recruiting for the Army, and petitioning for foreign military intervention. From their perspective, all served the goals of Syrian liberation.

Still in São Paulo, Jurj and Salwa Atlas invested themselves in fundraising for the American Red Cross, focusing particularly on medical aid and cash donations to provide food to the hungry in western Syria and Mount Lebanon. As elsewhere in the Americas, philanthropic endeavors were central to Syrian social life, and war relief expanded the institutional infrastructure connecting

migrant communities to one another. Atlas's group, *Homs al-Fatat*, collected relief to be sent to Homs, working together with ʿAbd al-Massih Haddad (editor
of *al-Saʾih*) and the United Syria Society of New York City; the Syrian Youth
Relief Committee in Buenos Aires; and several clubs in Chile, Mexico, and elsewhere in Latin America.[124] When Atlas learned that his friend and former parliamentarian ʿAbd al-Hamid al-Zahrawi was hanged in Damascus, he declared
his own rebellion against Istanbul. *Homs al-Fatat* raised funds for Syrian groups
collaborating with Emir Faysal's Arab Revolt. In addition to their cultural publication, *al-Karma*, Atlas founded a new serial called *al-Zahrawi*. Named for the
slain parliamentarian and printing Hashemite propaganda, *al-Zahrawi* carried
the tagline "Independence or Death."[125]

As the war progressed, the pages of the Syrian mahjari press grew crowded
with reports of starvation, epidemic, and political repression; calls for rebellion
led by former Ottoman officials; and heated exchanges between competing
cells of activists calling one another traitors. The cacophony of voices calling
for revolt against Istanbul or, conversely, demanding pro-Ottoman loyalty
made navigating the mahjar's geopolitics very difficult. Everyone demanded
loyalty of Syrian migrants: host societies (particularly the United States as it
entered the war in 1917), nationalist parties, the Ottoman state and its consular surrogates, and the pro-CUP loyalists who seemed to comprise a silent
majority.

Because Syrians found themselves subject to heightened political scru-
tiny by their host states, Ottoman loyalists avoided the public sphere
out of self-preservation. In the United States, for instance, the Bureau of
Investigation worked tirelessly to root out "pro-German" sympathies among
Ottoman immigrants, and they translated the Arabic periodicals regularly.
Consequently, it is in the archives of the US Justice Department that pro-
Ottoman migrants appear, within the context of criminal investigations linked
to smuggling, draft evasion, and acts of political violence. What these records
show is that new divisions appeared within Syrian migrant communities
over questions of loyalty, thus progressively making the diaspora a more
dangerous place.

The Syrian colonies of the Americas were historically blended; migrants
from towns, villages, mountains, and plains from all sects on the sifting principle of shared origins and language. Coming from distinct traditions (religious
and political) and from a variety of class backgrounds, Syrians crowded into the
urban tenements of places such as Washington Street in New York City or São
Paulo's Rua 25 de Marzo that were beset by the crimes that accompany urban
crowding.[126] But the additional passions of the war, the humanitarian crisis, and
the emergence of nationalist societies produced a new type of violence: politically motivated shootings, stabbings, assassination attempts, and mob affairs set

off by charges of betrayal. These confrontations could combust into street brawls involving hundreds at a moment's notice.

In Santiago, Chile, two merchants known for their outspoken criticism of the Ottoman Empire found their shops targeted by an angry mob in early 1916. Both men were dragged from their counters and beaten, and their storefronts destroyed by a group of thirty Syrians from the neighborhood, presumably Ottoman loyalists. A bystander named Ibrahim Bulus retrieved his pistol and shot into the crowd, tipping off a gunfight that he did not survive. Another merchant named Ilyas Qara'uni was badly beaten but survived the ordeal. Qara'uni told Chile's *al-Murshid* newspaper that, once recovered, he would leave Chile forever to join his family in Mexico.[127] A week later, a second mob converged on another Syrian storefront, leaving the owners badly beaten; *al-Murshid* questioned whether Chilean authorities were doing anything to protect the rights of Syrian immigrants from such brutality.[128]

The Syrian communities in Argentina also witnessed a spate of murders that set the community on edge. In one particularly grim example, a peddler named Zakariyya Zoghby disappeared in Buenos Aires in March 1916. His body was discovered in town a month later, stripped naked, stabbed, and showing signs of torture and posthumous mutilation. The discovery set off rumors among Syrians in that city that Zoghby was the victim of Ottoman spies working to root out Arabist sympathizers.[129]

Violence against merchants or activists who supported one or another Syrian political party was common. Sometimes the perpetrator was an Ottoman loyalist; sometimes it was the work of a competing group of activists. Syrians who engaged in relief work were particularly at risk as targets. The passions around humanitarian work also ensured that any violence directed at relief workers could potentially escalate into riots. In the United States, relief organizations such as the American Committee for Armenian and Syrian Relief, the American Red Cross, and the Turkish Red Crescent partnered with Syrian American activists to publicize their efforts in mahjari religious institutions, reading rooms, and ethnic clubs.[130] Although both these relief groups and the US Department of State attempted to frame this work as apolitical, neutral, and humanitarian, the arrival of Syrian relief workers in immigrant neighborhoods was widely understood as part of a broader pro-Entente campaign against the Ottomans. Syrian activists representing US relief employed patriotic rhetoric of saving Syria from the Ottomans, thereby positioning humanitarianism as a resistance act. For immigrants who supported Istanbul, these campaigns constituted evidence of foreign collusion and conspiracy, an intolerable political affront.

This pattern was exemplified in an event in Cleveland, Ohio, where two hundred Syrian immigrants formed a Syrian American Red Cross Relief committee in 1917. Although the committee was exclusively Greek Orthodox, they appealed to the Syrian community at large (around 2,000, around 10 percent of which was Muslim) for donations, framing the drive as proof of the immigrants' pro-American patriotism. This bred conflict among Syrians in the neighborhood, and on April 27, 1917 the fundraiser's chairman, "Saah," got into a fistfight with an Ottoman loyalist named Abden Majeed. Apparently, Abden Majeed encountered Saah in the street, insulted the American flag and "spat upon the Red Cross button worn by Saah." Saah punched Abden Majeed and was beaten down by Majeed and an onlooker, Abdel Aziz, according to the arrest report. The fight tipped off a round of reprisals, and police reported "some twenty fights between Christians and Mohemmedans" in the days that followed.[131] The situation continued to escalate until the Bureau of Investigation was called in to meet with Syrian leaders from all religious communities to "impress upon them the necessity of avoiding quarrels about the war."[132] The Cleveland conflict reveals the degree to which relief work was experienced as a political act among Syrians in the United States. It also hints at the tendency for support for the Entente against the Ottomans to fall along ethnic and confessional lines. The identification of Syrian and Armenian Christians as humanitarian subjects reinforced long-standing American stereotypes about Islam, but it also offended Ottoman immigrants concerned about the sectarian character that some Syrian resistance work was taking.[133]

In addition to humanitarian relief, some Syrian activists pursued the possibilities for military cooperation with the Entente. In Buenos Aires, local Alliance Libanaise officer and editor of *al-Jadid* newspaper, Najib Trad, approached the city's French consul to discuss the enlistment of Syrian men into the French Army in 1916. He secured assurances that France would welcome Syrian volunteers as irregulars or in the colonial regiments.[134] Trad then visited Rosario, São Paulo, and Rio de Janeiro, looking for young men to volunteer for service under the French flag. As Trad visited each place, the news that France would enlist Syrians—still Ottoman subjects—outraged Ottomans still loyal to the empire. They correctly surmised that the campaign would turn into a new arm for French imperialism in the Middle East.

It was in this context that Najib Trad arrived at a Maronite Church in Rosario in April 1916. Flanked by a representative from the French consulate, Trad pitched his idea. Local Sunni leaders opposed the meeting and, joined by the empire's loyalists from Rosario's migrant community, they confronted Trad and his attendees as they exited the church. A brawl ensued and evolved into a riot involving hundreds of men. One Ottoman supporter (a Syrian Muslim) was killed, sixteen people were hospitalized, and dozens more were arrested. The event was reported widely in the mahjar press, reverberating in Arab communities across the Americas. In New York City, rival papers offered wildly different interpretations of what caused the violence. Na'um Mukarzil's *al-Huda* reprinted the story from Argentina's Maronite paper, *al-ʿAdl*, and described the riot as Muslim incitement of fanatical violence against Christians. Mukarzil's report mentioned neither Najib Trad nor the French recruiters.[135] ʿAbd al-Massih Haddad's *al-Saʾih*, by contrast, drew upon the Buenos Aires Syrian Union's organ, *al-Zaman*. It mentioned the recruiters but did not reveal the riot happened outside a church.[136] The construction of rival narratives fed a broader pattern of polarization of the press, exacerbated by the very cross-diasporic connectivities that made it a potent political tool.

Episodes like this notwithstanding, military recruitment transformed into a favored means for activists seeking to oppose the Ottoman Empire from abroad. Najib Trad's first successful recruit was a young Homsi named Hafiz Khizam, a member of São Paulo's *Homs al-Fatat*. The club's founder, Jurj Atlas, reportedly accompanied Khizam to Buenos Aires, where he enlisted at the French consulate.[137] Trad paid Khizam's passage across the Atlantic, and in return Khizam remitted regular letters to Argentina as he fought alongside French troops, making him the first embedded war correspondent of the Syrian mahjar.[138] Khizam's letters appeared in Buenos Aires' *al-Jadid*, in New York City's *al-Saʾih*, and in Paris's *Correspondance d'Orient*.

Conclusion

Ultimately, the CUP's work in the mahjar following the 1908 Revolution helped cement the very transnational networks that later facilitated nationalist politics among Arab émigrés. The post-revolutionary Ottoman state courted Syrian clubs in a short-lived politics of embrace, hoping to harness the mahjar's economic and diplomatic vitality for the good of Ottomanism. The CUP's stark diplomatic disengagement, censorship of the press, and repression of the Arabist movement did less to cut the ties that bound Syrian activists to their mahjari counterparts than to cede control of these societies to the diaspora. Newspapers produced in the Syrian colonies—many stridently anti-CUP in tone—were sometimes halted at Ottoman ports but also sometimes found their destination. Greater repression in Beirut and Damascus ensured that emigrants were the ones left with space to contest Ottoman policies from abroad; access to foreign powers was this equation's second half.

The idea that it was incumbent on emigrants abroad to complete the unfinished work of the 1908 Revolution ignited anti-CUP politics across the entire ideological spectrum. Arabist, Syrianist, and Lebanist associations largely lacked the programmatic components of nationalism until after 1918, and instead proposed Syria's liberation as a realization of goals first articulated in 1908. They continued to work within the framework of Ottomanist constitutionalism, even when confronting the CUP government on its policies and propagandizing an end to Ottoman rule in Syria altogether. Even in working with the Entente powers against Istanbul, the émigré societies believed they were preserving the legacy of 1908. When political violence erupted in the Syrian neighborhood, its targets were usually those perceived to be complicit with foreign interests and goals. The daily passions of the war divided immigrant communities internally, fueled by a yellow press and especially when the Entente powers were involved in supporting one side of the neighborhood. Longtime neighbors began to warily eye one other from across the avenue. It was from within these intimately local struggles that the more divisive elements of the mahjar's nationalist politics emerged, set against a backdrop of emigrant anxiety and skepticism.

Military recruitment, nevertheless, emerged as an important symbol for the Syrian mahjar's contributions to the war. The Entente powers understood the propaganda value of Arab migrants fighting for their side; as it turned out, so did many Syrian activists. Perhaps as he read Hafiz Khizam's letters from his office in Paris, *Correspondance d'Orient* editor and Syrian activist Shukri Ghanim imagined the possibilities for migrant military recruitment on a larger scale. Together with George Samné, Ghanim wrote to the French Foreign Ministry to inquire about the possibilities for congregating Syrian volunteers in an ethnic legion destined for the Ottoman front. Ghanim and Samné offered France access to the transnational infrastructure enjoyed by the United Syria Society and their own political party, the *Comité Central Syrien*.[139] Within a year, France gifted Ghanim a substantial subsidy to raise this corps. The United Syria Society—a club that only recently celebrated the July Revolution—was one among many Syrian societies moving money and manpower across the diaspora for Syria's liberation.

Former Ottomans in the Ranks

Pro-Entente Military Recruitment in the Syrian Mahjar,
1916–1918

In September 1916, a Syrian soldier named Jibraʾil Bishara was pulled out of a trench in the French countryside. Originally from the village of Bazʿun in Mount Lebanon, Bishara was a Syrian migrant fighting with a Canadian regiment on the Western Front. Shrapnel struck him in the neck and jaw; he lay dying in a London hospital when fellow soldier Gabriel Ilyas Ward visited him some weeks later, on January 15, 1917.[1] Ward and Bishara had both left Syria for New York City in the 1890s and had since naturalized as American citizens. Frustrated by America's neutrality in the war, they joined up in Canada, landed in France, and became friends at arms. They believed that they were doing their part "to complete the salvation of Syrians and Lebanese from the suffering of this War under the Turkish yoke."[2] But Bishara's final thoughts on the world at war were more bitter. Ward recorded his last conversation with Bishara (jotted in notes because Bishara's injuries preempted his speech),

> You listen to me, dear Gabriel, do not risk yourself recklessly as I have, for my prize will be that I die in this strange, foreign place, without seeing my family, my friends, or my neighbors once more. Write to them in the mahjar and tell them how I have been killed.[3] Tell them that I have gone in martyrdom back to my homeland, where I pray there will soon rise a liberated Syria and Lebanon, free from nations of Genghis Khan.[4]

Sending his recollection to colleagues in New York City, Gabriel Ward returned to the trenches, until a gas attack robbed him of his sight in his left eye and he was reassigned.[5] But Bishara's dying words about fighting a dubious war for Syria's freedom from the wrong side of the world stuck with him. Convinced that the world war was a just one but wanting to help Syrians take their war directly to the Ottomans, Ward spent the next two years working as a military recruiter in Marseilles, London, and New York City on behalf of Naʿum Mukarzil's Lebanon League of Progress (Jamʿiyyat al-Nahda al-Lubnaniyya).[6] This chapter tells the story of recruiters and soldiers like Gabriel Ilyas Ward, men of Ottoman nationality or recent American citizens who fought for the Entente powers or recruited on their behalf. In two years, they funneled an estimated ten thousand Syrian men from the American mahjar into pro-Entente military service.[7] The political networks that they constructed, moreover, formed enduring conduits for diasporic nationalist activism, networks that outlasted the 1918 armistice.

Syrian émigré recruiters presided over a transnational, largely clandestine mobilization of volunteers from the migrant communities in the United States, Brazil, Argentina, and elsewhere in the Americas. They helped Syrian troops navigate the complex legal terrain between the Ottomans and the Entente. The enlistment of Syrian migrants required a significant amount of work: medical testing, new travel documentation, and often changes in nationality to ensure legality. Each facet of this work brought recruiters into close relationships with foreign government officials, most notably the French Foreign Ministry and the US Department of State, and recruiters mediated between foreign governments and migrant labor to exact favorable terms for their men. At the same time, the Syrian agents who managed the screening process worked in liminal legal spaces the Entente powers informally sanctioned but did not oversee.

These recruiters promoted Syrian participation in Allied efforts based on the belief that the war would liberate their Middle Eastern homeland from Ottoman rule, an idea deployed similarly by British, French, and American policymakers.[8] The enlistees, for their part, saw military service as a practical means of achieving a post-Ottoman nationality status. Syrian men who deployed (almost always to European, not Ottoman, fronts) described their status as a partnership with America fighting for Syria's liberation. Although such sentiments would later be touted as evidence of an authentic nationalist spirit in the mahjar, the reality was that this wartime activism was neither purely sentimental nor entirely nationalist in content. Military mobilization was a political act that recruiters linked closely with ideas about Syria's liberation from the Ottoman government. It was not just about patriotic sentiment, longing, or emotional connection to the homeland, however, but about the definitive action they inspired.[9] This distinction is important because, by casting new responsibilities upon migrant men on behalf of "martyred Syria," recruiters did not merely "imagine" the existence of a Syrian national community.[10] Rather, they worked toward Syria's armed reclamation from Istanbul and used the enlistment campaign to build partnerships with foreign governments to enforce it.

Recruiters helped enlistees obtain passports and documentation to distance themselves from the Ottoman Empire, which formally claimed them as subjects, but Syrian migrants also expressed fears that joining the military would expose them to prosecution by Turkish authorities. On one hand, charges of treachery; on the other, American nativist accusations of immigrant cowardice, "slackerism," or disloyalty. Syrian enlistees faced a difficult legal quandary, which one prominent recruiter described as being caught "between treason and cowardice."[11] Simultaneously compelled and forbidden to join the fight, many remained in a liminal station between Ottoman and American citizenships, fueling wider conversations about political belonging in the mahjar. Whether these men would be remembered as patriots or traitors depended largely on the war's outcome, and Ottoman nationals fighting for the Allies risked the possibility of statelessness as thanks for their efforts.

As Syrian American troops shipped abroad in 1918, the Syrian press published soldiers' images, biographies, and letters home, using them as material evidence of their patriotism and of the diaspora's political contract with the Entente. Nationalist political parties used the soldiers as symbols, folding them into Wilsonian narratives about self-determination through service and action. The connection between soldiering and nationalism persisted through the 1918 armistice.

The French Légion d'Orient

The Syrian diaspora's experience with pro-Entente mobilization began in 1916, with the formation of a French irregular corps called the Légion d'Orient. A mixed infantry regiment composed largely of Armenians (who numbered around 4,000) under French officers, the Légion d'Orient employed 550 Syrian and Lebanese migrants recruited from Egypt, Europe, and the Americas.[12] Heralding the corps as "saving the East from the claws of barbarism," Syrian fraternal societies promoted French war aims, identified new recruits, and sponsored their passage to France's enlistment sites in Bordeaux, Marseilles, and Le Havre.[13] The employment of Syrian irregulars dovetailed with France's larger use of colonial troops in combat, but the Légion d'Orient was not a unilaterally French project.[14] Although nominal in size, its value was touted by French Foreign Minister Georges-Picot as a symbolic manifestation of Syrian collaboration and support for France's Levantine ambitions.[15] The Légion d'Orient was deployed to Palestine in 1917, where it helped British forces under Edmund Allenby to secure Nablus for the allies.[16]

Syrian recruiters in São Paulo, Rio de Janeiro, Buenos Aires, Havana, and New York City enlisted migrant men for the Légion d'Orient between late 1916 and 1917. The Paris-based Comité Central Syrien (hereafter CCS) under Shukri Ghanim and Georges Samné led the effort, and, as a result, historians have understood the project as an extension of the CCS's pan-Syrian nationalist politics. Ghanim promoted Greater Syria's separation from the Ottoman Empire and its placement under direct French tutelage in the name of national development.[17] Although the CCS was perhaps the diaspora's most popular nationalist movement during the war, Ghanim's influence waned swiftly in 1919 as France endorsed the creation of a Lebanese state (the *Grand Liban*) at the expense of CCS demands for territorial integrity.

Although the Légion d'Orient had been Ghanim's idea, both Syrianists and Lebanists recruited for the corps and claimed the legionaries as symbols of their alliance with France.[18] Indeed, the mahjar's most successful recruiters did not share Ghanim's politics: in New York City, São Paulo, and Rio de Janeiro, the Lebanon League of Progress (hereafter LLP) provided most of the Légion d'Orient's recruitment services.[19] Like the CCS, the LLP endorsed French tutelage, but they also lobbied for the creation of a Lebanese state distinct from Syria. The party's leaders were prominent Lebanists Naʿum Mukarzil in New York City and Shukri al-Khuri in São Paulo, men who otherwise described Ghanim as their political rival. Although trenchant and intensifying ideological divisions between Syrianist and Lebanist leaders boiled over in 1918, the difficult work of diasporic recruitment demanded that they collaborate, and they did so on the practical belief that "France will liberate [our] country and break the heavy Turkish yoke that has treated us so severely, subjecting us to famine and starvation."[20] Mukarzil described mobilization as one half of a political contract he would later bring to the Americans: manpower in return for partnership in liberation. But the ideological content of Syrian and Lebanese patriotism remained less immediately relevant than the drive to build functional political alliances.

In the United States, Mukarzil's LLP raised $100,000 to assist migrants in joining the Légion d'Orient in 1917, a large portion of which came from the French government.[21] With this funding, he presided over a new migration network linking his Brooklyn office to recruiters in São Paulo, Buenos Aires, Havana, and Mérida, Mexico. Each city hosted chapters of the LLP, which furnished recruits with French passports and passage to New York City. After medical testing and vetting by Mukarzil, the men were given steamship tickets to Bordeaux.[22] Citing its own neutrality in the war, the US Department of State allowed the recruitment of foreign troops on its soil (not their enlistment). While all the work of vetting new soldiers was done in New York, their formal enlistment took place only after arrival in France.[23] Syrians from South America, the United States, and Canada made this lateral migration through New York City, facilitated in part by shipping lines managed by LLP partisans and Mukarzil's relatives in South America.[24] The piecemeal nature of the process and its management by private émigré recruiters made New York a locus for the diaspora's

الوفد البارليسى فى سان اولو

Figure 3.1. Légion d'Orient recruitment meeting in São Paulo, Brazil in 1917. *Comite Central Syrien* delegates from Paris Jamil Mardan Bey and Dr. Qaysar Lakah flank French Consul General, Paul Claudel (seated at center). Jafet, *Na'imi Yafith*, 104.

mobilization, but it also created opportunities for enterprising men seeking free passage across to Europe. Occasionally, they deserted upon arrival.[25]

The LLP printed daily calls for recruits in Mukarzil's newspaper, *al-Huda*; similar announcements appeared in São Paulo's *Abu al-Hawl*. The call to arms placed emigrant soldiers within a very specific political project:

> For recruitment and jihad in the name of humanity. Pay heed, oh sons of Lebanon! The Turks are dividing your land . . . it is our goal to expel the Turks from Syria, to cut the cords from those gallows once looped over the heads of [Lebanon's] men who dared talk about independence, the honorable, intelligent effendis of the nation. Oh sons of the nation, [we] advise you move to the places French soldiers are. The Lebanon League of Progress is ready and prepared to help volunteers enlist, and to dispatch them under the protections and liberties afforded to them by the government of France.[26]

As private recruiters working in neutral hemisphere, the league's management of a lateral traffic in recruits across the Americas was unprecedented, but even with the provision of passports, transatlantic passage, and guaranteed diplomatic protections, their recruitment stream was more trickle than torrent. The mahjar's Syrian legionaries never amounted to more than 550 in a predominantly Armenian force.[27]

Several factors mitigated the campaign's success. Critics pointed out that, although France supplied foreign soldiers with passports, it did not offer them French citizenship or permanent residency rights. Syrian volunteers of Ottoman nationality placed themselves into a complicated legal position, opening themselves up to treason charges in a moment when the Ottoman government enthusiastically prosecuted such crimes. Deployed soldiers wrote to *al-Huda* to "address the concerns of Syrians who fear their legal attachments to the Turks [and] of being potentially disgraced as traitors" by arguing that holding French passports would protect them from prosecution.[28] At the same time, others feared (correctly) that the Légion d'Orient would become a tool of French colonial policy aimed at exacerbating new and painful divisions between Syrian Christians and Muslims.[29]

The perception that the Légion d'Orient served French colonial interests prompted some Syrians to seek other means of enlistment. In New York City, a smaller stream of naturalized Syrian Americans migrated north to enlist with the Canadian Expeditionary Forces (hereafter CEF). Canada prohibited Ottoman nationals from serving in its military but encouraged its own Syrian immigrants to naturalize as Canadian citizens and join up. The CEF also welcomed Syrian Americans into its ranks, encouraging those who had achieved US citizenship or declared their intent to naturalize to enlist.[30] In his memoirs published in 1919, Gabriel Ilyas Ward recounted his own enlistment experience. By World War I, Ward had already serviced in the US army, deploying to the Philippines and Cuba.[31] He was working as a dry goods wholesaler between New York City and Nova Scotia when the war broke out in 1914. He, Jibra'il Bishara, and several other friends went to Montreal to enlist, arriving at the French trenches in late 1916.

Ward's enlistment appears to have been spontaneous, but Canada also hosted active recruitment networks managed by Syrian immigrants. From Montreal, recruiters Ilyas Yusuf and Shakir Karam advertised widely for new volunteers in New York's Arabic newspapers, where they competed with Mukarzil's LLP for manpower.[32] In a 1917 letter in *al-Bayan* addressed to the Syrians of New York, Karam announced his partnership with British officials to levy Syrian volunteers on behalf of the CEF.[33] The campaign particularly encouraged Muslim volunteers; although the recruitment of Syrians in the French and US militaries was almost entirely limited to Christians, Karam passed along assurances from the Canadian Minister of Justice, A. L. Newcombe, that his country "draws no legal distinction between Christians and Muslims" in matters of eligibility.[34] Syrian volunteers made strategic decisions when opting for military service within French or Canadian units, weighing desires to work in service to French or British interests and more practical issues such as the terms of service, quality of provisions, and pay. The United States' entry into the war in 1917 largely

Figure 3.2. Gabriel Ilyas Ward in 1919. A military intelligence officer and recruiter, Ward is seated in profile to obscure injuries sustained at the French Western Front. Evelyn Shakir Collection, Arab American National Museum, Dearborn, MI.

stymied both recruitment flows, but small numbers of Syrians continued to enlist with French or Canadian units through 1918.

Choice of destination also influenced enlistees' decision making. Syrians fighting for France could opt for the front against the Ottomans, as the Légion d'Orient deployed to Palestine. Those in American or Canadian units were limited to the European theater, overwhelmingly destined for the French Western Front. Most of the mahjar's recruiters stated a philosophical preference that Syrians should be deployed against the Ottomans, but the option to fight with the US army also represented an attractive opportunity to cultivate alliances. Recruiters of Lebanese, Syrian, and Arab nationalist persuasions all engaged in US army recruitment, vying with one another for available men. Mukarzil's propaganda in *al-Huda*, for instance, recommended the US army and the Légion d'Orient simultaneously until June 1917, when Mukarzil became suspicious of the French legionaries after the CCS sent its own delegation to South America. Dr. Qaysar Lakah and Jamil Mardam Bey toured Brazil looking for new recruits, but Mukarzil suspected that the tour was designed to undercut his own recruitment work and to solidify the Légion d'Orient as a Syrianist project. In response, in *al-Huda*, Mukarzil hastened to support enlistment in the US army instead and even deployment to alternative battlefields:

> This publication looks favorably on Syrian and Lebanese volunteerism for the homeland's recovery... but it also supports Syrian and Lebanese volunteers being deployed to alternative fronts and battlefields. If compelled to duty, we will report to the African Sahara, the European trenches, or anywhere else, for we have one single purpose, and that is to fight until freedom [hurriyya] is victorious.[35]

al-Huda was not the only Arabic paper to endorse enlistment in the US military as an alternative to the Légion d'Orient; New York's growing community of Syrian and Arab nationalists also did so, in a bid to curry favor with the Wilson's administration for their respective movements. The most notable such group was the Syria-Mount Lebanon League of Liberation (Lajna al-Tahrir Suriya wa-Lubnan) under Ayyub Tabet, Amin al-Rihani, and N. T. Tadross. Shukri al-Bakhash, a former member of the LLP in Brazil, had moved to New York, assumed editorship of *al-Fatat* newspaper and became the League of Liberation's primary recruiter.[36]

America's Selective Service Draft and Syrian Migrants

In April 1917, President Woodrow Wilson committed his country to war and announced that the United States would raise 4 million soldiers to join Allied troops on the Western Front. Most came from the largest compulsory draft in American history to that point, the Selective Service Draft of 1917. President Wilson's commitment to fighting "for the liberation of nations and oppressed peoples around the world" against "the spirit of autocracy that has shattered the weak peoples under its yoke" prompted Syrian migrants to support the call to arms, and it made President Wilson one of the most revered personalities for Syrian, Lebanese, and Arab nationalists alike.[37] In the United States, the same newspaper editors who endorsed America's war effort also led the first campaigns to enlist Syrians in the army: Na'um Mukarzil (*al-Huda*), Shukri al-Bakhash (*al-Fatat*), Ibrahim al-Khuri and Wadi' Shakir (*Fatat Boston*), among others. Of course, the draft's implementation raised questions about Syrian eligibility for service. While recruiters saw Syrian enlistment as a natural extension of work already being done with America's allies, US Provost Marshal Enoch Crowder was reticent to include Ottoman nationals in the army's ranks. Could Syrian immigrants be compelled to serve? What about those who retained their Ottoman nationality and were thus allied with America's enemies?

Like native-born American citizens, all male foreign-born immigrants and foreign nationals were required to register with the Selective Service boards, which then chose eligible men for compulsory military service. Unnaturalized foreign-born registrants were classified in one of three categories: declarant (having submitted a Declaration of Intent, the first papers required of immigrants seeking to naturalize), non-declarant (retaining a foreign nationality), or enemy alien. Enemy aliens were ineligible for conscription by virtue of international law, since they would be placed in a position of fighting their own countrymen.[38] But the legal standing of Ottoman immigrants was particularly murky, especially for Ottoman non-declarants. Because the United States never declared war on the Ottoman Empire, Ottoman subjects living in the country became "neutral

Figure 3.3. Shukri al-Bakhash, editor of al-Fatat, in 1917. A recruiter for the US Army and a War Department propagandist, al-Bakhash called his efforts a "literary jihad" against the Ottoman government. Ward, *Kitab al-Jundi al-Suri*, 115. James Ansara Papers, IHRC208, Immigration History Research Center Archives, University of Minnesota.

allies of the enemy," which meant they could not be compelled to serve (like enemy aliens), but they could volunteer or opt into service if mistakenly drafted. On the face of it, this granted Ottoman migrants a legal status distinct from that of German, Austrian, or Czech immigrants.[39] In practice, however, Syrian non-declarants were routinely drafted, unpredictably dismissed from the army (or conversely, denied dismissal), and misclassified in draft documents as "alien enemies" alongside other ineligible foreigners. Such ambiguities surrounding Ottoman military eligibility worried Syrian recruiters as they sought to widen the pool of available troops.[40]

Recruiters, nevertheless, found room to navigate the process and place men in the US army. A common strategy involved starting the naturalization process just prior to enlistment. In *al-Huda*, Mukarzil reported that, although all Syrian men between the ages of twenty-one and thirty-one had to register with the Selective Service Board, only those bearing their "first papers" (that is, a Declaration of Intent to Naturalize) would be eligible for voluntary induction. Only two years had passed since the landmark court case, *Dow v. United States* (1915), which had assured Syrian immigrants access to US citizenship. In readying Syrian men for enlistment, Mukarzil helped them submit their "first papers" before they registered with the Selective Service board. The move bolstered their chances at US citizenship by serving America as declarant immigrants, rather than as "neutral allies of the enemy."

Building on Dow, a new law further bolstered an American legal consensus that Syrians, though Ottoman subjects, were of contested Ottoman nationality. Responding to some of the draft issues raised by Syrian recruiters, Congress passed legislation in May 1917 which legally distinguished "Lebanonites or Syrians claimed by Turkey as a subject" from Turks and other Ottoman nationals. The law functioned as an early national origins category. In lieu of a Syrian or Lebanese state, Arab migrants could identify as legally Ottomans-but-not-quite in order to smooth the enlistment or citizenship process, or conversely, to exempt themselves from the mounting regime of restrictions faced by other Ottoman nationals in America.

The law also convinced nationalists that Americans saw Syrian and Lebanese aspirations for independence as legitimate and would support them. Writing in 1917, Mukarzil claimed, "the war has prompted the American government to distinguish the Syrians and Lebanese from those who are clearly Turks."[41] He did not mention the racial and religious connotations behind these labels in *al-Huda*, but it is worth noting that, in American legal parlance, the conflation of "Turk" with Muslim and "Syrian" with Christian was never far from the surface. Another outcome of *Dow v. United States* was the creation of a Syrian ethnicity that was racially white, Christian, and eligible for American citizenship on those bases.[42] The wartime distinction between "Syrians" and "Turks" presented an extension of this logic, and it opened military service up to Arab Christian immigrants while offering them a means of establishing a post-Ottoman nationality status and recognition as simultaneously American and "Syrian" (or "Lebanese," as Mukarzil characteristically insisted).

One significant obstacle persisted: US immigration law required that all new declarants reside in-country for five continuous years before applying for their "second papers," the petition for naturalization. Critically, Syrians who entered this waiting period remained subjects of the Ottoman Empire. In cases where Syrian declarants fought for the American military, they risked statelessness or prosecution by the Ottoman government. Mukarzil wrote to Provost General Crowder to inquire whether Syrian volunteers could be excused from the requirement, a system of sponsorship could replace the waiting period, and naturalized Syrians could vouch for their compatriot soldiers.[43] Such a change, he argued, would transform Syrian soldiers into American citizens overnight, mitigating legal problems arising from their option to serve.

The idea to offer citizenship to Syrian volunteers fell on deaf ears in 1917, as Crowder remained wary of the diplomatic issues that instant naturalization could raise. In May 1918, the army would revise its enlistment policies in just this way, but until that time the majority of Syrian volunteers levied were either second-generation Syrian Americans (American citizens by virtue of birth) or long-time declarants who took the final step to naturalize as they joined the army. Recruiters for the Légion d'Orient and the US army competed for immigrant attentions throughout 1917, and Mukarzil, al-Bakhash, and their partisans filtered manpower through US, French, and Canadian channels on the basis of citizenship status and soldiers' preferences about destination.

Campaigns for Migrant Recruitment

After President Wilson declared war, the Syrian mahjar hosted several mass recruitment fairs, complete with patriotic public square meetings with the feel of a carnival. In the United States, *al-Huda, al-Fatat,* and *Fatat Boston* newspapers celebrated deployed soldiers, and Syrian associations hosted festivals open to the community at large. The LLP sponsored one such rally in Boston in May 1917. Some 2,000 Syrians attended, among them the rector of Brooklyn's Our Lady of the Cedars Maronite Church Joseph Yazbek, Syrian American Club (al-Muntada al-Suri al-Amriki) recruiter and *Fatat Boston* editor Wadiʻ Shakir, and French consul Joseph Flamand. Speakers emphasized the immigrants' obligation "to enlist under the Stars and Stripes, and to fight for the greatest democracy in the world."[44] One of the community's enlisted men, Elias F. Shannon, appeared in uniform and addressed other second-generation Syrians.[45]

In recounting these festivals, the Syrian press juxtaposed speech transcripts with Liberty Loan advertisements, notices by Committee for Public Information, and hagiographic accounts of Syrian soldiers. According to a 1918 ad in New York City's *al-Nasr* newspaper, purchasing Liberty Loans was the best way to "prove that you are 100% American."[46] Syrian migrants in that city raised $300,000 in Liberty Loans by the war's end; the Boston-based Syrian American Club raised another $18,750.[47] "This organization is only as strong and radiant as its membership," wrote Mukarzil in June 1917, and "those of us who are strong must use that strength in national service; those who are not strong must inspire the mighty and powerful."[48] Syrian displays of pro-Entente patriotism signaled the community's proud participation in American political life, but they also linked support for American war aims with the liberation of the Syrian homeland. "Establishing the right of peoples to determine their future" remained the recruiters' primary goal.[49]

American-born children with Syrian parents played a unique role in soliciting manpower from their communities. Eager to boost its voluntary enlistment numbers, the army sent these men back into their communities as recruiters before deploying them abroad. One of these young men was twenty-three-year-old Albert Hatem. In addition to being the nephew of Na'um Hatem, a respected Syrian American author in Brooklyn, Albert was an heir of Hafid 'Id Hatem, a deputy in Mount Lebanon's Administrative Council before the war.[50] With funds from the LLP and the Syria-Mount Lebanon League of Liberation (hereafter SLLL), Hatem toured the southern United States in 1917, giving appearances in uniform with fellow soldiers Yusuf 'Abdu, Rashid Hajjar, and Ilyas Najmi, as well as Costa Najour and Dr. Mitri Mas'ud.[51] At a Syrian Greek Orthodox church in Atlanta, Hatem collected a dozen new men, destined for the Western Front, including Tanyus al-Najjar, Mihka'il 'Azzar, and Bishara Ma'luf. Hatem's colleague, Yusuf 'Abdu, reported to *al-Fatat* newspaper that the church also gave them a substantial cash donation for Syrian famine relief.[52]

Clergymen in both the Maronite and the Greek Orthodox churches sponsored recruitment events and provided men like Albert Hatem space for their activities. The Orthodox clergy took a particular interest in America's war effort and circulated statements in support of enlistment and its theological implications. Brooklyn's Orthodox archpriest at St. Nicolas' Cathedral, Basilius Kherbawi, summed up his stance in *al-Sa'ih* newspaper in 1917: "The present war has consumed the Christian world. Has it not been said to give unto Caesar what is Caesar's, and to God, what is God's? . . . If a Christian is called to military service, he must give his country what is asked of him."[53] The justness of America's involvement provided additional reason: "if the German nation and its Allies spread madness upon humanity, then isn't it upon every Christian to strike back at them for [the security of] their religion, civilization,

Figure 3.4. Albert Hatem in 1917. In 1918, he was deployed to France with the 28th Iron Division, where he was promoted to sergeant. Ward, *Kitab al-Jundi al-Suri*, 12. James Ansara Papers, IHRC208, Immigration History Research Center Archives, University of Minnesota.

and humanity?" Kherbawi endorsed "this recruitment campaign, and the Syrian Colony of America [which] leads the charge."[54]

The clergy's involvement influenced the communal composition of Syrian immigrant enlistees: the Légion d'Orient was widely seen as a Maronite project, while enlistment in the US army stoked competition between Orthodox and Maronite leaders. But clerical support also produced complaints that the mobilization effort served sectarian agendas, particularly among émigré Sunnis and Druze, for whom continuing loyalty to the Ottoman Empire combined with a distrust of foreign ambitions in Syria.[55] Their fears about sectarian discord linked directly to larger anxieties about foreign (particularly French) interference in Ottoman politics.

Diasporic military mobilization also created new political fissures between rival recruiters and among the immigrant troops they levied. The most common source of conflict lay in recruiters' preferences of foreign allies, as rival groups of Syrianists, Lebanists, and Arab nationalists each sought to raise their profile in Wilson's army.[56] In New York City, Mukarzil's LLP invested significant time cultivating American sympathies for Lebanese independence. But Mukarzil's primary competitor, Shukri al-Bakhash, worked for the US army in hopes of securing American support for the Arab nationalist project of complete, immediate independence for a federated state including Syria, Mount Lebanon, and Palestine. "The recruitment and deployment of fighters [mujahidin] for the Syrian cause," al-Bakhash wrote in *al-Fatat* newspaper in December 1917, was for ultimate liberation from foreign occupation, Ottoman or otherwise.[57] His sponsor in New York was the Syria-Mount Lebanon League of Liberation, which promoted Arab cooperation with US policymakers in the interest of transforming Syria into "a useful member in the society of civilized peoples . . . under the separate and direct protectorship of a democratic Christian nation." The SLLL's president, Ayyub Tabet, was at odds with the mahjar's many Francophile organizations because he promoted another vision: that the United States of America could reconstruct war-torn Syria. In the first of many petitions to President Wilson, Tabet described his own preference for an American mandate there, but "it is our sincere belief that the United States may not care to assume [this] responsibility."[58]

Intense political rivalries formed around these competing visions for the homeland, and they sometimes culminated in acts of sabotage. In 1917, for instance, Shukri al-Bakhash departed for Argentina for a recruitment trip. Visiting Syrian clubs in Mendoza and San Martín, he quickly levied forty recruits, scheduled to accompany him back to the United States.[59] Back in Brooklyn, Na'um Mukarzil took advantage of al-Bakhash's absence to report his newspaper, *al-Fatat*, to the US Postmaster General, Albert Burlson. A brash nativist, Burlson had recently been empowered by America's Espionage Acts of 1917 to censor the city's ethnic press.[60] He required all foreign-language publications to remit regular English translations to his office for inspection, and *al-Fatat*'s failure to do so in al-Bakhash's absence led to his indictment for sedition, along with two colleagues, Ilya Abu Madi (also at *al-Fatat*) and 'Abd al-Massih Haddad (editor of *al-Sa'ih*).[61] al-Bakhash rushed home from Argentina to sort out the matter, leaving his recruits behind. He was later acquitted after Ayyub Tabet prevailed on the French ambassador, Jean Jusserand, to write the US Department of State on his behalf.[62]

Since migrant troops in the US army were, without exception, sent to France, Syrian recruiters faced ongoing pressure to present the European front as a valid theater in the war against the Ottomans. At the same time, however, these recruiters pushed for opportunities to deploy Arab troops to the Middle East. Returning from another recruitment trip to Brazil in late 1917, al-Bakhash concluded that "it is significant and important that Syrians may struggle for their own emancipation from the Turkish yoke" rather than awaiting liberation at the hands of European powers.[63] Syrian battle deaths in faraway places such as the

Somme and Château-Thierry weighed heavily on him. He feared that the "un-acknowledged and uncounted disappearance" of Syrian war dead in the mass carnage dissolved their symbolic significance and undermined the political contract he believed Syrians had made with America.[64] Even as recruiters scoured the Americas looking for eligible men, they lobbied for two changes in army policy to enhance Syrians' visibility: an end to the five-year residency period, which discouraged some Syrian declarants from volunteering, and a reconsideration of the US stance on irregular corps of co-ethnic immigrants.

Although the US army refused to loosen its eligibility requirements for foreign-born soldiers in 1917, circumstances changed dramatically the following year. What had seemed like an elegant classification system dividing immigrants into declarants, non-declarants, and ineligible aliens proved messy and unworkable. Because the Selective Service Act required all immigrant men to register despite their actual eligibility, hundreds of thousands of ineligible aliens were mistakenly drafted into the army, among them thousands of Ottoman subjects. Some filed grievances through the foreign consular system; in the United States, the Spanish Consulate handled exemption claims on behalf of Ottoman immigrants.[65] But the exemption process was difficult and required drafted men to actively petition for exemption. Exemption fraud also became a problem.[66] If some immigrants used phony papers to claim exemption from the draft, many more opted to serve despite being legally ineligible.[67]

Meanwhile, ethnic leaders in several immigrant communities pushed for a loosening of restrictions, while nativists complained about "alien slackers" who had been excused from military service.[68] Congress revisited the issue of immigrant military service in 1918, drafting a new law that waived the five-year residency requirement for immigrant volunteers in the armed forces. The May 9, 1918 Act

> entitles all aliens in the service (including enemy aliens) to citizenship whether they have their first papers or not. Before the application is granted, however, it should be understood that the application is wholly voluntary and is a privilege which can only be granted to those producing evidence of loyalty. When the application is granted, the soldier will immediately become a citizen, with all privileges and immunities of citizenship.[69]

This instantaneous citizenship was available only to immigrant soldiers, regardless of declarancy or nationality status. A single witness, usually the recruit's commanding officer, was the army's standard for "evidence of loyalty." After signing a naturalization petition and a loyalty oath renouncing their previous nationality, the soldiers proceeded to base camp as new American citizens.[70]

The May 9 Act bolstered a new wave of enlistment enthusiasm among Syrian migrant activists. The Syrian American Club had long focused on "forging ties of love and reconciliation between the Syrians, assistance [to Syrians] in obtaining American citizenship, and the defense of Syrian Americans from all classes in either of these endeavors," but in summer 1918 it sponsored dozens of new applications aimed at joint naturalization and enlistment.[71] Its recruiters in the Boston area, Wadiʿ Shakir and Ibrahim al-Khuri, promoted military service as the best means of achieving American citizenship.

Almost invariably, nationalist elites and newspaper editors managed the recruitment process into the US army. The enlistees, themselves, by contrast, represented the diaspora's full class spectrum but none more fully than the urban working class. Most of the Syrians inducted in 1918 were textile workers from the mills of New England, and it appears that improved access to US citizenship appealed more to proletarians than it did to peddlers, merchants, and intellectuals. A prewar textile boom had led Syrians into industrial weaving, leatherworking, and heavy manufacturing. But even though cash wages reached an all-time high in these industries, unnaturalized workers were paid substantially less than US citizens. First-time army privates earned only $15 a month, a paltry sum compared to the $25–30 that skilled textile workers made. But Syrian enlistees who fulfilled at least one term in the army could then leverage their new citizenship status into higher wages at the factories that employed them. Those who stayed longer quickly advanced in rank, commanding monthly salaries as high as $50.[72] The men who came to Shakir and al-Khuri did so in groups from the shop floor, having resolved to join the army together.[73] In one case, a shop foreman named Jurj Maʿtuq brought several employees from a Boston-area shoe factory. Maʿtuq was an American citizen by virtue of birth; born in Boston to Syrian parents, he sponsored new enlistment applications until his own deployment as an army translator in 1918. Maʿtuq's name also graces the naturalization papers for several Syrians (all leatherworkers) under the May 9 Act.[74]

The US army also revised its policies regarding ethnic corps in mid-1918. Historically the Americans had resisted the use of irregular legions like the French Légion d'Orient because of concerns about the diplomatic entanglements that such units could produce. An early effort to levy an all-Syrian legion in Fall River, Massachusetts, failed to secure army approval. In this small mill town in 1917, a naturalized army veteran named Mitri Jabbur raised an informal column of 300 Syrian men running daily drills at the police academy. It is unclear whether Sgt. Jabbur had army authorization, but Fall River's municipal authorities endorsed the project as a show of immigrant patriotism. In his appeal to the US army's Provost Marshall, Sgt. Jabbur stated that his goal was deployment to Mount Lebanon. Upon learning of the exercises, Provost Marshal Crowder ordered the corps to disband.[75]

Several immigrant groups lobbied for new ethnic corps in 1917, and the US army systematically denied these requests, typically referring them to one of America's allies. Vladimir Jabotinsky's efforts to recruit American Jews for the Zion Mule Corp (later the Jewish Legion) are instructive. With volunteers from New York, Boston, and Chicago, Jabotinsky petitioned for American sponsorship to bring the company to Palestine on behalf of Jewish settlers there. When President Wilson declined to support the project, Jabotinsky obtained British backing and landed in Palestine with 10,000 recruits. Notably, half of the Jewish Legion's fighters were American citizens granted service exemptions by the US government.[76] Naturalized Syrian immigrants who served under the French flag in the Légion d'Orient were similarly exempted from the American draft.[77]

The May 9, 1918 Act prompted the US army to experiment with a variety of ethnic legions for the first time, changing the nature of immigrant mobilization as Syrians motivated by a desire to renounce their Ottoman nationality and gain US citizenship joined in larger numbers. In the summer of 1918, eight new battalions began training at Camp Devens in Massachusetts.[78] The regiments—Italian, Russian, Polish, Lithuanian, Greek, Albanian, Syrian, and Armenian—trained and spoke in their own languages and comprised immigrants given naturalization in return for service.[79] Sergeant James Habib 'Attara, a leatherworker originally from Aleppo, supervised the Syrian column. 'Attara's group was earmarked for France but did not deploy because the war ended before they completed training. The Syrian legion's naturalization paperwork was so hastily drawn up (and so slowly processed) that many of the men training under 'Attara formally remained Ottoman subjects until after the Armistice. Sgt. 'Attara's own citizenship papers, for instance, were not processed until November 22, 1918, two weeks after the war ended.

Syrian American Draft Evasion and Desertion

The 1917 Selective Service draft's inarticulate manner combined with the legal ambiguities marking "Syrians and Mount Lebanonites claimed by Turkey as subjects" to make migrant enlistment a complicated business. Syrian volunteers navigated not only legal uncertainties but also vague and changing documentary regimes granting them travel rights. Perhaps one of the greatest ironies surrounding the discussion about whether Syrian Ottoman nationals could enlist was that many more Syrian migrants were mistakenly drafted. Syrians who retained their Ottoman nationality could claim exemption from the draft, but they ran into difficulty when they tried.

The larger nativist atmosphere in wartime America placed Syrian immigrants under the same cloud of public suspicion that other Ottoman migrants faced, and these tensions were especially acute when Syrians sought exemption from the military service. "These real men without a country," bemoaned a nativist op-ed in the *Boston Daily Globe* in 1918, "are not Americans and won't be." Describing the Syrians, Turks, Kurds, and Armenians as "pestering the legal advisory boards with manifold excuses," the *Globe* damned their "keen black eyes" before exclaiming that "never before, have so many races gathered under one roof for the same purpose [as evading this draft]."[80]

The accidental drafting of foreign-born ineligibles was widespread, and it caused the US State Department considerable diplomatic problems. Already overburdened with exemption petitions by registered enemy aliens, Secretary of State Robert Lansing's office received complaints from foreign consulates concerning the conscription of their nationals in the first place. Entrusted with overseeing Ottoman affairs in America, the Spanish Ambassador, Francisco Javier de Salas, complained to Lansing that the army has unlawfully conscripted Ottoman nationals. The Secretary of State offered a standard exemption form in late 1917 in an attempt to fix the problem. Any Ottoman subject who was registered under the Selective Service Act of 1917 and subsequently called to service could obtain this document at the Spanish consulate, present it to the exemption boards, and be excused from service. The exemption boards were instructed to handle the Spanish Ottoman exemptions in a manner similar to men unfit for service through medical malady. Thousands of Ottoman subjects, including Syrian Arabs, successfully obtained these draft exemptions, but the process required individual inductees to seek the paperwork and remit it properly. The process was extraordinarily confusing and ineffective, resulting in exemption denials, draft dodging, and new opportunities for exemption fraud.

For Syrian and Lebanese immigrants, the exemption process was especially messy, owing to the United States' history of unpredictably classifying Arab immigrants as "Turks," "Syrians," and less commonly as "Mount Lebanese" in arrival papers, naturalization petitions, and in draft laws. In some sense, Syrians were simultaneously eligible for enlistment but (in theory) were exempt from the draft. These contradictions were confusing enough when it came to processing Syrian volunteers for the US army; they only multiplied when Syrians who did not want to fight sought draft exemptions claiming themselves as Ottoman nationals, sometimes belatedly.

The introduction of the Spanish exemption process in 1917 produced an almost immediate flood of applications from Syrians already inducted into the army, who applied for exemptions after the fact. The army's handling of these exemptions illustrates how frustrating the process was, especially amidst heightened nativist scrutiny. A range of unpredictable outcomes resulted. In New York City, one Alex 'Assa was among the first Syrians to claim exemption using Spanish documents in September 1917. His exemption was denied and he quickly appealed it, but he was ordered to report to base in the interim. Soon after arriving at Camp Upton in New York, ʿAssa was relocated to Atlanta, Georgia, where he spent the next eleven months awaiting the result of his appeal. In October 1918, he was finally exempted as a "recognized alien enemy" (not the correct terminology but employed widely of Syrians seeking exemptions) weeks before the war's end.[81]

Some inductees succeeded in getting exemptions in 1917 only to be drafted again as the Selective Service Boards issued additional calls to service. This is what happened to ʿAzeez Boulous, originally from Ramallah, Palestine. Boulous was inducted in 1917, then again in July 1918, and a third time in August 1918. In the final instance, Boulous was ordered to Camp Dix to await review of his exemption appeal. He was still at Camp Dix in November 1918, when he was discharged because his unit was disbanded following the armistice.[82]

Some Syrians saw value in participating in the draft and initiated exemption claims when deployment abroad was imminent. This strategy was popular following the May 9 Act which granted Syrian soldiers a fast track to American citizenship. The typical conscript's enlistment process began with weeks or months of training at one of several depot camps build across the eastern seaboard, primarily Camp Dix (New Jersey), Camp Upton (New York), and Camp Devens (Massachusetts). Many Syrian inductees never deployed but instead worked at these camps as privates, kitchen staff, machinists, or chauffeurs. The opportunity to get citizenship in return for such work was appealing enough that some claimed exemption only after being moved to an infantry unit destined for combat. Halim ʿAzar, for instance, served at Camp Upton from his induction in April 1918 until being moved to the 106th Infantry being sent to France. He filed his appeal and, though not formally exempted until after the armistice, was relocated to another unit not headed for the front.[83] Another man in his unit, Dickran Azarian (an Armenian from "Turkey in Asia"), exercised the same strategy and was excused "by reason of being an alien enemy."[84] For officials granting exemptions to these men, however, the perception that they were cheating the system produced resentment. The bureaucrat whose signature invalidated one Awaid ʿAzeezah's service card, for instance, included the commentary "enemy alien, hon[orably] dis[charged] for convenience of government."[85]

A few Syrian soldiers sought belated exemptions because of ill treatment by officers on base. Speaking with the Bureau of Investigation in 1918, Naʿum Mukarzil explained that a friend of his, Dr. A. Khairallah, "was drawn into a draft and served awhile," but that he "does not feel friendly toward this Government, because he feels he was not treated fairly in the matter of his commission."[86] Mukarzil claimed Khairallah took an exemption from the Spanish consul in New York and never returned to base. On the other side of this coin, several draftees applied for exemptions and were summarily denied, leading them to desert their posts and seek help fleeing the country. Such was the case for two privates in West Virginia, Faris Ayyub and Saliba al-Basit, who were denied exemptions in April 1918. Ayyub remained on base and was called for questioning when al-Basit disappeared in the middle of the night.[87] After interrogating Ayyub and several others on base, the Bureau of Investigation believed al-Basit had hired smugglers to escape to Mexico. None of them ever saw him again.

Because the exemption process was hastily enacted and difficult to police, it created new opportunities for fraud. The authorities looking for Saliba al-Basit were part of a federal dragnet investigating Spanish exemption fraud. In early 1918, the Bureau of Investigation discovered two Syrian employees at the Spanish consulate who were supplying exemption questionnaires with false answers to assist naturalized Syrian Americans in evading the draft. Joseph Solomon and Sa'id Joseph fled to Boston where there were arrested and charged with conspiracy.[88] At the same time, the Bureau stepped up security measures at the US border with Mexico, screening the Syrian merchants who crossed it regularly and barring the entry or exit of Syrians holding passports from countries they were not legal citizens of.[89]

Perhaps fearing a loss of respectability, Syrian and Lebanese recruiters in New York City participated in the crusade to prosecute draft dodgers. Even though they resented one another, rival recruiters Ayyub Tabet and Na'um Mukarzil both offered information concerning fraud to the Bureau of Investigation in 1918.[90] Special Agent L. Perkins was dispatched to the Syrian colony in Manhattan to interview local recruiters. One "Mr. Zaloom," a recruiter for the Syrian American Club, told him "the Spanish Consulate has been quite active in aiding local Syrians to evade the selective draft. Many of them come to me for assistance in making out their questionnaires, as I speak both Arabic and English, and that is how I learned of it."[91] Unsure of how widespread the phenomenon was, Zaloom could account for "only one case, Naceep Mallouf, who was aided by the Spanish to get a discharge; but I suppose that was according to international law."[92]

Investigators located and interviewed Mallouf, a printer living in Brooklyn. When they spoke with him, Mallouf readily admitted that he had filed a Declaration of Intent two years earlier, confirming Agent Perkins's suspicions that he was an unlawful deserter. But Naceep Mallouf's status as a declarant immigrant was not so clear-cut, because even though he had begun the naturalization process, he was still legally an Ottoman subject. "A Turkish newspaper here published a notice from the Spanish Consulate that Syrians, being Turkish subjects, were not liable for Unites States military service," explained Mallouf. "I went to the Spanish Consulate to see about this matter, as I did not wish to serve. I met a man at the Consulate . . . who told me to make affidavit as to my

Turkish citizenship and send it to the War Department, and I did so, and claimed exemptions." Mallouf produced his receipt proving his exemption. Perkins asked whether Mount Lebanon was a Turkish possession. "Yes, Mount Lebanon has had some sort of autonomy, but only since 1866," claimed Mallouf, but "the Turkish Government abrogated that when the European War drew it into the conflict."[93]

Mallouf's argument about Mount Lebanon's relationship with the Ottoman Empire was a common one, used simultaneously by pro-enlistment recruiters and by Syrians claiming exemption from the draft. In emphasizing the CUP's abrogation of the Lebanese mutasarrifate, Mallouf strategically reclaimed his Ottoman nationality and, with it, his ineligibility for compulsory service in the United States. This claim directly contradicted, however, the recent US law distinguishing "Syrians and Mount Lebanonites claimed by Turkey as subjects" as a contested nationality, a law that was itself erected on American assumptions that the Lebanese mutasarrifate was disputed territory guaranteed autonomy by foreign powers. Herein lies a conflict. Lebanist activists like Mukarzil argued that the United States should not recognize the CUP's abrogation of the 1861 Règlement Organique; by this logic, he convinced Congress to open voluntary enlistment to Ottoman nationals of Syrian or Lebanese extraction.[94] Mukarzil, Ayyub Tabet, and Shukri al-Bakhash all argued that draft laws could be extended further to justify induction of Syrians and Lebanese as wholly distinct from other Ottoman subjects and thus not entitled to draft exemptions. This belief inspired them to report Syrian deserters, regardless of those deserters' declared nationality. Indeed, this was what happened to Naceep Mallouf.

Wary about imposing draft orders upon Ottoman nationals regardless of the Lebanese mutasarrifate's status, the US government granted exemptions to any Syrian and Lebanese migrants who proffered their Ottoman nationality as proof of their ineligibility. Federal investigators did, however, subject Syrian declarants to heightened scrutiny. Mallouf's exemption was awarded on the basis that, though declarant, he was still an Ottoman subject by virtue of the mutasarrifate's 1914 abolition.[95] In his interview report, federal agent Perkins admitted to wishing he could arrest Mallouf on sight, but he settled for lecturing him instead:

> I could not forbear telling Malloof that as he came here to make money and to find a safe place to live, being protected by the American flag, he showed very poor spirit in hunting up an excuse for evading service under that flag in a crisis like this. Young men like him will either be put to work for the nation or sent back to where they came from.[96]

Weeks later, however, Bureau of Investigation chief Leland Harrison reported that Mallouf's understanding of the law was perceptive and "that according the Spanish Consulate's understanding, the citizens of Mount Lebanon are Turkish subjects and as such, they are under Spanish protections."[97]

The Bureau of Investigation could not confirm rumors that Turkish language newspapers had printed information about Spanish exemptions, but the city's Ladino language *La America* certainly did. The paper's editor, W. Moise Gadol, testified that Spanish consul general Francisco Javier de Salas had compelled him to print a letter in November 1917 reminding Syrians of their Ottoman nationality "even if they have taken out their first papers" and were awaiting naturalization.[98] Agent Perkins then interviewed Mukarzil, who told him "we [the Lebanon League of Progress] know that the Spanish Consul of New York has been sending circulars, especially to the Druses and Moslems of Detroit and West Virginia, warning them that as Turkish subjects they must not serve in the American army." When asked to produce such a letter, Mukarzil lamented "we have tried to get ahold of these circulars, but they have been destroyed by those who received them."[99]

Agent Perkins was unable to find systematic proof of massive exemption fraud in 1918, but rumors circulated through the Syrian community that Ottoman smugglers and spies could help conscripts escape. Some unscrupulous Syrians capitalized on drafted immigrants' desperation: in Cleveland, Ohio, a dozen Druze men were defrauded of $75–125 each by an agent promising them new passports in late 1917.[100] Rumors about itinerant smugglers also abounded. One smuggler named Muhammad al-Hajjar reportedly had access to both Spanish exemptions and fake passports. The Bureau of Investigation pursued Hajjar for months, aided by regular reports from Ayyub Tabet, who translated newspaper clippings about the man from the Syrian press.[101] Hajjar's principal aim, explained Tabet, was to assist Muslim deserters and particularly "those who had taken their first citizenship papers. Once the money was in his possession," Tabet continued, "Hajjar would tell them that he would use the services of the Spanish Consul to get them out of the service."[102] Because Hajjar was never apprehended, it remains unclear whether he was an Ottoman spy (as Tabet insisted) or purely an entrepreneurial fraudster.[103] But Tabet's motivations in reporting him stemmed from his belief that "the actions of Muhammad Hajjar and his like will lead to a wrong impression of our loyalty to this country which has given us all what we have in the world."[104]

The scandal at the Spanish Consulate also provided recruiters with a chance to settle political scores. In mid-1918, Naʿum Mukarzil again accused Shukri al-Bakhash of malfeasance, this time of being involved in Spanish passport falsification.[105] Having just recovered from his indictment at Mukarzil's hand a year before, al-Bakhash decided to fight fire with fire. al-Bakhash told Spanish consul general Francisco Javier de Salas about Mukarzil's accusations, and Salas issued an open letter to Mukarzil denouncing his poisonous rhetoric about al-Bakhash as "a whole tissue of falsehoods, which I ask you to rectify." The consul reminded Mukarzil that whatever his own goals for Mount Lebanon, "my mission is to protect the interests of Turkish subjects . . . whatever their race, creed, or political inclination is, and at the present moment, the Lebanonites are Turkish subjects, whether they like it or not."[106] Shukri al-Bakhash printed Salas' letter in *al-Fatat* every day for a month. The following week, Salas contacted the Bureau of Investigation to clear al-Bakhash's name and to instead report Mukarzil for "pro-German activities."[107] The vaguely articulated boundaries that marked draftees from deserters presented certain opportunities, but accusations of disloyalty also became an occupational hazard.

Syrians on the Western Front

Despite the recruitment obstacles that Ottoman immigrants faced, many Syrians and Lebanese successfully enlisted and deployed to Europe under French, Canadian, British, and American flags. The Syrian press in the diaspora printed their images, biographies, and letters, eagerly documenting Syrians on their "*hajj* to break the German empire."[108] A genre emerged that folded soldiers' stories into a pervasive narrative about Syrian liberation from abroad, serving the ends of recruiters and a variety of migrant nationalists. But Syrian and Lebanese deployment experiences illustrate a variety of responses to life in combat, undermining the confident patriotism imposed on them by the mahjar press. Mounting casualties, the drudgery of trench life, and brazen attempts by nationalists to appropriate the soldiers as political symbols indelibly marked recruits' perspectives of the war. For them, the simultaneity of "Syrian" and "American" patriotism, so important during the enlistment process, began to break down.

Writing home from the Western Front, deployed Syrians frequently reported their discovery of compatriots on the battlefield. Sometimes this was a source of glee: Gabriel Ward reported to Ibrahim al-Khuri and the *Fatat Boston* newspaper that some of the Syrians fighting in Britain's regiments were Ottoman draft-dodgers who "had been offered refuge in Britain" in return for their service.[109] Although few in number, Ottoman deserters who joined the Entente served the Syrian press a powerful symbol for partnership against Istanbul. Discussions about the empire's eroding military morale accompanied images of Syrian troops and advertisements calling for recruits.[110] To encounter an Ottoman deserter in Europe was not typical; the British principally employed them in the Hejaz as saboteurs with Emir Faysal's Arab forces.[111] But the Syrian émigré troops stationed in Europe often met others blended together in ways that facilitated new discussions about what it meant to be "Syrian," "Lebanese," or "Arab" as opposed to "Ottoman" in the context of war.

By 1917, Gabriel Ward's injuries had rendered him unfit for combat. Reassigned to London, Ward worked as an intelligence officer monitoring the city's Syrian periodicals, ethnic societies, and cafés and reporting "pro-German sympathies" to his superiors.[112] Writing to *al-Huda* newspaper in 1917, Ward described an afternoon interaction in one London café known as a haunt of Arab soldiers. Sipping coffee with a group of uniformed Syrian Christians, he was discussing Mount Lebanon's famine when the café owner, a Muslim named Saʿid who identified as a supporter of Emir Faysal's Arab Revolt, commented to the group: "the famine, the war; they are all signs of God's wrath." Ward replied, "the wrath of God, as you say, or that of Government?" The coffeemaker interjected, "God curse the Unionists . . . no Muslim starves or hangs his own people." Noticing the men's uniforms, Saʿid asked if they were "those men recruited by the Lebanon League of Progress?"[113] Ward denied this but voiced his support for Mukarzil's campaign as a means of "Syrian and Lebanese emancipation." Ward's distinction of "Syrian" from "Lebanese" reflected the diaspora's emerging nationalist idioms, but it was a distinction that Hashemite Arab nationalists sharply rejected.[114] Unimpressed by Ward, Saʿid appealed for pan-Arab unity:

> Brother, after this war we will all be together, not as 'Syrian' or 'Lebanese'. Please, I ask you to pass on my words to every colony and corner of your diaspora: that they are not Christian, nor Lebanese, nor Syrian. All of us are Arabs in a Turkish house . . . we are all under a single shadow, and no work can be done [about it] unless we do it together.[115]

Among soldiers, the experience of recruitment, enlistment, and deployment effectively changed what it meant to be Syrian or Lebanese as opposed to Ottoman subjects abroad. By 1918, new national signifiers took on more rigid ideological content.

At the same time, soldiers' writings betrayed a countervailing resistance to nationalist ideas, as well as a mounting belief that the war would destroy, not create, new nations. The war's global character and the Western Front's massive mortality alienated Syrian troops from the nationalist goals reported by activists abroad. Gabriel Ward's report of Jibraʾil Bishara's 1917 death was itself made in complaint over a central promise that recruiters made in the mahjar: that Syrian soldiers fighting anywhere contributed to their homeland's independence. When Ward tendered Bishara's dying words to *al-Huda* and *al-Shaʿb* newspapers in New York, he noted that Bishara's death (not his deployment) delivered him home. As the war wore on, his dispatches to *al-Huda* reveal his frustration with the suffering he encountered on the European front. In another letter to *al-Huda* he described a conversation with an Ottoman deserter hiding out in France. The man "had death in his eyes. He had witnessed true alienation and had a severe, strained countenance" as he asked Ward for help in joining the French infantry. Ward reported that, when he asked why he wished to join the Allies, the deserter chillingly replied, "Are we not all alienated? Are we not, all of us, fighting together? As this war heaps ever greater numbers of us, corpses and fleeing soldiers, atop one another, we shed our contrasting colors and are joined in mutual fear."[116] If Ward's account of Bishara's death had any quality of homecoming through martyrdom, this exchange comes to a grimmer conclusion: mortality as the means by which men cast off their nationalist raiment and rejoin an undifferentiated, suffering humanity.

Back on the American home front, Syrian newspapers were undeterred. They continued to celebrate deployed troops and facilitate the ongoing recruitment efforts of their editors. But soldiers' experiences abroad differed significantly from the expectations of the mahjar's nationalists, producing moments of friction when the latter appropriated recruits as nationalist symbols. After enlisting with a group of Syrian leatherworkers in Boston, Jurj Maʿtuq deployed to northern France in 1918, working as a translator for the 101st Engineer Corps. Once abroad, he wrote home to *Fatat Boston* to ask the immigrant community send care packages to his deployed compatriots.[117] The newspaper featured Maʿtuq's note on page 1, with the biographies of "entrenched Syrians" on the Western Front.[118] Its editor, Wadiʿ Shakir, also wrote a full-page editorial applauding Maʿtuq and plugging his Syrian American Club recruitment work. "We Syrians," Shakir began,

> We grow up abhorring the military lifestyle, and we live timid lives in fear and bitterness. Then there are those of us who go to service and face a world of death. Those feelings of fear and timidity are in the hearts of every young Syrian because of the Turkish government's brutality, of shortages and starvation . . . [but] they can draw on these hatreds to fight off eons under the Turkish yoke.[119]

Shakir left no room for ambiguity: these soldiers were engaged in a battle against the Ottomans on behalf of Syrians around the world. He probably thought that Maʿtuq would approve of his narrative; instead, Maʿtuq was outraged.

Upon reading about his unit in *Fatat Boston*, Maʿtuq penned a deeply critical letter to Shakir and the Syrian American Club. As a Syrian American, he saw himself as principally engaged in "a fight to the end for the stars and stripes, that flag of liberty and democracy."[120] He resented his name being attached to a discussion of homeland politics, and he felt that Shakir had capitalized on the lives of his fellow soldiers:

Figure 3.5. George Abraham Matook, photographed in Boston before his 1918 deployment. "Photograph of G. A. Matook, Co. E, 101st Engineers," Globe Newspaper Company, photograph 359, State Library of Massachusetts Digital Collections. My thanks to Omar Duwaji for this image.

> You are acting as Americans, in America, [but] are you really Americans, or are you only Americans for your busnis [*sic*]? I just wonder what your idea was in taking our name, our company's name and regiment address. I gust [*sic*, "guessed"] it was so you could remembre [*sic*] us when we die. Or was it to write to each other and attach your club to us, same as all the other [immigrant] clubs? I would just like to find out . . . what kind of Americans you really are. We [are] in France doing our bit, what are you fellows doing?[121]

Ma'tuq invoked what he saw as the fundamental distinction between Syrian soldiers and the émigré nationalists responsible for recruiting so many of them. For the nationalists, soldiers were a symbol of Syria's liberation and redemption. For Ma'tuq, by contrast, they were agents of liberation: "We [are] not fighters only where we were [*sic*] born but we are fighting for Syria too and Liberty. God is leading us to Liberty, our flag on his Right and France on his left, heading us towards Liberty." Maʿtuq challenged Shakir to use his pen to write to deployed Syrians in solidarity, rather than about them in the press: "even if they are not a member of your club, they are your own nationality, your kind, the same as the Italian, the Jew, and the Polish . . . why should we let somebody else [be] better than us?"[122]

Ironically, Maʿtuq's multilayered patriotism—as simultaneously Syrian and American—had already started to fall out of style among nationalists like Wadiʿ Shakir in favor of programmatic nationalist agendas concerned with the Syrian Question, Wilsonian self-determination, and the emergence of new national borders on the Middle Eastern map. The recruitment of emigrants had depended on a flexible, multi-layered patriotism appealing to desires for both Syrian liberation and American inclusion. The postwar movement, by contrast, would depend on unambiguous claims to national territories, histories, and identities. At the precise moment that Syrian soldiers grew frustrated with the limitations of nationalist discourse, activists abroad promoted these same nationalisms to policymakers in the Entente.

Conclusion

The First World War ended in the Ottoman Empire's defeat in October 1918 and with Syria's occupation by British, French, and Arab troops. The victorious Entente powers announced that the postwar settlement would be decided at the Paris Peace Conference in 1919, prompting dozens of Syrian migrant recruiters-turned-nationalists to shift focus from mobilizing the mahjar's military manpower to harnessing its representative voice through petition campaigns. In their production, circulation, and presentation to the Great Powers, petitions on the Syrian Question followed the same routes that once delivered Syrian troops to enlistment centers. Often, these documents passed through the same networks of men whose hands had stamped foreign passports, drawn up naturalization papers, and provided steamship tickets to migrant troops a year earlier. Those hands continued to shape the politics of the eastern Mediterranean long after the Wilsonian moment, into and through the interwar French Mandate.

For these activists, military recruitment was a significant form of war work, illustrative of a symbolic compact between Arab migrant communities and the host societies they lived in. Enlistment sat at one end of a broader spectrum of pro-Entente cooperation, the other side of the humanitarian work promoted by US organizations then raising funds in Syrian colonies across the Americas. Humanitarian politics depended on a rhetoric of depoliticized relief, but when taken from the perspective of the Syrian émigré aid workers these committees relied on, relief work became intensely political. In the

Syrian neighborhoods of the mahjar, then, both proponents and opponents of relief understood it as one among many resistance acts, including military contributions. This, too, continued through the interwar period, inflecting the mahjar's philanthropic tradition and its fraught relationship with homeland nationalisms.[123]

The Entente powers had different attitudes about the role that immigrants should play in the war effort, as well as in what immigrant soldiers could expect after being decommissioned. The French saw the symbolic value of stationing Arab troops along the Ottoman fronts, and employed colonials within confined units, ineligible for French citizenship. The Americans, by contrast, treated the US army as a site for immigrant Americanization, offering them legal naturalization for service but confining post-Ottoman troops to European fronts. The papers these men were offered in exchange for their service impacted their individual political fates, but also those of their homelands. The passports given to Arab soldiers fighting for the French did not entitle them to French citizenship, but they did function as a post-Ottoman nationality document in the interstitial years between the 1918 armistice and the Treaty of Lausanne. In 1923, Syrians who fought for the United States, similarly, presented that government with the challenge of codifying "Syrian" national origins during the war. US immigration regulations on who could claim Syrian nationality, in turn, impacted French Mandate laws determining nationality rights in the Middle East. If the mahjar's soldiers were forgotten by history after a generation, the legal legacies of this recruitment campaign go on.

Émigré nationalists understood the soldiers' symbolic significance and were eager to exploit the documentary opportunities that the recruitment campaigns had opened up after 1918. But as nationalists pressed forth with claims for repatriation, nationality rights, and new national borders, most of the soldiers they claimed to represent could no longer identify themselves within nationalist rhetoric. Most of them instead secured American citizenship, remaining abroad but maintaining a fluid, situational political identity: simultaneously Syrian and American, and as migrants with familial, commercial, and affective ties to the new states of Syria and Lebanon. 1919 would be a year full of ironies. Decommissioned Syrian troops across the Americas would pick up the newspaper, side-eye the nationalist politics playing out at Paris, and perhaps scoff at the constructed nature of homogeneous, exclusive concepts of national identification: Syrian, Lebanese, Palestinian, American, but never all of these at once. Even as one-time homeland liberators, such contrived categories had never much suited them.

4

New Syrians Abroad

An Émigré Project for a United States Mandate in Syria,
1918–1920

It was a cold January day at the wharf, *Fatat Boston* newspaper reported, when Ibrahim al-Khuri and Wadiʿ Shakir awaited the steamship that could carry Rev. Abraham Mitrie Rihbany to France. Only eight weeks had passed since the Ottoman Empire signed the Armistice of Mudros—news that reverberated in telegrams, newspaper columns, and personal correspondence across the Syrian mahjar. al-Khuri, Shakir, and Rihbany spent most of those weeks travelling between Boston and New York City, discussing strategy in Syrian affairs with the New Syria National League (Jamʿiyyat Suriya al-Jadida al-Wataniyya, hereafter NSNL), an Arab nationalist committee with Wilsonian, pro-independence leanings.

Though al-Khuri and Shakir were both US Army recruiters, they accompanied Rihbany to New York's port on a different errand. A Syrian Protestant reverend from Shwayr in Mount Lebanon, Rihbany was headed for France, where he would petition the 1919 Paris Peace Conference as the NSNL's delegate. As a well-known advocate for Syrian immigrants in America, Rihbany was an obvious choice for this task: during the war, he published extensively on the benefits of Americanism and "East-West" cultural exchange, he promoted US Liberty bonds, and he worked diligently to raise relief with the American Red Cross.[1] Under his arm, the reverend carried petitions bearing signatures from "thousands of Syrians who are members of the New Syria National League (of New York City) and the Syrian Union (of Boston)." If admitted to the conference in Paris, he was to deliver the petitions and lay out the aspirations of Syrian émigré activists for national self-determination and opposition to French tutelage. "America is free from personal ambitions and has demonstrated its disinterest in this war," Rihbany was quoted in *Fatat Boston*; "it has earned the respect of the Syrian people."[2] Having garnered the endorsements of powerful men such as Henry Cabot Lodge, head of the US Senate Foreign Relations Committee, the Syrian reverend believed he would be welcomed at the peace conference.[3]

The First World War ended in the Ottoman Empire's defeat at the hands of the Entente Powers. Ottoman troops evacuated Syria and Mount Lebanon, leaving them in the hands of Arab, British, and French forces. Syrian activists at home and abroad shifted their attentions to the Paris Peace Conference, where gathered representatives of the Entente would hear appeals by former Ottoman subjects clamoring for independence. Two tensions defined the peace conference and the international forum it wrought. First, the ethos of Woodrow Wilson's Fourteen Points raised expectations among Middle Eastern nationalists that they could petition the great powers and be heard. Second, the ongoing competition between Great Britain and France for supremacy in the Middle East led them both to employ procedural tactics to undermine the goals of imperial adversaries and nationalists alike.[4] The Wilsonian moment had arrived, and it brought with it all of the contradictions and imperial double-dealings that defined the prewar moment.[5] In one significant departure, however, the United States of America presided over the conference, and its American delegation demanded that its proceedings place the political claims of the world's "small peoples" at the fore.

For organizations representing Syrian, Palestinian, and Lebanese migrants living in the mahjar, the postwar negotiations represented a major opportunity to establish independent Arab states in the homeland. Migrant activists who spent the war working for the Entente as recruiters, smugglers, and propagandists quickly reorganized themselves into nationalist political committees aimed at the creation of new states in the eastern Mediterranean. Already in control of the press, émigré societies allied with the Arab nationalists under Emir Faysal, with the Syrianists under Shukri Ghanim, and the Lebanists under the Alliance Libanaise (Hizb al-Ittihad al-Lubnani) and the Lebanon League of Progress (Jam'iyyat al-Nahda al-Lubnaniyya) all vied for the attentions of a global Syrian public.[6] These parties circulated pamphlets and petitions endorsing a dizzying array of political visions, literally papering the mahjar and hoping to harness the power of its numbers.[7] For the nationalists, the Syrian mahjar was a political frontier to be claimed for the purposes of Middle Eastern nation-building.

Mahjari petitions arrived at the peace conference via telegram or under the arms of Arab delegates seeking to present their views to the assembly. The great powers admitted a few of these delegations, including those who came from the Americas. Historians have diligently restored the history of the mahjar's delegates to the conference, stressing the role diasporic actors played in the "Syrian Question" negotiations, especially in the decision to partition Greater Lebanon (the *Grand Liban*) from Syria and place both under French Mandate.[8] But the histories of those locked outside the halls of power remain a dim curiosity despite the multitudes who came to Paris only to be denied entry to the conference. Men like Abraham Rihbany, whose petitions were left unread by the conference, have been subsequently unaddressed by histories of this moment. Examining stories like Rihbany's and of his organization, the NSNL, fundamentally shift prevailing views about the mahjar and its relationship to the emergent French Mandate.

The conference's hierarchical structure and its system of great power sponsorship undermined the meeting's professed goal to adhere to the principles of self-determination. Significant work went into determining which delegates would be granted an audience, and Great Britain and France employed procedural tactics to block appearances by delegates with goals contradicting their own regional claims.[9] As a result, the petitions heard by the peace conference represented a fraction of those circulated in Syria and its mahjar. The conference therefore constructed a significant legal fiction: that the Arab Middle East lacked a viable means to independence and required foreign tutelage, and that Syrians and Lebanese—especially those living in diaspora—supported the Mandate principle.

From 1918 through the 1920 Treaty of San Remo, the French government went to considerable lengths to present themselves as the protectors of Syrian migrants abroad, who they depicted as political exiles awaiting the French-led liberation of their homeland. French consulates in the Americas produced reams of paper promoting this narrative about the mahjar, working with clients to subsidize Francophile Arabic publications, draft pro-French petitions, and amplify pro-French Syrian voices through delegations to the peace conference.[10] The mahjar's political realities were far messier.[11] Syrian and Lebanese migrants protested French rule, boycotted French businesses, condemned French attempts to censor them, and threatened the safety of pro-Mandate activists in the Syrian colonies.[12] Far from colonial middlemen, the diaspora Syrians were instead a restive population that could only be partly contained through travel restriction, punitive diplomacy, or revocation of national status.

The legal fiction that the mahjar supported the Mandate elides evidence of diasporic anticolonialism and consequently frames the French domestication of the diaspora—its "mandating" of the mahjar—as a partnership of mutual collaboration. The reality was closer to a forceful pacification of a transnational frontier. To write a history of mahjari protest during the Wilsonian moment requires pursuing men whose parties were denied entry into the 1919 Paris Peace Conference. Abraham Rihbany, the scorned delegate of the NSNL, was such a man. Rihbany and his contemporaries represented a transnational network of "New Syria" clubs joining nationalists in Egypt, the United States, Argentina, and Cuba. Rejected by the conference, the New Syrians lobbied instead for greater Syria's unity (including Mount Lebanon and Palestine) and independence under an Arab government and a limited American Mandate.

The idea for a US Mandate in Syria was one of dozens of proposed plans for the former Ottoman province in 1918–1919. Like the others, it was forgotten after France took control of the territory, but its momentary popularity illustrates that, for Syrians abroad, French rule was a challenge to be vehemently protested. For many emigrants, a French Mandate promised division within the homeland and permanent legal separation from it: Syrians abroad feared expulsion, denationalization, and permanent exile. The idea that the United States could be persuaded into taking control over a greater Syrian state momentarily proved a credible alternative. Syrians fitted the US Mandate idea into well-established theories of American "benevolent empire," suggesting that the specter of French rule in Syria could be dispatched through careful lobbying in Washington.[13]

American Exceptionalism and Arab Nationalism

The vision of an American role in Syria's postwar reconstruction emerged late in the war, promoted by American expansionists, Protestant missionaries, and Syrian émigré elites from Beirut, Cairo, and New York City. The connection to the Protestant mission and particularly the Syrian Protestant College is significant, as many of the Syrian intellectuals promoting US intervention were alumni with abiding connections to the school.[14] The New Syrians' link to America's expansionist lobby was of more recent vintage, developing during the war and especially in the contacts that Syrian American activists made as US Army recruiters.

Invoking wartime military partnerships and a historical legacy of American educational activity in Syria and Mount Lebanon, the New Syria activists built their vision for Syria on the ideological foundations of evangelical American exceptionalism and on the multicultural mythology accompanying this exceptionalism. Drawing on recent memories of America's "benevolent" interventions in the Philippines and Cuba during the Spanish-American War, the Syrian activists presented their homeland as the next American frontier. Some of them had served America in 1898. New Syria propaganda narrated, for instance, Gabriel Ward's experience of deploying to the Philippines after answering President McKinley's call for volunteers.[15] Before Dr. Najeeb Saleeby returned to New York City to assume a role as the NSNL's general secretary, he served the American colonial administration in Manila and was a specialist on the Moro people and their nationalist resistance.[16]

New Syrian propaganda blended the rhetoric of Wilsonian self-determination and independence from colonial rule with that of American expansionism. Abraham Rihbany, for example, captured the attentions of policymakers, diplomats, and missionaries with his 1918 *America Save the Near East*. An

Figure 4.1. Gabriel Ilyas Ward in 1898, enlistment photography from the Spanish-American War. Ward, *al-Jundi al-Suri fi-Thulath Hurub,* 187. James Ansara Papers, IHRC208, Immigration History Research Center Archives, University of Minnesota.

attempt to "voice the desire of an oppressed people for deliverance" and a "plea to America to undertake the reconstruction of Syria," Rihbany's book argued for a US Mandate in Syria and proposed a partnership with Syrian émigré clubs to rebuild the country.[17] He situated this project as completing work unfinished by the Young Turk Revolution:

> When the "Revolution"' of 1908 took place in Turkey, a gleam of hope flickered for a time in the land. The intelligent classes *loved* to hope that a better day was dawning upon a people that have suffered long and

silently endured that liberty and justice and enlightenment were on their way to revive and strengthen the soul of a people which had dwelt so long in the valley of the shadow of death. But that political enterprise proved to be a failure.[18]

Rihbany's reading of 1908, the expectations it raised, and the disenchantment that followed fits his work squarely within Arabist narratives. His assessment of why the revolution failed expanded on this idea while illustrating the need for foreign intervention: it failed

> because it was not a revolution of the people, but of a few army officers . . . and in reality there was no government behind the army and no united people. Whatever the original intentions of . . . the Young Turks who inaugurated the 'Revolution' may have been, the test of experience proved them to be no greater lovers of freedom and justice than the miscreants whom they had overthrown, nor half so able as those to direct the affairs of the Empire.[19]

Because it was not the popular revolution it set out to be, the Young Turks had been incapable of constructing either a universal Ottoman patriotism or a liberal constitutional system. Instead, the Unionist military leadership pursued a centralist trajectory that carried Syria into a disastrous world war.[20]

Rihbany also argued there was a natural confluence of interests between Syria's Arab nationalist movement and America's foreign policy objectives, particularly in combatting "the imperialistic machinations of the Old World" that had caused the war and destroyed his homeland. US influence in the region, by contrast, had been "a wise and great service to humanity," but Rihbany feared that isolationist impulses might keep the United States out of the Syrian Question:

> [America] has something to give which they [the Syrians] need to receive. She did wisely to shun the "game of kings." But now the new impulses are agitating human society all over the world. Not the game of kings, but the legitimate rights of peoples to gain their lawful rights now occupy the stage of social evolution. Our active sympathies must be allowed, nay, must be directed, to flow beyond out national borders to reach the uttermost parts of the earth.[21]

In appealing to the American spirit, Rihbany argued that the United States must "be the champion of liberty not only in word, but in deed." For Syria, this meant coming to "do the work of a liberator and educator" in reconstructing the decaying social structures after the war's end. Describing a US Mandate as a work of reconstruction rather than one of tutelage was part of Rihbany's strategy to appeal to American political sensibilities, particularly to American exceptionalism. America's westward frontier had been closed for a half century, but Rihbany exclaimed, "America, go East!"[22]

Race played an interesting role in Rihbany's ideas. *America Save the Near East* depicted the United States as a youthful nation with a recent colonial past and successful (although imperfect) experience of integrating immigrants from multireligious and multiethnic backgrounds. Rihbany borrowed such notions from Americanization educational projects, some of which he had participated in as a social worker in Boston and which he put to work here as a model for post-Ottoman Syria. Concerning Syria's own diversity, Rihbany explained that "notwithstanding the fact that the dominant blood in it is the Semitic, Syria has never developed a racial identity."[23] America's historical "experiment of racial amalgamation" could provide a model for confronting the divisions within Syria's ethnic and confessional communities:

> America . . . could go into Syria as a friend and helper, not only as a Power that is free from the age-old European complications and without the craving for a "sphere of influence" for herself, but with the tangible fruits of a vast and successful experiment in peaceably welding together many racial elements together and making them one free and enlightened nation.[24]

Assimilation programs like those targeting immigrant communities in New England, he proposed, would remake Syrian national identity while managing this diversity.

Rihbany's utopian appeal to American racial harmony would have appeared quite foreign to immigrants and, indeed, to many of America's citizens, since Arab Americans at this time were dealing with Islamophobia and acts of racist violence, including robbery, rape, and lynching.[25] Nevertheless, Rihbany believed that as the world's anticolonial power, the United States could rebuild Syria in her own constitutional, federalist image without simultaneously colonizing it.

Nor would America have to go it alone. Arab American immigrants—a quarter million of them by Rihbany's optimistic assessment—would repatriate to Syria to do the work of reconstruction, modernizing its economy, and granting the new state a pro-American technocratic class. By suggesting that emigrants would happily "return to the country of their birth to share in its rebuilding," Rihbany depicted every Syrian American as a respectable model minority that "makes a very creditable use of the ballot, is an ardent lover of his adopted country, and, as present military records show, a sacrificing patriot."[26] Other New Syria leaders echoed this expectation that the emigrants would repatriate home. In 1919, for instance, Dr. Philip K. Hitti planned a Syrian American educational mission to Syria to rebuild the country's educational infrastructure "because of the special connection America has with the revival of the Syrian intellectual scene."[27]

Rihbany's manifesto echoed in serials across the mahjar and found its way to activists working in the Middle East. "I believe I have advocated that which the majority of enlightened Syrians in this country and the much-afflicted 'old home' would approve," he concluded. That the NSNL elected him to serve as its representative in Paris illustrates that perhaps he was right.[28] *America Save the Near East* was not the first or only plan for a US Mandate in the region; several variations of the idea also floating around in Armenian, Kurdish, and Turkish intellectual circles. What is clear, though, is that Rihbany's text found its way into diplomatic cables from informants representing America in Egypt, and they reported the idea had found favor among Syrians there.

Working in Cairo as a missionary, American Samuel Zwomer discovered an Arabic translation of *America Save the Near East* circulating in intellectual circles close to *al-Muqtataf* and *al-Muqattam*, periodicals owned by Faris Nimr and Ya'cub Sarruf. Retitled "The Future of Syria," the pamphlet reproduced sections of Rihbany's work and described an American-led reconstruction of the homeland. Translating it back into English, Zwomer sent the pamphlet to Secretary of State Robert Lansing, opining that a US Mandate was an interesting (if improbable) proposition. Was not America's own historical experience in "assimilating a worse mixture of races" like that of Syria's sectarian divisions? Looking at the Near East through the eyes of a missionary, Zwomer concluded, "It has been aptly remarked that the Syrians are the Americans of the East. Like them they are a mixed race and highly enterprising, with this great difference however that instead of evolving under a free and forward system of government, they have degenerated under a tyrannical and backward rule."[29] Zwomer did not name the party responsible for the pamphlet but suggested that Syrians close to Egypt's British administration printed it, a likely allusion to Faris Nimr, the city's most prolific printer who had outspokenly endorsed the idea. Zwomer also suggested Great Britain might view a US Mandate with favor.[30]

In addition to repeating Rihbany's claims that American intervention in Syria would be driven by the principle of nation-building and "not by the lust of conquest and domination,"[31] Zwomer's Cairo pamphlet offered more details on Syrian American immigrants and their contributions to such a project. "There are in the U.S.A. some 75,000 Syrian voters ... [they] would be the chief factors in the regeneration of the country and have amassed their wealth in the U.S.A." The new generation of Syrian Americans would provide capital investment, and this investment would be matched by a large majority of [Syrian emigrants] expected to return to Syria once the odious Turkish yoke is lifted off. They will not wish anything better than to continue to breathe the same strong atmosphere of American liberty in their own country, and develop under the same free institutions.[32]

All in all, the Cairo pamphlet demonstrates the density of the intellectual linkages across the Syrian mahjar and the emerging idea among Syrian émigrés that America could be an ally. The vision for who America's partners in Damascus would be remained inchoate, however; neither Rihbany nor the Cairo pamphlet described a relationship with Emir Faysal. But in drawing a rough sketch of US expansion into Syria, this propaganda energized Syrian activists following the 1918 Armistice. The New Syria National League of New York and its partners in Cairo, Buenos Aires, and Boston capitalized on these ideas, turning them into a coherent political platform in early 1919.

The New Syria National League of New York City

Syrian migrant societies in the Americas tried to avoid being seen as overtly political institutions during the war, lest they ignite nativist suspicions or investigation into the community's loyalties. The idea that wartime work might yield broad US support for Syrian national aspirations, though, was never far from the surface. Syrian committees raised relief for the Red Cross and the American Committee for Syrian Relief, translated US propaganda into Arabic, purchased Liberty bonds, and recruited soldiers, wrapping each of these activities within a project for Arab-American alliance. War work was not only an expression of American patriotism but often an expression of Middle Eastern nationalisms.

Immediately following the 1918 armistice, Syrian American societies took a decisive step toward direct political intervention on Syria's behalf. On November 22,1918, activists founded the New Syria National League, with headquarters in both New York City and Boston. The party's executive board included the migrant community's most recognizable activists, most of them invested in partnerships with US policymakers or the Army: Dr. Philip Hitti, Dr. Najeeb Saleeby, Rev. Abraham Rihbany, Habib Katibah, Wadiʿ Shakir, and Ibrahim al-Khuri. The League swiftly elected a chairman, Jurj Ilyas Khayrallah. After establishing its slogan, "Syria for the Syrians, Independent and Undivided under American Guardianship," they drafted an urgent telegram to Secretary of State Robert Lansing: "The New Syria League anxious to see the United States take active part in the reconstruction of Syria. Appeals to you to grant an interview to its representative, Reverend Abraham M. Rihbany."[33]

The NSNL demanded the preservation of a "Syrian homeland, federated and independent," including Mount Lebanon and Palestine (which the party described as "southern Syria"). It rejected the foreign tutelage or "protection" offered by European powers and sought instead limited "technical assistance by the United States."[34] It stressed the ability of Syrian migrants abroad to deliver postwar reconstruction through capital investment and repatriation programs targeting the young Syrian American generation (typically preceded by party-sponsored college education).[35] The repatriation of Syrian Americans would help ensure that, in the words of Habib Katibah, "the burden of guardianship would not be heavy (for America). The Syrians only need a little assistance to get back on their feet again," especially through the founding of national schools.[36] Citing America's "honor in its dealings with foreign nations under its guidance" and unique capacity to "leave when it becomes clear that the people can rule themselves capably,"[37] the NSNL commanded Syrian migrants in the diaspora to "follow the flag (home) as America's great gift to the East."[38]

Having established its project, the NSNL lobbied American policymakers to generate support for American intervention. Receiving Rihbany's telegrams, US Secretary of State Lansing invited him to Washington for a meeting, along with Henry Cabot Lodge, then head of the US Senate Foreign Relations Committee.[39] A long-standing American expansionist, Senator Lodge agreed with Rihbany's reasoning that Syria could be reconstructed through a US intervention on the order of the Philippines, and on December 16, 1918, Lodge presented the NSNL resolutions to Congress for consideration. As attentions shifted to Paris in January 1919, the NSNL submitted its resolutions to the State Department in the hope that America would support a delegation to discuss their vision with the assembled powers.[40]

The Syrian Question was among the most contentious issues debated at the Paris Peace Conference of 1919. France pushed her claim to spheres of influence in Syria and Mount Lebanon, competing with Great Britain for political supremacy and border territories bisecting the former Ottoman territories of the Arab Levant. Secret documents leaked by the Bolsheviks in 1917 revealed Britain and France had planned to divide the Middle East between them, infuriating Arab leadership. The revelations of the 1916 Sykes-Picot Agreements made the prospect of a US Mandate in Syria politically desirable in the eyes of Arab nationalists. That the United States of America would preside over the conference gave Arab nationalists hope that the principle of national self-determination would be abided. Indeed, on the surface it appears that even the Great Powers believed the same thing: all petitioners at Versailles had to have the legitimating sheen of representing the will of the Syrian people. As a result, both Britain and France charged into the mahjar in search of Syrian voices that would justify their policy goals.

The mahjar's nationalist societies were acutely aware of how the diaspora's demographic weight could be leveraged at the conference. For that reason, they all made overtures to French, British, and American officials; the great powers, in turn, sought to harness unclaimed voices from among them. When the French Foreign Ministry learned about an émigré campaign in the Americas in support of a French Mandate in early 1919, for instance, they granted pro-French petitioners office space in the French consulates, paid them to collect signatures, and asked French officials in cities with Syrian populations to promote them locally.[41] These campaigns joined, of course, France's practice of subsidizing Francophile Arabic newspapers in the Americas and of pro-French propaganda.[42] Syrian and Arab nationalist camps opposed these measures but contended with a powerful and well-financed network of Francophile activists, particularly those affiliated with the Lebanon League of Progress (hereafter LLP) and the Alliance Libanaise.[43] Petitioning was a particularly high-stakes practice because it was upon these documents that the powers sponsored national delegations to the peace conference. As it turned out, France was also deeply committed to filtering out groups whose appeals contradicted French goals in the region.

Though facing a formidable Lebanist opposition, the NSNL was confident that their message would be carried by the American delegation because, in the words of the party's Boston-area secretary, Wadiʿ Shakir, America's politicians "will solve the Syrian Question through international compacts" rather than through dodgy secret treaties like Sykes-Picot. "Because America favors Syrians' honorable democratic intentions . . . only they will hear our appeal for unity," Shakir concluded in January 1919.[44] The party's delegate, Abraham Rihbany, boarded a steamship bound for France. But in the three weeks it would take to traverse the Atlantic, the odds of the New Syrians' plan for a US Mandate irrevocably worsened.

Abraham Rihbany was not the only émigré delegate to come to Paris hoping for an audience with the world; the arrival of his rival, Naʿum Mukarzil, in February 1919 illustrates he was not even the only one coming from New York.[45] Paris was also the headquarters of the Comité Central Syrien (hereafter CCS), Shukri Ghanim's and Georges Samné's organization; its Syrianist delegates milled around the city in a perpetual search for influence. An established French ally, Shukri Ghanim sat at the head of a global network of Syrian migrants who believed their collaboration would yield a greater Syrian state under some degree of French tutelage.

Ghanim's wartime bloc was so well represented that even activists who loathed his pro-French politics worked with him on humanitarian endeavors. But in early 1919, his fortunes changed swiftly under the fickle winds of French imperial priorities. The disclosure that France had planned a partition of the region, for instance, polarized the nationalist positions of clubs previously under the CCS's umbrella and damaged Ghanim's credibility in the mahjar. Goodwill toward Ghanim further eroded when he met with French policymakers at the Marseilles Congress in January 1919, presenting a CCS plan for a French protectorate over greater Syria as the majority will of all Syrians, at home and in the mahjar.[46] He also told his French interlocutors that a new system of secular education would be required, specifically to win over Syrian Muslims who remained wary of France's overtures to "protect" the region's Christians.[47]

Syrian and Arab nationalist leaders abroad reviled Ghanim's representation of the mahjar and its aspirations, and the emigrant mood shifted decisively against Franco-Syrian partnership and toward complete and unfettered independence (with or without American assistance). Migrant leaders published statements protesting that Ghanim had misrepresented their interests and those of the Syrian people. From Cairo, Faris Nimr addressed the Paris Peace Conference directly:

> the Comité Central Syrien have told the European press that "the Syrian people unanimously demand a close Franco-Syrian Union." This is sheer myth, a disgraceful bluff. The sincerest friends of France and of the Lebanon . . . are with a country which wants to stand on her feet alone.[48]

Together with Ya'cub Sarruf and Khalil Khayyat, Faris Nimr founded the Moderate Syrian Party (al-Hizb al-Suri al-Mu'tadil) in January 1919. Growing out of the Syrian Union Party then active in Cairo, the Moderate Syrian Party promoted the goals of Arab nationalism and a US Mandate among the Syrians of Egypt. In his letter protesting Ghanim's Francophilism, Nimr laid out his party's goals for Syria: a decentralized, federated Syrian state "possessing National Arab Unity," immediate "full independence under the aegis of the League of Nations," a new constitution with a secular civil code and laws to guarantee the rights of minorities, and a formal partnership with the United States of America in Syria's reconstruction.[49] "The attitude of Syrians, who have the interest of the homeland at heart, tends to secure for Syria the soundest freedom with the help of the most impartial Power," Nimr reasoned, and even more, "the Syrian Colony of America have openly asked the United States to reorganize Syria."[50] Nimr's support for a US Mandate elicited some distrust among his partisans within Cairo's Syrian Union, but also produced a trans-Atlantic alliance with the NSNL of New York. He kept a correspondence with chairman Jurj Khayrallah for much of 1919.[51]

The French Foreign Ministry kept close surveillance on Faris Nimr and his contemporaries, suspecting the Moderate Syrian Party was actually an Anglophile cell working with the British to deny France its stake in the Syrian Question. These suspicions were not entirely misplaced: both *al-Muqtataf* and *al-Muqattam* were openly pro-British in their outlook. And in both Cairo and Washington, DC, British military officials leaned on the United States to consider taking the Mandate in Syria as a means of curbing French regional influence.[52] From his office in Paris, Shukri Ghanim warned French War Minister Georges Clemenceau that groups like Nimr's Moderate Syrian Party were popular enough to threaten French goals in Syria.[53] But with so many Syrians reviling Ghanim in the press, the French grew nervous about whether he was a political liability.

Ghanim's Syrianist coalition progressively fell apart over the question of France's role in the Middle East, prompting rival Lebanist organizations to capitalize on this moment, lobbying French policymakers toward their goals for a Lebanese state. France spent the war suspicious of the goals of the Lebanese independence movement, or at least, of the secular nationalism of Cairo's Alliance Libanaise (Hizb al-Ittihad al-Lubnani), which it accused of being a British front as late as November 1918.[54] But following the Marseilles Congress, the French Foreign Ministry pivoted sharply toward endorsing a greater Lebanese state under French Mandate and endorsed the platform of the Alliance Libanaise. Originally a part of the decentralization movement, the party sought the creation of a greater Lebanese state (the *Grand Liban*) separate from its Syrian hinterland, its territories enlarged from historical Mount Lebanon and Beirut to include Tripoli, Saida, and the fertile Bekaa Valley. Initially opposed to the principle of foreign mandates, the Alliance Libanaise endorsed the French Mandate as the path to independence after securing French backing for Greater Lebanon.[55] The decision had not been without its drama; party chairman Iskandar ʿAmmun resigned in protest, leaving the party under the leadership of Auguste Adib Pasha and Yusuf Sawda.[56]

France's endorsement of Lebanism was, of course, strategic. Upon securing this new instrument for French policy in the Levant, they reassessed their relationship with Shukri Ghanim and the CCS generally. Ghanim's frustration grew as his many letters went unanswered or returned replies full of condescending platitudes.[57] In summer 1919, he resolved to travel to Syria, only to have his passport request rejected. Meanwhile, the French Foreign Ministry sponsored two Lebanese delegations at the Paris Peace Conference. The first was led by Daud ʿAmmun and presented the Alliance Libanaise's plan for a greater Lebanese nation-state, simultaneously published as *Le Liban après la guerre* in February 1919.[58] The second came later that year, when Maronite Patriarch Ilyas Huwayyik confirmed both his support for a Lebanese state and his belief in France's historic obligation of protecting Lebanese Christians. The two Lebanese delegations played a significant role in the League of Nations decision to award the mandate over Syria and Mount Lebanon to France in April 1920.[59]

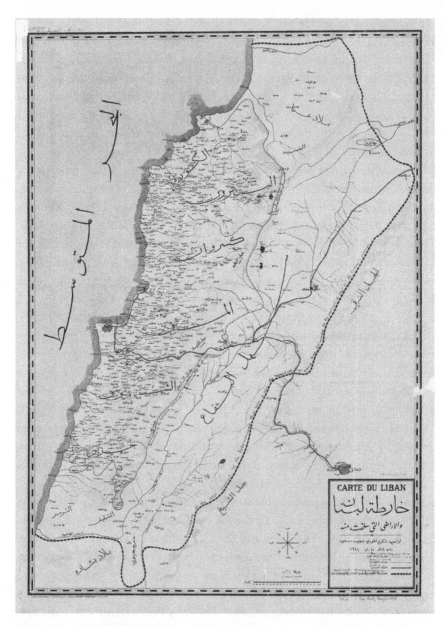

Figure 4.2. 1918 Map of Lebanon and claims to its expansion, adapted from French maps by Shukri al-Khuri and Habib Mas'ud for the Lebanon League of Progress [Jam'iyyat al-Nahda al-Lubnaniyya], São Paulo, Brazil. The map was presented to the Paris Peace Conference by the First Lebanese Delegation in 1919. American Geographical Society Library, University of Wisconsin, Milwaukee. My thanks to Zayde Antrim for this image.

Syrian activists in the mahjar watched their political fortunes change at Paris in 1919, as several parties previously allied with Ghanim broke ranks and endorsed the American Mandate idea and its public face, the New Syria National League. Ghanim repeatedly begged France to abandon the greater Lebanese idea, arguing that rival petitions for an American role in Syria would dissipate into irrelevance if France endorsed Syrian unity.[60] And there was something to his rhetoric, because it was France's endorsement of the First Lebanese Delegation that alienated its former partners in the mahjar and bolstered the popularity of Arab nationalism there. In New York City, for instance, the chairman of the Syria-Mount Lebanon League of Liberation (Lajna Tahrir Suriyya wa-Lubnan), Ayyub Tabet, shifted toward an American partnership in building an independent Syria. Writing on his change of heart in al-Sa'ih newspaper, Tabet argued that that the United States of America—also a nation "in its childhood"—was best positioned to give Syria the technical assistance it required without also submitting it to imperial tutelage.[61] He proposed assisting the NSNL in drafting a formal treaty of friendship between a Syrian federation and the United States of America. Tabet's statements incensed French Minister Lefèvre-Pontalis, who scoffed at the concept of an allegedly "anti-colonial" America taking Syria in an internal memo before dismissing the New Syria National League as likely British agents (a favorite refrain).[62]

All this time, Abraham Rihbany was in Paris, doing his best to keep up with the changing circumstances of his proposal. On one hand, Rihbany mistrusted the rise of Lebanism and its new preeminence at the peace conference. On the other hand, these same shifts bolstered the appeal of pro-American Arab nationalism among emigrants abroad, a needed buttress against French occupation in Syria. Nevertheless, Rihbany's request to attend the Paris Peace Conference was rejected. He tried to appeal the decision for naught; he spent several weeks awaiting a new decision that never came. His efforts frustrated, he joined a Palestinian delegation also in Paris lobbying to secure US support against foreign colonialism.[63] Rihbany also described how he befriended the Emir Faysal, boarding with him for a time and negotiating the possibilities for a US relationship with Faysal's emerging Arab nationalist state in Damascus.[64]

The Syrian Congress of Buenos Aires

News that Daud 'Ammun's first Lebanese delegation would propose separating greater Lebanon from Syria prompted a wave of protest in the mahjar, led not only by Arab nationalists but also by Lebanists who opposed French rule. The NSNL challenged the partition proposal as an instrument not of self-determination but of French imperial designs; "Those Syrians who call for French protection are ignorant of the desires of the Syrian people," opined Ibrahim al-Khuri in *Fatat Boston*. "We do not deny that France and its allies have worked to the betterment of the Syrian people, nor that they have played an historic role in protecting them," he continued, but the Sykes-Picot agreements also definitively "demonstrate that France and England have in mind to make Syria into a French colony, just one among many in its Empire."[65] Contesting ʿAmmun's presentation of Franco-Lebanese partnership as rooted in a deep history of protection and conservatorship, al-Khuri concluded that the pressures of the war had perverted French goals in the region. "Only America," by contrast, "has a record of freeing people from bondage and helping them on the path to true democracy."[66]

The NSNL also criticized the foreign sponsorship of national delegations at the Paris Peace Conference. It was not lost on the chairman Jurj Khayrallah that France collected signatures in the mahjar to use them as evidence of popular support while barring New Syrian petitions from consideration. Khayrallah criticized the futility of petitions, calling them a hopeless "protest of pens"; instead, he advocated for direct politics, either in the streets or through bilateral lobbying. *Fatat Boston* correspondent Jibraʾil Mansur described his frustration with petition politics in an April 1919 letter to the Syrian everyman. After "centuries of oppression" under Ottoman rule, argued Mansur, the Syrians were threatened by a compliant politics that led them from one imperial power to the next: dependency on elites, and a passive faith in the petitions these elites carried under their arms into the halls of power. Rather than follow ʿAmmun into a French protectorate, he challenged the Syrians of America to take to the streets in a show of numbers for independence. "We must tell them all that we want is our due—our Independence—to be returned to us," Mansur continued, "we are the Syrians who served America. We served its armed forces in war. Our unshakeable hope is now that America will not prohibit us from serving her further in Victory."[67] Mansur defined victory as a partnership between America and Arab nationalism. "Our only alternative," he warned, "is to allow Europe to give Palestine to the Zionists, and let France plant itself atop Syria. The word 'independence' would then never be realized."[68]

Amid such rhetoric, mid-1919 witnessed a rippling of popular anger across Syrian and Lebanese communities in the Americas. The New Syria clubs rallied against the hypocrisy of the Paris Peace Conference, sometimes confronting demonstrations by pro-French Lebanist organizations like Naʿum Mukarzil's LLP. Hopeless or not, Syrian clubs continued to seek signatures but they also drew on older patterns of activism, joining Young Turk-style mass participation with claims for national self-determination. It was in the context that the Syrian Union Society (Jamʿiyyat al-Ittihad al-Suri) of Buenos Aires announced it would host a General Syrian Congress in February 1919. Modelled after the 1913 Arab Congress that occurred in Paris before the war, its goals were to draw

pro-independence activists together, to establish demands and a functional network of nationalist parties in the mahjar, and to raise the movement's profile in
the international forum.

Buenos Aires was an apt city to host the General Syrian Congress. It had
only been four years since the Ottomans fired Amin Arslan, but the renegade
consul kept himself busy. During the war, Arslan joined the city's Syrian Union
Society, an organization founded by Dr. Khalil Sa'adih. Like Abraham Rihbany,
Sa'adih was originally from Shwayr; he had also attended the Syrian Protestant
College with Faris Nimr, who had gotten Sa'adih his first journalism job writing
for Cairo's *al-Muqattam*. Sa'adih crossed the Atlantic in 1914; though destined
for the United States, his ship was turned away at Ellis Island over fears about trachoma. Rerouted to Buenos Aires, Sa'adih initially resolved to stay in the city only
a few months, but the war's outbreak that August kept him in Argentina, where
he founded a number of serials including the Arab nationalist *al-Majallah*.[69]

Founded in 1916, Khalil Sa'adih's Syrian Union Society raised humanitarian
relief destined for US Red Cross, and though he had serious doubts about
French interests in Syria, he also recruited legionaries for the Légion d'Orient.[70]
Additionally, the Syrian Union ran a school for Syrian youth, enjoyed close ties
with the Syrian Masonic Lodge, and developed institutional tied with Arab
philanthropic organizations across multiple Latin American contexts. After
the war's end, the organization endorsed the NSNL's pro-American platform
and rechristened its political wing the Free Democratic Nationalist Party (al-
Hizb al-Dimuqrati al-Watani al-Hurr).[71] It was this political party that hosted
the Syrianist and Arab nationalist delegates in Buenos Aires in 1919; delegates
from Argentina, Brazil, Chile, Mexico, Cuba, and the United States were all
represented.

Sa'adih timed the Syrian Congress to meet in Argentina the same week that
the First Lebanese Delegation was in Paris, hoping that the press would report
the gathering of those Arab activists who were locked out of the conference.
Together, the group drafted a series of demands to issue to Paris and the Great
Powers: that greater Syria should be granted complete independence (al-istiqlal
al-tamm), without French "protection" (himaya), and the new, integral Syrian
state should be immediately granted a seat at the League of Nations. Written
into the preamble, the Congress asserted the "rights of barbarians" (huquq al-
barabira) to self-determination and independence, contesting European visions
about the Mandates as a civilizing exercise. Sa'adih argued that national "sovereignty precedes civilization," not the other way around.[72] If any connection to
a foreign power was needed, the Syrian Congress wanted partnership with the
United States of America. In a similar vein, the Congress protested against the
Syrian Question's framing in terms of sectarian terms, arguing that this framing
abetted French colonialism and debates about partition. Did they not, the men

gathered at the Syrian Congress, represent every class, sect, and political tendency? Saʿadih told his audience, "We are no longer Muslim, Christian, Druze,
nor Jew, for the gallows were erected for all of us together; the famine killed all
indiscriminately. We must now form . . . a single coalition. We are now Syrians,
Lebanese, and Palestinians, without factions, religions, or sects."[73]

Though they were sent to Paris for the conference's consideration, the Syrian
Congress's 1919 resolutions were couched not in the rhetoric of seeking ad-
mission to the conference but as a popular claim to the national aspirations
of 110,000 Syrians living in South America (a figure that represented every
Syrian living in Argentina but which the French challenged). Authentic self-
determination, the letter argued, did not require Great Power sponsorship. The
memo did request, however, that the demands be read alongside those of Emir
Faysal's Syrian delegation planned for later that year.[74] Amin Arslan additionally
offered to bring the demands to the attention of the American Commission in
Paris, and make the case for a US Mandate in Syria.[75]

Along with Saʿadih and Arslan, cotton mogul Naʿimi Jafet made the trip
from São Paulo to Buenos Aires, along with two of his brothers, Basilius and
Antunius. Though the Jafets had been committed French partners during the
war and even once supported the French Mandate in principle, Naʿimi Jafet
endorsed the demands of the Syrian Congress in 1919, including a US Mandate
against French colonialism.[76] Jafet also spoke about grabbing the imagination
of Syrian youth in Latin America, tapping into the same rhetoric of diasporic
responsibility toward the homeland that had been prevalent during the war.
He broached the idea of migrant repatriation, opining that the mahjari second
generation (Syrian youth born in diaspora) could return to the Middle East to
"teach them (the Syrians) about independence, how to progress in national life
with true independence, and to live their lives in the spirit of freedom. For that
reason, it is necessary that we demonstrate patriotism to them to guarantee a true
national independence. We must build a patriotic mission."[77] Jafet's São Paulo
"mission" stood at the central office of his organization, the Syrian Lebanese
Patriotic Society of Brazil (Sociedade Patriótica Síria Libanesa), established in
1917.[78] At the Syrian Congress he proposed that well-cultivated Syrian migrants
could return to Syria to reform its national schools, offer commercial expertise,
assist with public works and administrative oversight, and reinfuse the Syrian
economy with remittances.[79] These Syrian "missionaries" would reintroduce
their homeland to the political principles of Arabist parliamentary democracy,
with a somewhat American face.

The Syrian Congress left vaguer, however, the relationship between its own
Syrianist ideas and those of Hashemite Arab nationalism, supposing that a partnership with Emir Faysal in Damascus was a possibility without more formally
endorsing him. Saʿadih proclaimed that "a Bedouin's independence is better than

civilized bondage," implying a connection with the broader Arab nationalist movement.[80] These same impulses are found in the propaganda of the NSNL and the Treaty of Friendship between Emir Faysal and the United States.[81] Still, the Congress included several Syrianists recently in Shukri Ghanim's coalition, men who remained reticent about supporting Faysal's Arab state in Damascus and who insisted on a tone of lateral collaboration with his movement as a way to repudiate French colonialism and partition in the homeland.

Nationalists of all stripes claimed to be the true representatives of the Syrian and Lebanese national body living both in the Middle East and in the mahjar, and in the context of the Wilsonian moment, such claims also prompted them to shore up these claims through propaganda. Their efforts papered the Syrian colonies of the Atlantic from Canada to Chile. The Lebanists were represented in this space by the Alliance Libanaise and the Lebanon League of Progress; the New Syrians by the New Syria National League, the United Syria Party, and Khalil Saʿadih's Free Democratic Nationalist Party.

Winning the fealty of the mahjar's smaller colonies took on new importance, particularly in Syrian communities that also hosted a French consulate. When a Syrian club founded by Amin al-Rihani in Mérida, Mexico endorsed the NSNL plan for a US Mandate in February 1919, the LLP hastened to open a pro-French group there to compete with the New Syrians on this new frontier.[82] In Cuba (then hosting a scant 15,000 Arab migrants), a French consul named Mr. Brillouin reported overwhelming new overtures by both the LLP and the NSNL. Having risked France's uneasy diplomatic equilibrium with Cuba during the war by subsidizing a Syrian club with ties to Shukri Ghanim's CCS, Brillouin was annoyed by the spike in Lebanist propaganda he saw circulating within the Arab community. He reported with dismay that two French expatriates recently separated from his consulate and purchased a newspaper, *Le Cèdre du Liban*. In "an all too obvious commercial move," they printed LLP propaganda with Naʿum Mukarzil's signature. In July 1919, these expats accompanied local Arab migrants to his office and presented him with a new flag for greater Lebanon, a French tricolor with the mutasarrifate's green cedar tree at its center. They told him their club created the flag to bolster Franco-Lebanese cooperation.[83]

By summer 1919, Brillouin seemed convinced that the Lebanists had won the propaganda war in Cuba. "Despite considerable expense and intense propaganda, the campaign by some Syrians demanding an American protectorate has failed completely." A major reason for this failure, according to Brillouin, was "that our majority—fervent Catholics—understand that this campaign was led by the New York branch of the American protestants," a reference to the New Syrians' enduring ties to missionary institutions like the SPC, the Red Cross, and the Committee for Armenian and Syrian Relief.[84]

New Syrian Support for the King-Crane Commission

After the Syrian Congress in Buenos Aires sent its resolutions to the American commission at Paris, the NSNL's delegate, Abraham Rihbany, realized he would never speak at the conference and returned to New York City. The parties would try a different tactic: approach America directly and, where possible, push it into assuming a supervisory role in Syria. If distance had been to the Syrian émigré parties' disadvantage with regard to Versailles, they hoped their proximity to Washington would bring them greater success. The New Syrians kept pushing for a United States Mandate for Syria (with or without a Hashemite partnership), but they also lobbied for the King-Crane Commission and used the power of their numbers—in actual bodies appearing before important men in D.C.— to push for change.

The formation of an Inter-Allied Commission to Syria under Henry Churchill King and Charles Crane originated in the doubts of the Americans attending the peace conference that the plans presented by sponsored Middle Eastern delegations represented the wishes of the people who lived in these territories. US diplomats and missionaries working in Beirut and Cairo, for starters, disputed the notion that territorial partition reflected Syrian political aspirations. Shortly after the first Lebanese delegation presented its vision for a greater Lebanese state, the Syrian Protestant College's president, Howard Bliss, submitted a request that the United States sponsor an "Inter-Allied or Neutral Commission" to Syria in March 1919 to determine the authentic desires of its people, reintroducing the principles of self-determination in a meaningful way while "def[ying] the imperial nature of both Sykes-Picot and the Balfour Declaration."[85] Then also in Paris, the Hashemite Emir Faysal sought entry to the conference with his Arab nationalist Syrian delegation. French claims that Faysal's delegates did not represent all Syrians and Faysal's counterclaims that France suppressed Arab nationalist sentiment in Mount Lebanon contributed to the Americans' sense that only an *in situ* commission would discern Syrian political desires.

As debate roiled in Paris, New Syria partisans in the United States worked in support of the King-Crane commission and drew closer contact with Arab nationalists in Damascus. In April 1919, Jurj Khayrallah corresponded with Faris Nimr about a possible Treaty of Friendship between Emir Faysal and the United States, setting up plans to approach the US State Department and to produce Arabic/English propaganda in favor of the treaty to appear in American newspapers. Writing from Cairo, Nimr instructed Khayrallah to "publish through associated press that . . . our party has been petitioning the Paris Peace

Conference that Syria be kept undivided and that ... the United States be named mandatory power for Syria. We must appeal to the American public and press to support our aspirations."[86] The NSNL obligingly printed an English-language pamphlet called "America and Syria" for circulation to US policymakers and the press. It endorsed American reconstruction of Syria and proposed Emir Faysal as a useful intermediary between the United States and the Syrian people. Copies, which appeared simultaneously in New York, Washington, DC, Cairo, and Alexandria, concluded,

> All right minded persons will confidently believe that America will not let the Syrians' call (for reconstruction) go unheeded. Indeed she has the lofty idealism and imagination to appreciate the privilege of returning on behalf of the West, the debt of the East, of helping in the restoration of the old glories of Jerusalem and Damascus and the land of immemorial cedars ... through that masterpiece, the League of Nations covenant.[87]

Khayrallah's goal was to influence the reception that Faysal received as he approached the Peace Conference, principally by encouraging the United States to support his delegation against French protestations or perhaps even by sponsoring it. In the end, this did not come to pass, and France predictably argued that Faysal's Syrian delegation was not representative of the Syrian people. After some deliberation, the conference dismissed Faysal without hearing his appeal.

Outraged by Faysal's dismissal, Jurj Khayrallah issued an April 1919 public letter in New York condemning the Great Powers for their behavior toward Arab nationalists. If the Great Powers truly wanted to find the political pulse of the Syrians, he argued, they would have to venture beyond their Paris hotel rooms. They certainly could not rely on printed materials arriving from Damascus or Beirut, because even "though Syrian Muslims quite plainly speak that they do not want France ... censorship is so rigid and strict that not a shred of paper in which a political idea is expressed is allowed to go out of the country."[88] Instead of deliberating the Syria Question in Paris, "the League of Nations [ought to] approach the Syrian people direct (sic) and ask them to speak for themselves." Speaking as chairman of the NSNL, he endorsed the idea of an American commission to discern the wishes of Syria's people:

> America is our best friend. She is the best friend of the weak peoples. America made it possible for dependent states to have justice and be free. Now is the time; now is our opportunity! ... Have the Syrians courage enough to ask for what they want? Have we, who live in the

United States of America, the land of freedom and free speech, the courage to speak our minds?[89]

Rather than continue to press his political claims in the international forum, Faysal left Europe and returned to Syria in April 1919. There he set his sights on building a viable Arab nationalist state capable not only of self-governance but also of defense against foreign occupation.

The King-Crane Commission arrived in Syria in June 1919, and travelled extensively through Syrian, Lebanese, and Palestinian territory interviewing local elites, clerical leaders, and political parties with the goal of establishing the representative will of each district. Its findings largely validated the arguments of Emir Faysal, Arab nationalists, and of the New Syria parties. The majority of Syrians wanted immediate, unfettered independence; if a foreign Mandate was to be imposed, American or British tutelage was preferable to French. Rejecting partition, most Syrians supported a single constitutional state including both Mount Lebanon and Palestine, and the majority rejected Zionist claims to a state in Palestine. The King-Crane commission submitted its report to the peace conference in August 1919; it was subsequently ignored it because its findings contradicted French and British regional designs.[90]

Although the King-Crane Report was not made public, piecemeal news of its findings leaked to the media, including that the "majority of Syrians . . . favor an American mandate," as the *London Times* reported in July 1919. "Reports as to the results . . . have called forth a sorrowful criticism by the French," claimed the *Times*, "who speak freely of British agents of propaganda in Syria and Palestine."[91] Reading such headlines while still awaiting results from King and Crane themselves, the American Commissioners in Paris opened a dialogue with American Consul General in Beirut, Paul Knabenshue, to inquire into local perceptions of the idea. "It may be unreservedly said that the only logical, practical, and internationally expedient and safe solution to the [Syrian] problem . . . is an American Mandate," replied Knabenshue.

> Public opinion in America seems opposed to the acceptance of any mandate, but the force of circumstance is demanding our acceptance of the mandate in Syria. If [France] is given even a limited Mandate over the Arab state, the Arabs will undoubtedly attack the French, and if opposed by superior forces, carry on guerilla warfare against them for many years.[92]

To Knabenshue, it was unquestionable that Syrians would submit to an American Mandatory to ward off French occupation of his district. Having invested himself in the idea, he further offered that British officials also endorsed the idea. Citing conversations with General Edmund Allenby, General Clayton, and Britain's Undersecretary of State Sir Ronald Graham, he concluded, "the British have nothing to fear from an American Mandate in Syria and are consequently supporting this program as a counter to French claims for the country."[93]

Notably, Knabenshue was silent on whether his British interlocutors felt similarly about relinquishing Palestinian territory to the United States. The Americans seemed readier to think about a US Mandate in Syria exclusive of Palestine, and the silence over which portions of Syria would be included positioned it within an Anglo-American understanding that British claims to Palestine were unimpeachable. After the King-Crane Commission, even the NSNL stopped claiming Palestine as part of its desired Syrian state, a move that signaled the New Syria parties' willingness to cater to Great Power politics and to target French colonialism specifically.

That the American public would likely not support the plan for an US Mandate in Syria presented a significant obstacle for policymakers who endorsed the idea. Writing from Beirut, Knabenshue opined that if Henry Cabot Lodge and the Senate Foreign Relations Committee wanted to move the American people on the issue, he would be better off making appeals on humanitarian and moral grounds:

> It is believed that the assent of the general American public could be secured only by an appeal on sentiment and humanitarian grounds. America would not come to Syria to colonize or exploit the country, which has been under the yoke of the despotic Turks for so many centuries, but to assist the people and develop for them their potentially prosperous land and guide them in the administration for a time until they would be prepared to take the reins of government.[94]

For Beirut's Consul General, Syria was America's next great frontier, another experiment in exporting democratic principles abroad in partnership with cooperative locals. The European approach to Mandates—particularly claims made by France—threatened to undo democratic development there and necessitated US intervention.

In sum, the King-Crane Commission's findings undermined both French and British aspirations in the Middle East while endorsing a more direct role for the United States that might risk diplomatic conflict and that most Americans would not support. The report was repressed, angering the Senate's most ardent supporter of expansion, Henry Cabot Lodge. Lodge quickly requested a copy for the US Senate Foreign Relations Committee, but was denied on the basis that it "contains confidential references to other governments."[95]

Meanwhile, the Paris proceedings continued, no longer bothered by claims about the popular desires of the Syrian people. Instead, in October 1919 another delegation came to present its stance on greater Lebanon: a French-sponsored second Lebanese delegation headed by the chief cleric of Mount Lebanon's Maronite Church, Patriarch Ilyas Huwayyik. Like Daud ʿAmmun's first Lebanese delegation, Huwayyik's delegates argued that the creation of a greater Lebanese state within enlarged borders was an economic necessity supported by the majority of Mount Lebanon's inhabitants. He argued additionally that France's historical role as protector of Lebanese Christians in an overwhelmingly Muslim region legitimated its claim to the Mandate.[96]

The Maronite Patriarch's admittance to the peace conference was controversial among Syrian and Lebanese emigrants, driving both enthusiasm from Francophile Lebanese clubs (most allied with the LLP) and also protest from Syrian and Arab nationalists.[97] The suppression on the King-Crane Commission's findings put the NSNL and its Egyptian and Latin American partisans on the defensive. Unable to access the League of Nations, Amin Arslan himself travelled to Istanbul and met with the American commissioners there in November 1919. Joining a delegation of Lebanese Druze to protest the partition of post-Ottoman Syria and, by extension, France's right to rule the territory, Arslan broached a treaty of friendship between the United States of America and Emir Faysal as an alternative.[98] It came to naught, for having already declined a more significant role for itself in Syria, the United States contented itself with the League of Nations' transfer of authority over Syria, Mount Lebanon, and Palestine to Great Britain and France. As the Paris negotiations concluded, it became clear that France would be granted Syria and Mount Lebanon, that it would swiftly establish a greater Lebanese state, and it would take a military confrontation with Faysal to conquer the rest of Syria.

By early 1920, the prospect of European Mandates in the Arab world was taken as a given by the great powers. The NSNL busily campaigned for an independent Syria under American guardianship, undeterred by the project's mounting improbability. Alarmed by French plans to forcibly wrest Syria from its Arab government, Dr. Najeeb Saleeby and Dr. Philip Hitti reminded the Department of State in a December 1919 petition that French efforts to impose themselves on parts of Mount Lebanon had "brought on a condition of serious unrest and grave dissensions and was met by serious opposition by the majority of the native population." Saleeby laid out the following rationale:

> Whereas, a decided majority of the Syrian people has declared emphatically for an undivided Syria under one mandate only . . . and whereas there will soon be convened a conference of the Allied and Associated Powers [at San Remo] for the purpose of settling the political future of

countries which were formerly included in the Turkish Empire . . . we
members of the United Syrian American societies . . . do earnestly be-
seech that the United States Government exert its influence in the next
session in such a manner as will guarantee to Syria her national unity
within her natural geographic boundaries.[99]

Syrian and Palestinian parties from New York, Boston, Detroit, and Milwaukee
signed Saleeby's petition, asking Americans to "maintain a watchful and kindly
attitude during this period of unrest," lest Syria fall victim to "the horrors of
another war."[100] Eager to gain further intelligence into the confrontations between French forces and local Syrians, Secretary of State Lansing again invited
Najib Saleeby to meet with him and William Sheridan at the State Department's
Division of Near Eastern Affairs. At that meeting, Saleeby further insisted that
Syria would not quietly acquiesce to French occupation. But the moment when
an American Mandate seemed a viable option had passed. The following April,
France was given the Syria Mandate, and the New Syria National League's battles
were lost.

Conclusion

The New Syrians were neither the first nor the only group to call for a US
Mandate over former Ottoman territory: plans for American guardianship over
Anatolian Turkey, Cilicia, and Armenia also floated around émigré groups, their
petitions arriving on the desks of US policymakers working in the diplomatic
corps.[101] Former US Ambassador to the Ottoman Empire Henry Morgenthau
described an US Mandate over Turkey, for instance, as a key means in staving
off mass deportations and massacres against Greeks, Assyrians, Armenians, and
other Ottoman minorities.[102] Writing to his superiors from Istanbul in spring
1919, American Commissioner Lewis Heck reported that the city's newspapers
favorably discussed the idea of an American-backed protectorate over Anatolia
as a safeguard against European domination. He lamented that French censors
controlling the mail out of the city regularly redacted editorials in *Le Courrier
de Turquie*, and were "especially inclined to object to any articles which are too
friendly to the United States and which tend to indicate a desire on the part of
the Turks for an American Mandate or control."[103]

Nationalist movements also grabbed onto the idea that America could serve
their interests as a League of Nations mandatory. In addition to Arab petitions
cited by the King-Crane Commission, the Americans received petitions for US
tutelage from Smyrna in early 1919 and from Sivas that August.[104] Meanwhile,
rumors swirled in the Smyrna press that the Americans were considering taking

Mandate over Turkey. An August 1919 issue of the French-language *La Liberté* even claimed that the US Senate had approved the idea and gathered investors to fund the project.[105] Armenian organizations in the United States also lobbied for an American Mandate over their ancestral homeland. The Armenian National Delegation's Miran Sevasly sent frequent petitions warning that "French ambitions to extend their influence beyond Syria and into the province of Cilicia" presented an immediate threat to Armenian self-determination.[106] Like the NSNL's plan, Sevasly's campaigning went nowhere: a letter from William Phillips summed up the Department of State's view that "such a campaign (for an American mandate in Armenia) would at this time seem to be premature and unwise."[107]

What these petitions reveal is that the idea of an American Mandate was a common one, articulated across several Ottoman communities and deployed as a buttress against European imperialism. Imperialism ultimately won the day in 1920; after receiving the Mandate for Syria and Mount Lebanon, French amassed troops in Beirut and the Bekaa Valley to meet Faysal's Arab nationalist armies. France defeated the Hashemites at Maysalun in July 1920 and occupied Damascus. They declared the establishment of Greater Lebanon in September 1920 and subdivided the rest of occupied Syria into five ethnoreligious cantons where they dealt with perennial acts of resistance, revolt, and protest against French rule. Both the seeming inevitability of this outcome and the violent resistance France encountered in Syria have contributed to a post hoc erasure of the mahjar's own resistance to imperialism. The Lebanese diaspora, in particular, is more often remembered for its support for the Mandate, its French-sponsored petitions held up in evidence in favor of foreign rule, partition, and complicity.

But petitions have a dark side. The image of a pro-French Syrian and Lebanese mahjar was itself a French construction, abetted by the Paris Peace Conference which systematically filtered out anticolonial voices—but none so completely as those emanating from the American mahjar. Émigré Arab nationalists were acutely aware of the legal fiction being constructed at Paris, and they invested themselves in undermining it, with limited success. In the end, as the spurned NSNL delegate Abraham Rihbany recorded in his memoirs, "we have a fine specimen of old diplomacy . . . the Conference dashed all hopes. It seemed to Easterners to uncover the moral nakedness of Europe."[108] After 1920, the mahjar's Arab nationalists represented both a political and symbolic threat to the French Mandate. Not only did they continue to protest French rule from abroad, remitting funds, propaganda, and repatriates to occupied Syria; they also undermined France's legitimating claim that Syrian and Lebanese exiles had supported their mandate. Early French policies toward the mahjar, moreover, demonstrate a desire to domesticate the diaspora through census registration, travel restriction, passport control, and selective repatriation.

The establishment of the French Mandate opened a new chapter for Syrian activism in the mahjar. If emigrants wanted to maintain their ties to their countries of origin, they would have to do so by mediating through the Mandate. But by claiming that the mahjar largely supported the Mandate, the French tacitly invited this diaspora to make claims against it. As officials constructed a functioning administration in the Middle East after 1920, they were also forced to contend with the political demands of a half million emigrants who began gathering outside French consulates across the Americas. They demanded the Mandate honor their right to travel, especially to repatriate to their homeland. They demanded full rights of nationality and citizenship, including passports, diplomatic protections, and full suffrage in national elections. In 1919, the vision of the mahjar as dominated by a pro-French political consensus proved illusory, a figment of an internationalist imaginary underwriting the League of Nations mandate system. The 1920s, by contrast, were a time of claims-making by Syrians and Lebanese migrants abroad, introducing a new politics of extraterritorial citizenship, its privileges, and its limitations which inflected the Mandate's legal structures.

To further complicate things, many of those emigrants making demands remained deeply displeased with the Mandate in principle, and with French rule in practice. A contradictory set of challenges emerged: the Mandate depended, on one hand, on continued political support by Arab emigrants, especially in relation to travel and return migration policies. On the other hand, the mahjar remained, for the French, a site of defiance, a place where pro-independence agitation threatened the Mandate's symbolic and administrative foundations. To confront these challenges, the early Mandate relied on an emerging documentary regime, papers that allowed officials to sort friend from foe. This sorting began with the passport, a document France had offered Syrians and Lebanese engaged in allied war work but which, in the weeks after the 1918 armistice, granted them the means to legally claim Arab emigrants as future French colonials.

5

Travelling Syrians, Immovable Turks

Passport Fraud and Migrant Smuggling at the Close of Empire,
1918–1920

On July 11, 1919, seventeen riveters from Worcester, Massachusetts arrived at the Boston French Consulate to apply for passports to leave the United States. The war industries were winding down; the naval blockade in the Mediterranean was lifted. Of Ottoman nationality, these riveters had applied for French *sauf conduit* (safe conduct) passports to permanently repatriate to their homeland. A legal anomaly, these special documents allowed Syrians to travel under temporary French diplomatic protection despite US laws banning cross-border travel by Ottoman subjects. In the months between the 1918 armistice and the San Remo Conference in 1920, the *sauf conduit* passport was the only legal ticket home for Syrians wishing to repatriate to the Middle East from America.

Boston's French Consulate processed hundreds of these applications in summer 1919, so the arrival of seventeen Syrians that day raised no suspicions. French clerks reviewed a heap of paperwork attesting to the riveters' Syrian identity through a multistep vetting process. Each man presented signed affidavits from two witnesses who knew them to be Syrian; papers notarized by James Fay's Aliens Bureau in Boston; and papers signed and sealed by Ya'cub Rufa'il, secretary of the Lebanon League of Progress (LLP; Jam'iyyat al-Nahda al-Lubnaniyya) in New York City.[1] According to these documents, the applicants were all legally Syrian, but when the clerk asked one to verbally confirm his nationality, "he replied very indignantly, 'No, I am a Turk!'"[2] French Consul General Joseph Flamand reviewed the names of other men granted *sauf conduits* that day: Suleiman Mohammet, Hasaan Ali, Mislim Mohammed, Jouma Ahmad, Ali Moustafa, Osman Zilfo, Hussein Juma, Fetah Apoch, Mohammed Yousouff. All of them were headed to Diyarbakır, an Ottoman vilayet (province) on the frontier between Syria and Turkey. Although their passports read

"Syrian," they were all Turkish-speaking Kurds.[3] Flamand contacted the US Bureau of Investigation; his office had uncovered a passport ring smuggling Ottoman Kurds and Turks out of the United States by transforming them into "Syrians" on paper.

The resulting investigation led to the arrest of James Fay, a US citizen previously fired by the French Consulate, and a dozen co-conspirators of Belgian, Greek, and Ottoman nationalities. Having made a sum charging exorbitant fees for their services, all were accused of conspiracy to defraud the United States government, as well as dozens of clients. But as Bureau of Investigation agent Robert Valkenburgh pursued James Fay, he got tangled in the legal tripwires concerning US legal understandings of "Syrian" nationality, its relationship to the other Ottoman immigrant nationalities, and the ambiguity of Syria's borders in the armistice moment. As it turned out, Fay and his smugglers had exploited incoherencies within wartime US laws written to exempt Syrians and Lebanese from the multiplying prohibitions that confronted other Ottomans migrants in America. The porosity of the border between greater Syria and Armenian and Kurdish districts in Cilicia, French ambitions to claim both places in the ongoing peace negotiations, and the inconsistency in US laws defining who was— and who was not—Syrian ensured that James Fay would never be indicted for his crime.[4]

Examining a series of smuggling cases involving the production of "paper Syrians" in the United States after 1918, this chapter reveals the transnational implications of US laws discerning Syrian as a distinct national origins category. During the war, US lawmakers decoupled "Syrian" identity from Ottoman national origins, creating a new category largely to facilitate the enlistment of Arab American troops. An emergent national origins classification, to be a "Syrian" in America increasingly offered Arab migrants exemptions from the mounting restrictions that faced their Ottoman co-nationals, especially restrictions on cross-border travel. Although created for wartime US domestic purposes, the same laws formed the basis for a new transnational sorting system immediately following the armistice. France granted Syrian and Lebanese migrants *sauf conduit* passports entitling them to cross US borders and repatriate to the Middle East. The passport program functioned with the US Department of State's blessing and over the protest of Ottoman diplomatic officials, and the French used the *sauf conduit* regime to claim Syrian and Mount Lebanese migrants as future French colonials.[5] Working with the French, Arab activists in the United States also used these passports to reclaim emigrants for the homeland. But because the passport system built on American foundations centered on Syrian as a racial category (and not a geographic one), it opened loopholes for smugglers. Émigré agents, French clerks, and smugglers all mediated what

Syrian nationality became in the mahjar, with real impact on who returned to the homeland, how they did so, and where that homeland's borders began and ended.

The months between the 1918 armistice and the establishment of the French Mandate in 1920 were tumultuous ones. In Paris, many competing delegates made claims on the Syrians of the diaspora, invoking them in their plans for a post-Ottoman Middle East, proposing mass repatriation projects, or otherwise putting emigrants to symbolic work for Wilsonian causes. But there was also a physical rush to the mahjar, a resurgence of state-led projects to assert authority over Arabs living abroad as a means of claiming new sovereignty over their homeland. This political pattern was not entirely new; the Ottoman Empire momentarily practiced it in 1908, grooming Ottoman subjects abroad through diplomacy, but had sharply disengaged in 1914. Now that the war was over, France endeavored to document and regulate Syrian and Lebanese repatriates, hoping to eventually follow them home.

In regulating the movements and nationality claims of Arab migrants abroad, the *sauf conduit* regime joined other French policies designed to transform this diaspora into leverage for an emergent French Mandate. At the same moment, the French Foreign Ministry funded petition drives in support of the mandate,[6] printed pro-French propaganda in the Syrian mahjar,[7] and sponsored national delegations to the Paris Peace Conference.[8] Although it was just one facet of a larger regulatory politics, travel regulation played a specific role in not only legitimating French authority but also in defining the territorial limits of Syria and Lebanon. Arab emigrants made up around 20 percent of Syria's total population, but their homeland's post-Ottoman borders yet to be defined. Stamping repatriation passports bolstered French claims that the Syrians and Lebanese had opted for foreign tutelage, suggesting also the geographic extremities of a possible French Mandate. This pattern, forged in the mahjar immediately after the war's end, came home to the Middle East during the interwar period and was practiced by both the French and British mandatory authorities.[9]

At the same time, however, France delegated the work of vetting and verification of travelers to its clients in the Syrian migrant community. These clients exercised considerable latitude in determining what made a traveler legally Syrian versus Turkish. The Syrian agents who processed the Kurdish passports in 1919 were not unaware of their own ethnic background, nor were they entirely lying when they argued in court that they believed these Kurds to be Syrian. What they had done, however, was use passports to extend French sovereignty over a contested Middle Eastern frontier, asserting it as a possible French Mandate and claiming its people as potential French colonials.

The 1918 Travel Control Act and the *Sauf Conduit*

As a ubiquitous identification document for crossing international borders, the passport is the result of countervailing impulses of securitization and facilitation that governed the world as a result of the First World War.[10] Before 1914, states seeking to regulate the mobility of their subject-citizens did so primarily through documents designed for internal use within the polity. Ottoman migrants typically carried the *mürûr tezkeresi* passport issued for the purposes of moving within the empire.[11] Although Istanbul made a few attempts to curb the departure of Syrians from the eastern Mediterranean in the 1890s, travel regimes and port regulations remained exceptionally liberal before the First World War.[12] The global shift toward using passports to regulate international travel began with the war; and in Europe and the United States, states used passport control to surveil foreigners or restrict the movements of migrant undesirables.[13]

For their bearers, passports also served important diplomatic functions: they were a statement of protection, a state-backed guarantee to certain extraterritorial rights. Travelers bearing a passport were theoretically protected from the danger of expulsion or the vulnerabilities of statelessness. In a world of multiplying borders, massive displacements, and, in the case of the Ottomans, imperial disintegration, passports offered Ottoman migrants the opportunity to travel under the auspices of a foreign power at a moment when the question of their nationality had not yet been settled.

The provision of French passports to Syrians in the United States cut against the grain of an American passport regime focused almost entirely on travel restriction. Like most of Europe, America's first passport measures emerged in the context of temporary wartime restrictions that later ossified into permanent regulations despite the intentions of their architects.[14] The first such regulation came in a 1915 executive order requiring all persons leaving the United States to carry a passport issued by that state and given a visa by US officials.[15] In 1918, Congress expanded this policy with the Travel Control Act of May 22, 1918, which imposed specific restrictions on citizens and foreign nationals seeking to exit or enter the country.[16] Among these restrictions was a prohibition of cross-border "travel deemed contrary to public safety," targeting German, Austrian, and Ottoman migrants as sources of political subversion.[17]

As a neutral immigrant population in the United States, Ottoman nationals in America found their community targeted by the Travel Control Act because of pervasive Islamophobic fears about Middle Eastern migrants as a particular type of public safety threat. In the case of Ottoman nationals (simultaneously "Turks" and "neutral allies of the enemy" in US legal parlance) exit from the country was prohibited, with exceptions given only to those who could prove medical incapacity or mental incompetence.[18] The 1918 act drew fire from the judiciary because it limited the departure of non-citizens from US territory, rather than purely arrivals. Although the Attorney General criticized the measure as contrary to international practice and diplomatic protocol, President Woodrow Wilson reimposed its terms in August 1918 by Executive Order 2932, which mandated that all "hostile aliens must obtain permits for all departures from, and entries to, the United States" from both their own consulates and the US Department of State.[19]

Certain Ottoman minority communities were exempted from both the Travel Control Act and Executive Order 2932. Armenians, Sephardic Jews, and "Syrians and Mount Lebanonites claimed by Turkey as subjects" each enjoyed certain exemptions, owing to their access to foreign diplomatic protections and US wartime laws mitigating Ottoman sovereignty over migrants and refugees. Syrian migrants, in particular, could obtain a French *sauf conduit* passport naming them as temporary French clients.[20] US lawmakers defined each of the groups eligible for exemption as religious minorities and granted them enhanced travel protections on that basis. On its face, Executive Order 2932 restricted Ottoman mobility on the basis of their "Turkish" nationality, but the issuance of exemptions specifically to Ottoman non-Muslims on the basis that they represented persecuted religious minorities meant the restrictions disproportionately impacted Muslim migrants. The travel ban was effectively a prohibition on Muslim travel into and out of the United States. The restrictions on Ottoman travel remained in effect until the conclusion of the Paris negotiations in 1920.

As the travel regimes of the prewar period were progressively replaced by wartime passport controls, the *sauf conduit* was a mechanism that seemed to paper over the problems created by increased migration restriction. Produced and recognized by the Allied Powers, safe conduct passports provided temporary protections to travelers, facilitating various types of neutral trade and travel across contested international borders. *Sauf conduits* were used in prisoner exchanges and refugee relocation, for instance, as well as in trans-Atlantic shipping and neutral merchant commerce.[21] They were used to smooth the military recruitment process: Arab volunteers in the French Légion d'Orient carried them across the mahjar to New York City and used them to exit the port for French enlistment sites. Syrian and Lebanese migrants also obtained them for cross-border commerce. French *sauf conduits* were the favored papers of Syrian peddlers, shippers, factory owners, and bankers during the war, proffered whenever US officials suspected these Syrians of "pro-German" (or pro-Turkish) sympathies.

Syrian migrants in the Americas had practical reasons to apply for the French *sauf conduit*. By 1917, merchants who conducted cross-border trades discovered that their status as Ottoman subjects represented an economic liability. Getting French diplomatic protection allowed Syrian traders (usually Christians from Mount Lebanon) privileged access to neutral markets across Latin America and the United States. Most of them were small businessmen, but a few larger houses exercised considerable diplomatic pull and profited mightily from cross-border commerce. Syrian cross-border commerce inspired the suspicions of US immigration authorities then policing the US-Mexico border and ports of entry from New York to Florida. Writing of one Jorge Chame, the US Consul in Rio de Janeiro opined, "all the Syrian traders of this city, which may always be distinguished by their more-or-less Arabic names, are small traders open to suspicion," and he requested that "export licenses be given to none in this class."[22] During the war's final months, the US Bureau of Investigation placed Syrian trading routes between El Paso, Texas and Mexico under heavy surveillance, distrusting the French documents offered them by Syrian traders but honoring them nevertheless.[23]

These papers protected their Syrian bearers as they worked across their colonies in the American mahjar, vouchsafing them as individuals known to France. France claimed this right to offer passports to Syrian and Lebanese migrants as part of her role as guarantor of the 1861 Règlement Organique, a treaty that created the mutasarrifate of Mount Lebanon as legally autonomous within the Ottoman Empire.[24] Like other foreign capitulatory agreements, the Ottomans had unilaterally abrogated the Règlement Organique upon entering the war in 1914, but this did not stop the French Foreign Ministry, its consulates abroad, or Syrian migrants themselves from invoking its terms to gain foreign diplomatic protections, avoid Ottoman military service, or renounce their Ottoman nationality altogether.[25]

The *sauf conduit* passport permitted Syrians to travel under French protection, but they were not given for purposes of individual identification, for registration, surveillance, or to grant Syrians full nationality rights of French citizenship. Although globally the modern passport was shifting into an all-encompassing document of nationality, the *sauf conduits* continued to operate more like a temporary letter of marque than as a total identification document.[26] The United States was then in the midst of a struggle to regulate migration, standardize compulsory identity documents, and process new citizenship claims through passport control. Within this shifting legal regime, the French Consulate used *sauf conduits* to embrace Syrian migrants as clients without simultaneously claiming them as citizens. On paper, this paperwork transformed individual Syrians into temporary—or perhaps potential—French colonials in the eyes of US officials. At the same time, France used the passports to legitimate its claims to Syria and Mount Lebanon and to expand the geography of a future French Syria from the territorial limits of the Lebanese mutasarrifate to a greater Syrian territory. By granting migrants from Aleppo, Homs, Damascus, and even Diyarbakır *sauf conduits*, France redefined who was Syrian in the mahjar while bolstering its self-professed role as historical protector of an enlarged Syrian territory.

In January 1919, the peace conference in Paris was under way, but it remained unclear who would rule the former Ottoman territories in the eastern Mediterranean or on what terms. France claimed Syria and Mount Lebanon as part of her war indemnity, invoking wartime agreements made with England by Mark Sykes and Georges Picot; she also claimed parts of Cilicia and Asia Minor as zones of French influence.[27] Arab nationalists organized under Emir Faysal contested French claims, however, as did Syrianist and Lebanist groups both in the Middle East and in the mahjar. As the conference roiled in claims and counter claims to Syrian territory, France quietly claimed Syrian migrants abroad through the provision of passports.

Although some Syrian migrants in the Americas had achieved citizenship in their host societies by 1919, the overwhelming majority of them continued to hold Ottoman passports and nationality. Whereas the wartime *sauf conduit* had functioned as a letter of marque, it transformed into a document in lieu of a nationality in 1919. Applicants were no longer working in neutral territories for economic reasons, but were instead returning to Syria for permanent repatriation. The French Foreign Ministry hastened to be the sole provider of repatriation documents, hoping to follow the returning migrants home, not merely to Beirut and Mount Lebanon but also to greater Syria, Cilicia, and Iskenderun. These papers granted Syrians the right to return to the Middle East by placing them under French authority. They also authorized France to vet returnees, making the *sauf conduit* the perfect instrument for France to claim some, reject others, and secure a monopoly over the legitimate means of movement between Syria and its mahjar.[28]

Although France exercised the right to extend its sovereignty selectively, Syrian migrants also had to opt into the arrangement. The choice between securing French travel papers or delaying repatriation was not an easy one for Syrians already wary about French ambitions. Some made use of the *sauf conduit*, but most would-be repatriates maintained their Ottoman nationality and awaited the outcome of the Paris conference. As they waited, they were denied the right to depart the United States. The fate of their nationality and citizenship claims hung in the balance.

Of the half dozen federal agencies tasked with managing passport control for foreign nationals, the Department of State was especially concerned about the departures of enemy nationals, "declarant" immigrants, and naturalized American immigrants from US territory to their homelands of origin. Practical concerns over the safety of naturalized citizens played a role, such as the concern that new Americans would be conscripted into foreign militaries or imprisoned

Figure 5.1. After receiving their passports, Syrian and Lebanese returnees await departure via A.K. Hitti Shipping Company in New York City, 1920. Mukarzil, *Tarikh al-Tijara al-Suriyya*, 140. James Ansara Papers, IHRC208, Immigration History Research Center Archives, University of Minnesota.

in a country lacking a treaty relationship with the United States.[29] But in the case of Ottoman subjects, the State Department wished to delay repatriations until the conclusion of the peace conference because the borders of former Ottoman territories remained uncertain and the fate of its nationalities unknown. The Ottoman Empire did not recognize the right of its subjects abroad to unilaterally renounce their Ottoman nationality, placing Ottoman migrants—Syrians among them—on legally tenuous ground.[30] The US government cited these among other public safety concerns for its own cross-border restriction of Middle Eastern travelers, but the ban also frustrated migrants wanting to return home to visit family or see to household affairs.

The specter of the repatriating Syrian migrant was more than mere trope. The diaspora's nationalist political parties were then actively calling on Ottoman Arabs to return home, including the Syrian committees of New York tasked with issuing *sauf conduits*. Some of these parties couched their claims that the mahjar would revitalize Syria through return migration, as did the New Syria parties. With shipping lanes opening up and migration out from Syria and Mount Lebanon resuming, many in the mahjar were eager to return home; indeed, as many as half of all migrants who left Mount Lebanon before 1914 repatriated in the interwar years.[31] The State Department endeavored to convince them to stay in America, using the Syrian American press as their instrument.

In a 1919 series published in New York City's *al-Fatat* and *al-Nasr* newspapers, the State Department published full-page advertisements imploring Syrian migrants to remain in America. The bilingual ads mirrored similar ads then appearing in several ethnic newspapers. This particular ad was translated by *al-Fatat*'s editor, Shukri al-Bakhash, and featured endorsements by the city's most economically powerful Syrians: president of the Syrian Faour Brothers bank, Daniel Faour; head of the Syrian Merchants' Association, T. K. Malouf; president of the Zaloom textile firm, G. Zaloom; and delegates from several of the city's Syrian committees. The ad argued that Syrian migrants could make the most positive impact by working in America: "it is America's duty to struggle to assist the countries devastated (by the war), and because you are a part of its strength, it is your duty to stay with America."[32] Why return to lands ravaged by conflict, rotting infrastructure, and famine? Instead, the ad called on Syrians to stay abroad, to work, and to send money home to finance Syria's reconstruction.

Interestingly, the same men delivering nationalist petitions to the Paris Peace Conference also signed this ad, including New Syria National League secretary Najib Saleeby and Lebanon League of Progress vice-president Mikha'il al-Khouri. The New Syria National League, in particular, questioned the *sauf conduit* as the means of repatriation, as Saleeby correctly believed these documents only furthered French pretensions and policy objectives in the Middle East. There were also Syrians who, noting this connection between French passports and French plans for a Middle Eastern mandate, petitioned the American commission at Paris to halt the practice or else afford "Syrians and Arabians residing in [American] territories . . . all facilities of travel by land or sea by issuing to them their own permits or passports *without reference to any other Government.*"[33]

Rarely did the French consulates of the Americas deny Syrian and Lebanese travelers the *sauf conduit*. When Syrians were denied the document, however, it was because France believed them to have ties to pro-independence or anti-French political parties in the mahjar, a trend that strongly suggests the French consulate used the repatriation regime to sort out undesirable repatriates.[34] Although no internal memos between French policymakers have been found definitively demonstrating this political sorting process was policy, it is clear that all parties in the mahjar—Syrian travelers, US policymakers, and French consular staff—understood the *sauf conduit* to be a part of a broader project of claiming returnees for a future French Mandate.

Repatriation to Syria was thus a deeply fraught project. Syrians in America gained a privileged right to travel not afforded other Ottoman immigrants, but they did so only as potential French colonials, a legal status few in the Syrian colony in New York were comfortable with. Nonetheless, the French consulate found ready partners to vet applicants, and they empowered six Syrian committees with approving *sauf conduits* in late 1918. Ayyub Tabet's Syria-Mount Lebanon

Figure 5.2. 1919 bilingual propaganda urging Syrian migrants to stay in America. Originally targeted at European immigrants, the State Department placed this in *al-Fatat* and *al-Nasr* newspapers with an Arabic translation by Shukri al-Bakhash. *al-Nasr* (New York, NY), 29 March 1919, 7.

League of Liberation, the Mount Lebanon Club, and Maronite clergymen in both New York City and Boston each authorized Syrian passports, but it was the Lebanon League of Progress (hereafter LLP) that processed more of these documents than the other Syrian committees combined.

The LLP's relationship with France was longstanding. During the war, Naʿum Mukarzil recruited for the Légion d'Orient and processed French passports for them. Mukarzil kept a stack of blank passports in a desk drawer at his Brooklyn office, and he was authorized to notarize travel papers for Syrians and Lebanese travelling under French diplomatic protection. This existing relationship explains why the French consuls who received *sauf conduit* applications bearing the LLP's seal processed them without a second thought. As during the war, the 1919 *sauf conduits* were a one-way ticket, and they required passage through Europe, where Syrian migrants would be again vetted by French officials. At LLP headquarters, Mukarzil and his executive secretary, Yaʿcub Rufaʾil, were instructed to be meticulous in screening applicants.

On its face, this system was pretty straightforward. Syrians applied for these passports regardless of their formal nationality; Ottoman nationals, naturalized US citizens, and Syrians who had obtained citizenship in another country could all apply. After being authenticated through some combination of witnesses, a language test, or an interview with Syrian club officials, their papers were stamped, and they proceeded to the French consulate for the passport. But each step in this process could be corrupted. Passport agencies, witnesses, the test, and the stamps of the Syrian clubs or of French officials could all be purchased. More often than not, ineligible Turkish and Kurdish returnees trying to return to Asia Minor ended up with *sauf conduits* and had no idea that they had been defrauded.

Trouble at Café Anatoli and the Incredible Disappearing Witnesses

After the discovery of seventeen "paper Syrians" in Boston in mid-1919, the Bureau of Investigation pursued the smugglers responsible for the fraudulent *sauf conduits*. Bureau agent Robert Valkenburgh spent months collecting the testimonies of Turkish and Kurdish migrants, mostly from Adana and Diyarbakır, who had obtained a French *sauf conduit* through James Fay's Alien Bureau. The Ottoman consulate remained closed, so a Spanish consular clerk, H. Kazas, attended to represent Ottoman interests in these interviews. The testimony of one Fatta Abbas establishes a pattern in whom James Fay sought out to repatriate to Ottoman lands. A Turkish-speaking Kurd from Diyarbakır who arrived in the United States in 1913, Abbas worked in heavy industry in Peabody, Massachusetts. The thirty-seven-year-old laborer had applied for repatriation at Boston's Spanish Consulate to care for a sick relative back home. The Spanish granted his passport, but it was quickly rejected by the State Department on the grounds that Abbas was a Turk and Ottoman national.

Abbas reported to Valkenburgh that as soon as he returned to Peabody, one of Fay's notaries, a man named Paul Asloglu, approached him and promised to get him a French passport for $20. Abbas only met the smuggler James Fay once and described the meeting thus:

> "Did you tell James Fay that you were a Syrian?"
>
> "No, I told him I came from Diarbekir (sic), I speak Kurd and Turkish, and I am a Kurd."
>
> "Did you know that Paul Asloglou made out your application as a Syrian?"
>
> "No, I cannot read English, and Paul Asloglou can speak Turkish, and knew that I was a Kurd."[35]

Not only did Abbas' passport claim that he was Syrian, but his name and address details had also been altered to avoid detection by State Department officials. Fatta Abbas became Fetah Apoch. His *sauf conduit* bore Ya'cub Rufa'il's signature and the LLP's official seal, but Abbas admitted he had never met Rufa'il or the two witnesses who legally attested to his Syrian identity. Spanish Consulate clerk Kazas produced a dozen Kurdish witnesses for Valkenburgh to interview as he built his case against James Fay. Like Abbas, each witness originally came from parts of Anatolia either under Allied control or claimed by France as part of her Mandate under the terms of the 1916 Sykes-Picot Accords. Most came from Diyarbakır; none of them spoke Arabic.

Because US laws governing who was "Syrian" lacked geographical specificity and were framed largely within racial constructions that only made sense in the American context, Agent Valkenburgh understood that indicting Fay would require proving that these Kurds were not, in fact, Syrians. US Attorney General Anthony Goldberg told Valkenburgh that the only way to try Fay for smuggling was to charge him with fraud rising to the level of "conspiracy to defraud the United States" under Article 37 of the criminal code. A conspiracy charge raised the burden of proof, however, and Valkenburgh's witness testimonies needed to prove that Fay and his partners knew their clients to be Turks and deliberately turned them into Syrians. The Spanish consulate brought Fay's clients to Valkenburgh's office for sworn testimony, but after these interviews concluded, an odd thing happened. One by one, Valkenburgh's witnesses began to disappear before the smugglers could be brought to trial. These men were, after all, still trying to go home, and many of them opted to do so clandestinely.

In Fatta Abbas's case, he returned to Peabody after meeting with the Bureau of Investigation to give his affidavit. In September 1919, Abbas and another witness named Mohammed Youssouf received letters from one Ali Nihad, the proprietor of a Turkish coffee shop in New York City called Café Anatoli. Nihad offered both men a chance to clandestinely leave the United States, enjoining them to come to his café where he would smuggle them through the port. Nihad even reportedly offered to subsidize their passage across the Atlantic.[36] Abbas and Youssouf went to New York to pursue this option. When the Bureau of Investigation discovered their absence, they placed the ports under surveillance to halt their departure. Bureau Superintendent George Kelleher believed James Fay was behind the Café Anatoli smuggling ring, and he informed his supervisors that "Fay is reported to have remarked to some Turks in Peabody, Mass. that he will be able to have all the witnesses out of the United States by the time the case is called to trial."[37]

In pursuit of lost witnesses, Valkenburgh decided to surprise Ali Nihad at Café Anatoli, only to discover that Nihad's establishment was not at the address listed in the smuggler's letter, but next door. Nihad was familiar with the smugglers and told Valkenburgh that a "fake priest who lives directly over a saloon" named Abdull Mached managed the scheme. Nihad emphatically denied being involved with Fay or Mached because they "are fooling the Turkish people and getting money from them by all kinds of schemes and promises."[38]

Convinced that Nihad had not authored the letter, Valkenburgh proceeded to the address listed and discovered a wholesaler named A. Abedin, who produced a list of witnesses Fay was planning to smuggle out of the country with Spanish passports obtained under assumed names. The authorities met the steamship *President Wilson* bound for Patras, Greece, and recovered five men, including Fatta Abbas, before the ship left port.[39] Several other witnesses, however, managed to disappear. Once in custody, Abbas reported rumors within the Turkish community that James Fay had been exonerated and that they were now allowed to depart. That the group had somehow secured Spanish documents made Abbas' claim credible in Valkenburgh's eyes. He implored Abbas to remain until Fay's trial. As added insurance, Valkenburgh asked the State Department for assistance in restricting the men from being allowed to depart.[40]

The Bureau investigated New York's Spanish Consulate more closely to try to understand how Fay—a known fugitive under federal investigation—obtained passports there. The Consulate's Turkish clerk, Shah-Mir Effendi, could not locate any valid passports processed in the names of the men Valkenburgh captured at the port. The clerk promised to cancel any Turkish passports coming his way but leveled accusations at the LLP: if the Bureau wished to track Turkish subjects leaving the country, he claimed, the LLP was well-known for that.[41] Intrigued, Valkenburgh spent some of his time in New York exploring the Bureau's archives, where he discovered that the LLP's president, Na'um Mukarzil, had been investigated for passport fraud just weeks before the Fay case. In Mukarzil's file, a letter written by the former Bureau Chief, A. B. Bielaski, laid out the State Department's formal attitude toward Syrian migrants of Ottoman nationality. Dated April 16, 1919, it read,

> With reference to Agent Perkins' report on N. A. Mokarzel and the activities of the Spanish Consul-General in New York,[42] I am advised by the State Department that according to their understanding, the citizens of Mount Lebanon are Turkish subjects and as such they are under the protection at the present time of the Spanish diplomats and Consular offices.[43]

Agent Valkenburgh had a new question: why was the United States allowing France to grant Syrians *sauf conduits* in the first place if the State Department regarded them as Turkish—and not French—subjects? He resolved to investigate the LLP and its role in mediating Syrian national identity more closely.

At the same time, Valkenburgh learned that three of his key witnesses—including Fatta Abbas—had secured paperwork documenting health concerns that cleared them for departure in accordance with US Customs laws.[44] The State Department delayed their departure considerably but by late October 1919, all three men had departed the United States for Asia Minor. The rumors swirled that Turks who wished to repatriate had only to have themselves declared medically infirm to be exempted from the travel ban. A Turkish informant in Cambridge, Massachusetts reported that "there are Turks leaving Peabody, Worcester, Lynn, Lowell, and Providence by filing health certificates . . . signed by a certain doctor in Peabody." The informant stated that "he knows these men to be able-bodied and not sick."[45] Valkenburgh never saw Fatta Abbas again.

Sykes-Picot, French Ambitions, and James Fay's Greater Syria

James Fay evaded federal agents for several weeks, fleeing Boston for New York City, then Providence before disappearing entirely. Agent Valkenburgh finally caught a break when, rather than approaching Fay's cagey neighbors to ask about his whereabouts, he mailed an attractive package to Fay's Boston office. Without delay, Fay's neighbors helpfully forwarded the box to an address in Detroit,

Michigan.[46] Bureau agents went there to arrest him, but Fay instead popped up again in Boston, ready to surrender himself with his attorney at his side.[47] Within his personal effects, Fay submitted a map of Syria and Asia Minor cut out from a magazine. Upon it appeared circles in pen noting all the places then occupied by Allied troops, as well as territories then claimed by France as her projected Mandate at the Paris Peace Conference. The shaded areas on Fay's map roughly corresponding to territories delineated in the Sykes-Picot Agreements of 1916.

James Fay gave a statement before being taken into police custody. When it came to French *sauf conduits*, he explained, "I only issue applications to people who come from Diarbekir and Kharput; these cities are under French control." Handing the agent his map "with proposed lines marked by the Syrian Committee at New York which shows what part of Turkey France wanted as her share of war indemnity," Fay claimed that he had disclosed to Ya'cub Rufa'il, the LLP's secretary, "that these men were Kurds but now under French control and they could visa their applications so that they could get safe conduct from the French Consul at Boston."[48] Agent Valkenburgh reminded Fay that these Kurds' exit applications had already been rejected by the State Department. Fay grew impatient and repeated,

> It did not make any difference, they were now under French control and were intitled [sic] to French safe conduct. Anyone coming from Diarbekir, Turkey is intitled [sic] to a French safe conduct after the armistice was signed as it is now called Greater Syria.[49]

Quite sure that Diyarbakır was Turkish territory, Valkenburgh was nevertheless concerned that there was enough truth in Fay's claim that the Kurds were French colonials to exonerate him or, at least, to muddy the juridical waters. "With this proposed map Fay has fooled these applicants, the French Consul at Boston, and possibly also the French Consul General at New York City," Valkenburgh recorded in his weekly brief. He sent a letter to the Department of State, asking them to decipher Fay's map and assess the veracity of his claims concerning French claims to Diyarbakır. As it turned out, the matter was far more complicated than Valkenburgh thought.

Before the war, the city of Diyarbakır sat at the center of an Ottoman vilayet of the same name. The vilayet hosted over a half million Ottoman subjects in 1914: 492,101 Muslims (Turks and Kurds) and 73,226 Armenians.[50] Diyarbakır experienced significant, repeated displacements during the war, initiated by the Unionist deportation orders driving the city's Armenian population into the Syrian desert in April 1915.[51] The Armenian Genocide changed the city's character further when the Ottoman Army then hastily resettled 30,000 Muslim refugees from Bitlis in the homes of 22,000 deported Armenians. Typhus, cholera, and famine hit Diyarbakır in successive waves, precipitating mass flight to the countryside. A 1917 German report described a dying city reduced from over 55,000 to a paltry 6,000 people.[52]

Turkish troops evacuated Syria in October 1918, moving through Diyarbakır province as they headed into Anatolia; many of the town's Unionist supporters continued northward with them, further emptying the town. In 1919, the Ottoman government formally claimed Diyarbakır but these claims were contested by France and by competing Armenian and Kurdish nationalist movements. The Kurdish migrants cited in the James Fay case, then, were seeking to reconnect with lost relatives, to assess property and estate claims, and to put inheritances in order at a moment when Diyarbakır's fate remained desperately

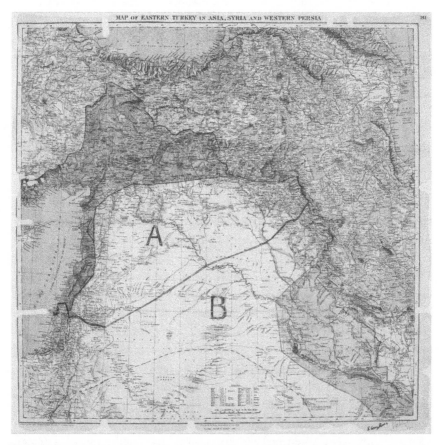

Figure 5.3. 1916 Sykes-Picot Map bearing "spheres of influence" negotiated by England and France shaded in pencil. Though Fay's map was not preserved in his casefile, it is likely he was drawing on information within this map, made public in 1917. Sykes-Picot Agreement, Eastern Turkey in Asia, Syria and Western Persia, FO 371/2777 (folio 398), MPK 1/426, Royal Geographical Society.

uncertain. The province's political limbo continued for two years after the 1918 armistice, as various parties pressed claims to Diyarbakır in the international forum. Most salient to the passport case were French claims on the territory, based on the agreements made with England in 1916. Citing these documents, France argued at the Paris Peace Conference that they were due control over Syria and Mount Lebanon but also over Adana, Diyarbakır, and other mixed regions on the frontier between Syria and Asia Minor.

Armenian and Kurdish nationalist groups also claimed Diyarbakır, placing the province at the center of their own proposed states. The Armenian National Delegation under Vahid Cardashian, for instance, presented its goals for an Armenian homeland in the territory in February 1919. Arguing that the genocide necessitated international sponsorship of a sovereign Armenian state, Cardashian concluded, "with the creation of an independent Armenian state, the majority of the Moslems that now remain in Armenia will follow the Turkish Government. This has always been the case when a Christian nation has been liberated from the Turkish yoke."[53] Less successful at lobbying the great powers, the Kurdish League pushed similarly for the creation of a Kurdish homeland in eastern Anatolia. Writing the American Commission at Istanbul, Diyarbakır's Kurdish League sought American support for their national aspirations and explained that "the Kurds [are] especially proud and exceedingly hostile toward any foreign yoke [and] never did submit to the Turkish administration except as an inevitable evil; they never gave up hoping for a better future."[54] Some US policymakers discussed the possibilities for an American sponsorship over a future Armenian state, opening questions about whether Diyarbakır would come under American political orbit.[55] The April 1920 Treaty of San Remo formally awarded Syria and Mount Lebanon to France but did not draw Syria's northernmost border. The border that definitively placed Diyarbakır in Turkey was drawn by a bilateral agreement between France and Turkey in October 1921. Following the length of the Aleppo-Mosul railway, the new border left many Arabs in Turkey and Turks within Syria. It also cut the city of Diyarbakır from most of its agricultural hinterland and consigned the town to comparative economic obscurity compared to Aleppo, the region's entrepôt.[56]

So, at the moment in mid-1919 when James Fay processed Kurds as Syrians, the fate of their home city was in flux, simultaneously claimed by the Ottoman and French states, petitioned for by competing nationalist movements, and momentarily coveted by American believers in benevolent empire. From his Boston jail cell, James Fay claimed his map was created in consultation with New York's Syrian committees and the French Consulate. In their petitions to the Paris Peace Conference, several of the mahjar's Syrian and Arab nationalist parties claimed Adana and Diyarbakır within the confines of greater Syria, among them one of the committees empowered by France to issue *sauf conduits*, the Syria Mount Lebanon Liberation League of Ayyub Tabet.[57]

Whether entirely fictional or just fanciful, Fay's map was the core of his defense against the charges against him. Fraud could only be proven if he knowingly lied or misrepresented these migrants, and it was only conspiracy if those migrants could testify to the pattern. Fay argued instead that he understood the would-be repatriates to be French colonials, at least, in the same ambiguous and tentative sense that Syrians were considered French colonials under US law. Surely if Kurds and Turks came from territories which France claimed as extensions to Syrian lands—Adana, Harput, and Diyarbakır—they had no less right to the *sauf conduits* than did their Arab neighbors.

Investigating the map, Robert Valkenburgh discovered that Fay had used it extensively to secure clients, compel co-conspirators, and fool French consular and US Immigration officials. Syrian boarding house owner A. Abedin, for instance, described how Fay approached him to serve as a sponsor for men seeking *sauf conduits*:

> [Abedin] asked Fay how he could do that when Dierbakir is in Turkey and not in Syria. Fay said it would be all right and showed Abedin a map on which Fay had marked with ink, a proposed lined of the new piece of Turkey which would be annexed to Syria, including Dierbakir, and remarked that Dierbakir is now under French control and anyone coming from there would now be a Syrian and not a Turk.[58]

Convinced by this argument, Abedin signed some of the documents attesting to the Syrian identities of Fay's clients. He continued working with Fay until being named a conspirator following Fay's arrest; this testimony cleared him in October 1919.

As Fay awaited his grand jury trial, the French Consul General in Boston, Joseph Flamand, visited him in jail. Flamand already knew who Fay was; he had briefly employed the man before firing him for misrepresenting the purposes of his private business at the Aliens Bureau. Bureau of Investigation Agent Peri Weise accompanied Flamand, hoping to ascertain whether Fay understood Diyarbakır to be Turkish territory. Fay told Flamand "that he was innocent and did not know that the men for whom he procured the passports were not bonafide Syrians." Weise remarked that Flamand angrily told Fay that "he should have known better than to get into this mess, that he had warned him on various occasions, and that if he was not a crook then he certainly acted very foolishly."[59]

Fay's map of Diyarbakır prompted the US Justice Department to ask the Department of State to clarify its positions on who rightly claimed Syrian identity. Bureau of Investigation Chief Frank Burke wrote to Washington to clarify whether Diyarbakır fell under Turkish or Allied sovereignty, and whether Kurds could be considered legally Syrian. After seven unsuccessful attempts, Burke instead sent a frustrated telegram to New York superintendent George Kelleher, "Repeated efforts have failed develop attitude Department State Turkish passport cases."[60] A handwritten memo in Burke's papers suggests "Mr. Winslow (counsel to the Department of State) will call about this case," but nothing indicates that such a call was ever made.[61] Miscommunications like this were common in the months following the armistice. Half a dozen federal agencies had been instructed to cooperate in passport control measures, but turf wars, jurisdictional issues, and a lack of resources checked against the efficiency with which the State Department worked with prosecutors.[62] Whatever the cause, the Bureau of Investigation would have to press its case against Fay without expert testimony concerning the veracity of his map of "greater Syria."

All of these factors weakened the Bureau's case against James Fay. It was clear that Fay had engaged in gross exploitation; his twenty-dollar fee was criminally exorbitant. But to prove he defrauded the United States government, the Justice Department had to amass more evidence. Fay's lawyers filed multiple continuances to delay the grand jury hearing, and key witnesses systematically disappeared.[63] Valkenburgh still had one more lead to pursue: the role that the Syrian committees played in determining who was—and who was not—Syrian in the eyes of the law. Why was a private migrant club like the LLP empowered with this role, and what was their litmus test? Had the group approved the Diyarbakır Kurds, and if so, had they also committed passport fraud?

Investigating the Lebanon League of Progress

By October 1919, the Bureau of Investigation had visited the Lebanon League of Progress in Brooklyn twice: once with a dozen captured Kurdish migrants to determine their national origins (which Ya'cub Rufa'il determined to be Turkish after discovering they could not speak Arabic), and a second time to interview secretary Rufa'il about his practices for processing Syrian *sauf conduits*. During that second visit, Rufa'il accused the LLP's Boston branch of forging his signature. Valkenburgh quickly discovered that to be untrue and learned that the League's Boston secretary, T. Shahal, was in a bitter political feud with the League's president, Na'um Mukarzil. Federal agents described Rufa'il as friendly but unhelpful; in the course of their interview, for instance, he told investigators that "the Lebanon League of Progress is unable to distinguish between a Syrian and Turk owing to the similarity of national traits and language."[64] The LLP's vice president, Mikha'il Khouri, agreed with Rufa'il and told investigators that he, too, "was unable to distinguish between a Syrian and a Turk."[65] For this reason the LLP required all comers to provide "an affidavit that he was a cit-izen of Syria," which was the "sole means of identifying an applicant as a Syrian subject."[66]

After obtaining Rufa'il's signature and the LLP's seal, Syrian applicants proceeded to the French Consulate in either New York or Boston. Boston's French consul general Joseph Flamand explained in his interview, "I did not give a Sauf Conduit to anyone unless the seal and (Rufa'il's) signature was on appli-cation."[67] Nevertheless, the State Department temporarily froze all Syrian *sauf conduits* coming through Boston and processed by the LLP pending investiga-tion into their vetting practices.

The Bureau of Investigation re-interviewed Ya'cub Rufa'il at the LLP head-quarters in October 1919. Showing him a list of known Turks, Valkenburgh asked him if he recalled signing *sauf conduits* for these men.

VALKENBURGH: "Did you O.K. these men for passports?"

RUFA'IL: "I do not know. I might have signed their application, but I do not remember."

VALKENBURGH: "Who sent the Fay applications?"

RUFA'IL: "Fay brought them himself."

VALKENBURGH: "Do you keep a record of applications you sign?"

RUFA'IL: "No."[68]

Valkenburgh suspected that Rufa'il was not telling the truth. The idea that the LLP would not keep records of applications they processed seemed improbable. That said, Valkenburgh had to limit his questioning to the case against James Fay. Rufa'il told the agent that Fay had no standing with the LLP and that he under-stood the man to be working for the French consulate. Of the applicants, "he claimed they were Syrians," was all Rufa'il could say of the men.

VALKENBURGH: "Do you investigate all the applicants?"

RUFA'IL: "No. I take it for granted that the witnesses who swear that the appli-cant is Syrian are reliable. Fay brings the applications to me and claim(s) they are all right."

VALKENBURGH: "Is Diarberkir in Syria or Turkey?"

RUFA'IL: "Diarbekir is in Turkey. It does not belong to Syria. It is quite a distance from the Syrian border."[69]

Rufa'il tendered samples of his signature for comparison with the *sauf conduits*. He also told Valkenburgh that no one at the League's Boston office was author-ized to sign his name.[70]

Ya'cub Rufa'il's argument than Fay had claimed his clients were Syrians contradicted Fay's own testimony that he had told Rufa'il that they were Kurds: "I told the Secretary of the Lebanon League of Progress . . . that these men were Kurds but now under French control and they could visa their applications so that they could get safe conduct from the French Consul."[71]

At the same time, investigators also interviewed two Maronite clergymen, Francis Wakim in Brooklyn and Joseph Yazbek in Boston, who both told them that the idea that the LLP could not tell Turks from Syrians was absurd. Shown the names of the Kurdish witnesses, "Father Yazbek declared positively (that they) were Mohammedan-Turkish names and surely not Syrians."[72] This opened a new question for the Bureau: what, exactly, distinguished a Syrian from a Turk (or a Kurd) in the eyes of US law? Other than signed affidavits, how did men like Fay, Rufa'il, and French consul Flamand determine who was Syrian enough to qualify for a passport? If examining a map obscured more than it revealed, what basis was used instead?

Syrian identity in the Americas was still broadly understood to be a racial identity established by immigration and naturalization court cases like 1915's *Dow v. United States*. "Syrian" identity was popularly connoted with Christian identity and distinguished from "Turkish" identity, which was simultaneously understood to be unambiguously Muslim. On these bases Syrian came to be understood as a legal category distinct from other Ottoman nationals, even when those same Syrians in America were still overwhelmingly Ottoman subjects. Similar exceptions existed for Ottoman Armenians, Greeks, and Assyrians, all Christian groups with migrant communities living in the United States.[73]

Though it was not a formal legal criterion for Syrian identity, competency in the Arabic language seemed to be a part of the passport sorting process. After discovering Kurds and Turks holding *sauf conduits* in the French Consulate, immigration authorities took them to the LLP headquarters to determine their national origins. "The Syrian Committee tried them in Syrian," agent Peri Weise reported to his superiors, "but these people naturally did not understand the language. They were then sent in the same building to a Doctor who spoke Arabic and who tried them in that language. They did not understand that either."[74] US Immigration officials prohibited the men from leaving the country on that basis. And as the Justice Department mounted evidence against James Fay, his business cards, printed in Turkish (and crucially not in Arabic) constituted a key piece of the prosecutor's evidence that Fay knew he was targeting ineligible Turks for repatriation.[75]

But as US Attorney General Anthony Goldberg pursued the language criterion as a means of establishing that fraud had occurred, he discovered that immigration laws defined "Syrian" as an ethnic and racial category, but not one with any linguistic markers. The Justice Department did not pursue, however, the question about whether "Syrian" identity in the United States was really a religious distinction. It certainly had been in the racial prerequisite cases like Dow, and in the wartime military enlistment laws.[76] France's investment of authority over the *sauf conduits* to Maronite clergy reflected a larger pattern of conflation between Syrian national origins with religious and racial content, a conflation also apparent in US law.

By November 1919, most of the witnesses against James Fay had left the country and the State Department had still not complied with requests for help parsing Fay's map of Asia Minor. Attorney General Goldberg began to question whether the Bureau of Investigation had marshalled enough evidence to convict, and whether Fay's acts had been explicitly illegal in the first place. Goldberg met with Fay's principal co-conspirators, Paul Asloglou and Spiros Kaliris, informing them that "if they can show that there was no violation of the law in the filing of these applications of French safe conduct," Goldberg would dismiss the charges against them.[77] Goldberg also dropped all charges against Walter Morell and Charles Booth, two men whose names appeared on several of the *sauf conduits* attesting to the Syrian identity of their bearers.[78]

After several delays, the grand jury convened to hear the case against James Fay in December 1919. They considered his map and heard testimony from an attenuated list of his clients as well as from his two notaries, Paul Asloglou and Spiro Kaliris. In the end, the grand jury declined to indict, and the case was unceremoniously closed. Problems with the case included the prosecution's inability to prove conspiracy or to prove that Fay had acted intentionally to defraud the US government.[79] Indeed, the Department of Justice could not definitively prove that Kurds from Diyarbakır were not Syrian or that their *sauf conduits* had been fraudulent at all, because the US laws governing Syrian national origins failed to provide meaningful limits on who among Ottoman immigrants qualified. The only crime that prosecutors could prove was that Fay overcharged his clients for his services. Guilty of being acquisitive, ungenerous, and perhaps even mercenary, James Fay's actions were not sufficiently criminal without a complaining witness to testify against him.

Conclusion

The James Fay case reveals inconsistencies in US law concerning Syrian national identity, and these inconsistencies influenced the degree to which Ottoman subjects from other parts of the empire (then under various degrees of foreign occupation) could claim rights after 1918. At different points during this investigation, Fay's lawyers argued that his clients were Syrians by virtue of being from geographic Syria, then by virtue of being future French colonials, and then by virtue of coming from places marked in the Sykes-Picot map. French officials argued they could not tell a Syrian from a Turk, and a few of the Syrian committees given precisely that task defensively concurred. Setting aside the men's vested interests in believing these things, they all operated in full conformity with an ambiguous US documentary regime that required only a signed affidavit and an individual decision to opt into Syrian nationality. One was Syrian if he said he was. Lawmakers had unintentionally built a pathway for Ottoman migrants to become Syrians from abroad.

The wartime connections between passport control laws and human smuggling networks in the Ottoman diaspora persisted after the 1918 armistice because the contradictions concerning Ottoman nationality had not yet been resolved. America's impulse to halt all cross-border traffic pending resolution at the peace conference contradicted the multiplying number of exemptions foreign nationals invoked to travel. US lawmakers remained deeply divided on whether America could even enforce a ban on departure of foreign nationals from its territory, and documents such as the *sauf conduit* allowed them to declare the ban while also providing a diplomatic means of obviating it. As the product of international compromise and a larger ambiguity around the modern passport, the *sauf conduit* was the perfect vehicle for post-Ottoman smugglers because prohibitions against its use were as unenforceable as the travel ban itself.

For migrants and their agents, the *sauf conduit* was a ticket home. Migrants facing the real possibility of having their property seized or claims to wealth negated by a collapsing Ottoman Empire felt intense pressure to repatriate before the postwar negotiations concluded. Travelers like Fatta Abbas were not concerned with which states legitimately claimed them; legally dubious or not, the passport was a means to an end. But for the French consulate, the *sauf conduit* served as documentary proof of France's historical protection over Mount Lebanon, Syria, and Middle Eastern Christians more generally. By assuming a diplomatic relationship with Syrians in the mahjar, France bolstered its claims upon their homeland.

Perhaps most striking in 1919 was the role of the Syrian committees in the United States as agents vested with the authority to determine the limits of Syrian nationality. The LLP, the Syria-Mount Lebanon League of Liberation, and other associations processed *sauf conduits* with no official oversight and no formal criteria for distinguishing Syrians from the rest. In passport investigations, no one openly questioned the use of informal agents in determining eligibility within a diverse documentary regime. The Spanish consulate, the US Departments of State and Justice, and the French consulate maintained an unremarked consensus that the Syrian committees were the best available agents for defining Syrian nationality, even as these committees were also actively petitioning in Paris on behalf of nationalist movements very much at odds with one another. This reflects a significant investment of sovereignty and its creation on a transnational network of non-state actors.

At the same time, the international forum was actively building a system that assumed nation states to be the unproblematic unit of political sovereignty, an assumption that contradicted the reality that Ottoman subjects in the Americas faced as individuals simultaneously claimed by many states and by none at all. To be sure, these Ottoman migrants were not stateless peoples; they had the legal right to appeal to the Spanish, the French, and the American governments, and they did so in turns. But while all three claimed varying degrees of diplomatic responsibility for them, no Ottoman migrants could claim full rights as citizens of any country. The establishment of the French Mandate and, more significantly, the 1923 Treaty of Lausanne theoretically remedied this problem for Arab migrants, entitling them to a post-Ottoman nationality status attached to the new polity their village of origin sat within. In practice, however, several obstacles confronted Syrians, Lebanese, and other post-Ottoman peoples seeking to assert their nationality. First among these were the imperial dictates of the French Mandate, its policies designed not to facilitate broad and inclusive provision of nationality to Syrian and Lebanese emigrants, but to limit its acquisition to perceived friends of the Mandate. This was particularly the case in the new state of Greater Lebanon, where the Mandate needed emigrants more than they could have initially known.

The French constructed a state with republican administrative structures in Lebanon, creating an elected representative council in 1922, a new nationality law in 1925, and a Lebanese Constitution in 1926 (none of which were similarly granted in neighboring Syria, nationalists pointed out in protest). Their claims to Lebanon hinged on France's historically protective relationship with Mount Lebanese Christians, particularly to the Maronite Church. Though officials initially presumed that Lebanon's enlarged borders contained a Christian majority, the annexation of the Bekaa valley, Tripoli, Saida, and Tyre challenged that assumption; by 1921, it appeared as though French claims to Christian demographic primacy were more fiction than fact. From his office in Beirut, High Commissioner Henri Gouraud weighed the costs and benefits of inviting Lebanese emigrants back into the post-Ottoman body politic. He was not the first state official to propose tapping into the mahjar in order to solve political problems at home. But when he signed an order in February 1921 commanding his consulates abroad to count emigrants for Lebanon's first population census, Gouraud set the Mandate up for a new politics of formally domesticating this diaspora through extraterritorial citizenship. Together with the passport, the 1921 census continued an early French Mandate tradition of documenting emigrants for Middle Eastern state-building purposes. The census and its uses irrevocably altered the politics of the interwar French Mandate and, after 1943, those of post-independence Lebanon.

6

Mandating the Mahjar

The French Mandate and Greater Lebanon's Census of 1921

On September 1, 1920, the Patriarch of the Maronite Church, Butrus Ilyas Huwayyik, took his seat in Beirut's central square. Next to him sat the High Commissioner of the French Mandate, General Henri Gouraud; opposite him was the Sunni grand mufti of Beirut, Sheikh Mustafa Naja.[1] A crowd gathered to hear Gouraud announce the formation of Greater Lebanon under French Mandate.[2] Greater Lebanon (*Grand Liban*) would be a confessional republic under French tutelage, built on France's claim as historic protector of Lebanese Christians in an overwhelmingly Muslim region.[3] Patriarch Huwayyik and Grand Mufti Naja were presented to the crowd, together representing a compact between Lebanon's religious communities and their cooperation within a republican structure. In the Mandate's early months, French officials invested themselves in establishing in Lebanon "equitable representation" among confessional groups while also "safeguarding the rights of minorities," particularly the Maronites who they believed were France's partners.[4] In Gouraud's vision presented that day, France had been invited to transform Lebanon's confessional diversity into a political asset, to build a nation that would protect the future of Lebanon's Christians who, although they were a religious minority in the region, would comprise a numerical majority within Greater Lebanon's borders.

The problem that immediately presented itself, however, was that Christians did not constitute a clear demographic majority in Greater Lebanon. The country's new borders considerably expanded beyond the limits of the Ottoman mutasarrifate it replaced, drawing in a diverse population who contested both Lebanon's new borders and France's right to rule them. At the 1919 Paris Peace Conference, Daud 'Ammun and the first Lebanese delegation had proposed Lebanon's expansion as a necessary precondition for its economic survival.[5] Incorporating the Bekaa Valley's fertile agricultural lands into a state centered on Mount Lebanon, he had argued, would grant Lebanon economic autonomy from the Syrian hinterland. He said less about the Bekaa's demographic makeup or that of Tripoli, Saida, or Tyre, framing his proposal in economic determinism rather than political self-determination.[6] A second Lebanese delegation visited Paris later that year, and, headed by the Maronite Patriarch, situated France as the best possible protector for Lebanon. Only through economic self-sufficiency and autonomy, Patriarch Huwayyik opined, could Lebanon also be a haven for Middle Eastern Christians in a Muslim region.[7]

Settling into his new role as High Commissioner of the Levant, Gouraud and his secretary general in Beirut, Robert de Caix, faced new questions about who belonged to Greater Lebanon. Who were the Lebanese? In a country where fully one-third of its population lived in diaspora, who counted as Lebanese, and on what terms?[8] Who among Lebanon's emigrants abroad were entitled to Lebanese nationality, to citizenship, or to suffrage? What if these Lebanese denied the viability of Greater Lebanon, or the validity of the French Mandate? Gouraud quickly resolved that a population survey was needed to assess the country's demography in preparation for building the Lebanese state. As the Mandate's first administrative point of contact with its new colonial citizenry, the census required a fastidious classification of Lebanese within a schema of rights, privileges, and responsibilities to the state. In a key decision, Gouraud ordered it would enumerate both Lebanese residents and Lebanese emigrants.

Lebanon's first census was completed in 1921, the first of only two population surveys in the country's modern history.[9] Within Lebanese territory, the French registered households directly, drawing on tax records and also relying on co-operative village *mukhtars* to report population data to Beirut. But counting Lebanese in the mahjar was trickier business. Lacking the colonial infrastructure necessary to conduct a formal census across transnational space, French officials relied on Lebanese clergy already abroad to do the counting. In 1921, High Commissioner Gouraud's office made a series of decisions that collectively ensured that Lebanon's census would yield a Christian majority: the decision to count Lebanese emigrants, to classify them according to sect, and to rely on clergy to count them. Although the census's findings represent another of the French Mandate's bureaucratic legal fictions, its officials employed this census data in shaping Lebanon's confessional republic, defining its legislative structures through independence.

From the mahjar's perspective, the 1921 census represented an instrument of French control. By counting migrants abroad, the Mandate fulfilled its obligations to the League of Nations, but it also used census data to control the movements and legal entitlements of its Lebanese subjects abroad. As they operated in the mahjar, census takers laid claim to Arab populations for whom national belonging remained unsettled following the Ottoman Empire's defeat. Like the passport agents of the armistice period (1918–1920), these census takers worked on the Mandate's behalf, but with little French oversight.

Whereas the census data influenced Lebanon's legislative structures at home, it also informed new French policies toward the mahjar designed to selectively encourage Lebanese repatriation, to embrace allies with nationality rights, and to cut ties with anticolonial troublemakers. Taken collectively, these policies reflect a pattern I call *mandating the mahjar*, a refraction of state authority to contain select emigrants within the strictures of citizenship.

But for Lebanese emigrants across the Americas, the census also represented their first chance at exercising a substantive post-Ottoman citizenship, a shot at claiming rights from the Mandate. They registered at the French consulates, at their churches, or sometimes remotely through family in Lebanon, expecting that the Mandate would grant them diplomatic protections, travel rights, Lebanese nationality, and voting rights in Lebanese elections. These expectations set the Mandate up for conflict with its emigrants in the 1920s. Although the French saw the diaspora as a convenient national constituency, necessary to ensure Lebanon's Christian demographic majority, the 1921 census encouraged new patterns of transnational claims-making by migrants abroad, refashioning Lebanese politics around the inclusion/exclusion of émigrés from the body politic.[10]

Who Counts?

The historiography of the Lebanese census commonly focuses on the census of 1932, the country's second population survey conducted by the French Mandate. This focus is apt, not only because at the time of writing, the 1932 census remains Lebanon's most recent recorded population data, but also because its findings underpinned the Lebanese political system through independence. The 1932 census's defining characteristics were built on the methodological bones of its 1921 predecessor. Both censuses, for instance, classified Lebanese citizens in confessional terms; both underreported Muslims; and both included a largely Christian Lebanese diaspora to arrive at a 6:5 electoral ratio (of Christians to Muslims) that scholars like Rania Maktabi argue reflected French desires for Lebanon more than it did the demographic realities of the state.[11] But remarkably little is known about the 1921 census except that its results were, at the time, considered "highly imperfect, for the reasons . . . of concealment, misunderstanding, falsification, [and] conjecture."[12] Even less is known about the census's impact on the Lebanese (and Syrians) in the mahjar.

The French High Commissioner employed census data to establish electoral districts and set up the confessional distribution of seats in the Lebanon's Representative Council, the administrative body that replaced the Ottoman-era Administrative Council in 1922.[13] The census's registrants were arranged along three planes, classified by sect, village (or village of origin), and heads of household.[14] Mandate officials borrowed this principle from their reading of Ottoman precedent. Before the Tanzimat reforms of the mid-nineteenth century, the Ottoman Empire had classified its subjects within the millet system, a useful method because tax rates, military service obligations, and other responsibilities exchanged between the Sultan and his subjects were in accordance with their belonging to a distinct millet.[15] Informed by Lyautey's colonial principle of association, which dictated that colonial peoples are best governed according to their own laws and traditions, High Commissioner Gouraud and his secretary, Robert de Caix, incorporated French understandings of religious sect into the Lebanese census.[16] Their focus on balancing confessional interests through accommodation within representative structures was rooted in the assumption that the Lebanon's religiously diverse groups had been, since time immemorial, in a state of constant religious conflict, particularly between Christians and Muslims.[17] The French Mandate also borrowed from Ottoman precedent in other ways: they almost entirely delegated personal status laws to the respective religious authorities.[18] But the High Commissioner's reshaping of Lebanon's first republican structures through confessional quotas fostered the modern sectarian system that continued to shape the country's politics through independence.[19]

Registration with the 1921 census was often an individual's first formal contact with the French Mandate. Within Lebanon, French officials registered Lebanese communities directly, but lacking access to émigré communities abroad, the French instead relied on three data streams to count migrants living in the mahjar. First, the High Commissioner's office in Beirut assessed municipal tax records, automatically entering tax-paying emigrants as though they continued to live in their villages of origin. Gouraud believed that tax payments reflected an ongoing investment in Lebanon, and he inferred that emigrants were likely future repatriates and should be counted. Including this data in the 1921 census had the effect of substantially boosting Christian numbers in mixed electoral districts, especially in the mountainous zones that had seen the most extensive emigration in the decade before the First World War.[20] Second, the High Commissioner corresponded with Lebanese clergy with ties in the diaspora, asking them to remit population data on the emigrants' behalf.[21] Finally, the French Consulates across the Americas were empowered to count Lebanese migrants directly on a voluntary basis, calling on the community to appear before French officials to be entered into the registry.[22]

Taken together, these three approaches represented the Mandate's first steps toward extending its legal authority over Lebanese emigrants. The French High Commissioner was particularly concerned about the ongoing departure of Lebanese Christians to the Americas, and he believed the census would set the foundation for policies designed to induce return migration to Lebanon.[23] In a

Table 6.1

Municipality or Caza		Maronites	Sunnis	Shi'is	Greek Orthodox	Druze	Greek Catholic	Protestants	Other	Total	Emigrants not paying taxes	Foreigners	Total present	Total emigrants	GENERAL TOTAL
Beirut	Present	17,573	32,844	3,273	12,422	1,514	4,225	535	4,906	77,292		14,206	91,498		91,498
	Emigrants paying taxes (p.t.)	190	38	1	250	9	31	9	1	528	2,406			2,934	2,934
Total		17,763	32,882	3,274	12,672	1,522	4,256	544	4,907	77,920	2,406	14,206			94,432
Tripoli	Present	1,687	24,738	3	4,060	1	171	148	704	31,512		838	32,350		32,350
	Emigrants p.t.	409	1,356	—	2,764	—	15	37	60	4,641	421			5,062	5,062
Total		2,096	26,094	3	6,824	1	186	185	764	36,153	421	838			37,412
Zgharta	Present	19,100	4,766	—	1,379	2	—	—	76	25,413		5	25,418		25,418
	Emigrants p.t.	2,233	4	—	54	—	—	—	—	2,291	9,160			11,451	11,451
Akkar	Present	6,847	16,839	—	9,576	2	435	293	740	34,732		—	34,732		34,732
	Emigrants p.t.	1,422	280	—	1,538	—	55	—	9	3,304	6,935			10,239	10,239
Koura-Batroun	Present	19,373	1,582	404	12,867	7	472	5	19	34,729		10	34,739		34,739
	Emigrants p.t.	3,654	103	47	3,518	—	—	—	—	7,322	12,597			19,919	19,919
Total		52,719	23,574	451	28,932	11	992	298	844	107,791	28,692	15	94,889	41,609	136,498

(continued)

Table 6.1 Continued

Municipality or Caza		Maronites	Sunnis	Shi'is	Greek Orthodox	Druze	Greek Catholic	Protestants	Other	Total	Emigrants not paying taxes	Foreigners	Total present	Total emigrants	GENERAL TOTAL
Matn	Present	31,149	742	3,857	6,650	6,464	2,561	187	298	51,709		336	52,045		52,045
	Emigrants p.t.	5,115	12	61	1,674	832	496	25	98	8,313	4,922			13,235	13,235
Chouf	Present	16,823	8,127	1,032	5,191	23,492	4,351	713	42	59,781		403	60,184		60,184
	Emigrants p.t.	2,700	168	32	710	2,168	787	228	2	7,245	8,227			15,472	15,472
Kesrouan	Present	34,395	200	2,639	1,010	—	208	36	128	38,636		2,368	41,004		41,004
	Emigrants p.t.	4,441	24	61	250	—	26	3	1	4,816	9,474			14,290	14,290
Dayr al-Qamar	Present	2,440	60	21	23	72	342	14	—	2,972		113	3,085		3,085
	Emigrants p.t.	305	—	—	1	—	19	1	—	326	254			580	580
Total		97,368	9,333	7,523	15,519	33,478	8,801	1,207	569	173,798	22,877	3,220	156,318	43,677	199,895
Saida	Present	2,698	6,533	21,160	201	29	1,199	64	370	32,254		180	32,434		32,434
	Emigrants p.t.	287	34	518	—	—	111	1	5	956	1,848			2,804	2,804
Sour	Present	2,432	735	34,694	137	11	3,063	96	46	41,214		80	41,294		41,294
	Emigrants p.t.	147	—	615	1	—	121	23	—	907	5,347			6,254	6,254
Djezzine	Present	8,241	272	2,122	76	252	4,520	354	9	15,843		50	15,893		15,893
	Emigrants p.t.	1,802	14	238	6	6	641	11	—	2,818	2,622			5,440	5,440
Marjayoun	Present	970	2,283	3,337	2,539	141	1,015	543	198	11,028		—	11,028		11,028
	Emigrants p.t.	111	1	82	465	—	124	91	—	874	2,241			3,115	3,115
Hasbaya	Present	511	3,392	30	1,910	3,012	270	253	1	9,359		—	9,359		9,359
	Emigrants p.t.	56	133	—	341	68	78	16	—	592	2,048			2,740	2,740
Total		17,255	13,397	62,796	5,673	3,519	11,242	1,434	629	115,945	14,106	310	110,008	20,353	130,361

Bekaa	Present	7,535	11,979	3,001	—	239	10,706	328	570	39,674	6	1,129	40,803		40,803
	Emigrants p.t.	448	402	98	5,316	1	1,041	19	—	2,515	8,621			11,176	11,176
Baalbek	Present	3,018	3,556	19,534	506	8	4,628	22	22	31,777		351	32,128		32,128
	Emigrants p.t.	134	4	79	991	—	200	2	—	461	2,583			3,044	3,044
Rachaya	Present	406	3,087	17	42	4,590	359	157	122	12,800		134	12,942		12,942
	Emigrants p.t.	26	251	—	4,071	259	58	10	9	1,485	1,481			2,966	2,966
Hermel	Present	414	227	8,124	883	5	25	—	—	8,795		47	8,842		8,842
	Emigrants p.t.	—	—	47	—	—	—	—	—	47	16			63	63
Total		11,980	19,506	30,900	11,789	5,102	17,015	547	723	97,562	12,741	1,661	94,713	17,549	111,964
TOTAL POPULATION		199,181	124,786	104,947	81,409	43,633	42,462	4,215	8,436	609,069	81,243	20,250	579,778	130,784	710,562

February 1921 letter to the consulates in the Americas, Gouraud instructed his staff to promote the tally as resting on "the interests and intentions to Syrians and Lebanese abroad to maintain a link with their place of origin." Census registration was open to "all Lebanese who so request it" anywhere in the mahjar, and Gouraud argued that the emigrants would prove a supportive and "numerically significant" constituency abroad.[24]

Appearing before a French agent, Lebanese migrant registrants proffered their Ottoman documents (*tezkeret néfous*) as proof of their origins in exchange for a receipt of registration, marking their first footfall into French Mandate citizenship.[25] The receipts given in exchange for registering became proof of relationship with the new Lebanese entity, and they were offered to emigrants with the expectation that they would ultimately return to Lebanon.[26] In the Americas, many Lebanese Maronites registered enthusiastically, eager to replace their antiquated Ottoman documents and claim a legal tie to home.[27] The French Mandate, meanwhile, collected rich data to be mined for the purposes of policy, particularly with regard to policies designed to regulate, control, and ultimately extinguish the Lebanese emigration.

The census project did not, however, provide significant resources to count emigrants; to accomplish that, French officials would have to tap into the transnational networks of trust and cooperation that connected Lebanese communities in the mahjar, networks that the Mandate did not control. Gouraud delegated the registration of Lebanese migrants to religious authorities already operating in the Americas, particularly the Maronite Church and its Patriarch, Ilyas Huwayyik. The Maronite Church cooperated with the census project for two reasons, embracing the opportunity to assist in reclaiming emigrants for Lebanon but also using the project as a chance to reorganize the Maronite Church and project its own influence into the Lebanese mahjar.

Who Does the Counting?

Letters between Maronite Patriarch Huwayyik and the High Commissioner's office in Beirut illustrate that the Patriarchate was intimately involved with the counting of Lebanese emigrants. Shortly after Gouraud's announcement of the census in February 1921,[28] the Patriarchate in Bkerke sent Maronite Bishop Shukrallah al-Khuri to the Americas to tour the diaspora's Maronite communities and report on the state of the Church. al-Khuri's trip lasted over two years and took him across the Americas; from his dormitory in Brooklyn, furthermore, the bishop corresponded with clergymen across the United States, Latin America, and Europe, consolidating a vast archive of information on Maronite colonies and religious practice in the diaspora.[29]

Bishop al-Khuri boarded a steamship in Beirut with the understanding that his mission was ecclesiastical in nature, and only after his arrival in New York did the French government seek the Church's assistance in registering Lebanese populations for the Mandate's own census project.[30] In April 1921, the French consul in New York sent al-Khuri a formal register, asking him to categorize emigrants according to confession, household, and village of origin, in addition to raw numbers.[31] The consul's letter explained that the Beirut High Commissioner also sought names of Lebanese heads of households where possible, a prerequisite for registration papers being prepared in Beirut. Such registration was necessary, the consul concluded, to help France "in everything it undertakes to protect your compatriots in the most effective way possible."[32]

Clearly the French consulate's assignment was a daunting one, and the bishop obliged, issuing a circular letter to Maronite clergy requesting information regarding their congregations be sent to Brooklyn's Our Lady of Lebanon Cathedral, where al-Khuri would assess it. The census data trickled to New York, arriving with staid letters by Maronite clergy describing the state of the church, ritual, and Maronite religious practice across the United States. Amalgamating the data as swiftly as possible in April and May 1921, al-Khuri remitted it to the French consulates in New York and Washington, D.C., as well as to the Maronite Patriarchate in Bkerke, where Patriarch Huwayyik planned a reformation of his church in the Americas. al-Khuri's role in the census was thus a joint effort, a partnership made by French authorities and the Church in the name of identifying Lebanon's non-resident constituents in temporal and spiritual matters simultaneously. This politics of embrace shaped both early Mandate policies toward the Lebanese mahjar and the Maronite Church's reorganization there, further cementing the partnership between the Church and the state.

At the same time, the correspondence between Maronite clergy in the mahjar and French officials reveals significant mismatches in goals and agenda. New York's French consul initially asked al-Khuri, for example, to count "all Syrians and Lebanese in our jurisdiction (the United States)," of all sects and religions, a massive project the Bishop returned as unworkable clarifying that his office could only faithfully record Maronite emigrant data for the Mandate. On the mahjar's other Lebanese sects, "I regret only that I can offer imperfect numbers, offering more exact figures for the Maronites, the object of my visit to America."[33] The bishop offered to assist French officials in locating Orthodox and Melkite clergy in New York, but "with respect to other, non-Christian Syrians—Jews, Druze, Muslims—I do not know for certain, but I think they are very few in number."[34] The bishop emphasized the demographic strength of Lebanese Christians in the United States and the Americas generally, but the exchange reveals also that the accuracy of the census data hinged on the French Mandate's ability to find willing census takers.[35]

Although Christians certainly constituted the simple majority in Lebanon's diaspora in 1921, there were numerous communities of Lebanese Muslims and Druze in the mahjar. They had their own political societies, welfare clubs, charities, and newspaper presses, and were visible participants in Lebanese political culture.[36] In New York City, for instance, the political daily *al-Bayan*, operated by Suleiman Baddur, had a distribution comparable to *Mirat al-Gharb*, *al-Sa'ih*, and *al-Sha'b* newspapers.[37] *Al-Bayan* had a Druze editor, a mixed Druze and Sunni set of columnists, and an Arab nationalist outlook that opposed the 1921 census project and French rule in Syria and Lebanon.[38] The publication ran continuously from the late Ottoman period through the early 1920s and would have been a visible focal point for the non-Christian immigrant population as well as those who opposed the Mandate.[39] It was unlikely, however, that French officials would find Muslim or Druze ethnic leaders to undertake the 1921 census; these communities were overwhelmingly elided from the Mandate's official record as a result.

A month into the census project, Bishop Shukrallah al-Khuri could personally account for 16,000 Maronites living in the northeastern United States, mainly in New York and Massachusetts.[40] For reasons not entirely clear, however, he submitted an estimate of 25,000 Maronites living in the northeastern United States to the French government on May 1, 1921.[41] He estimated a grand total of 55,000 Maronites for the entire country.[42] These numbers were speculative, rough estimates on the Bishop's part to conform to High Commissioner Gouraud's rushed May 1 deadline. By that date, many Maronite parishes had yet to actually reply to al-Khuri's request for data. al-Khuri's decision to round up based on an incomplete data set reflected his desire to build the case for his sect's numerical supremacy, and his belief that the numbers would bear out as clerics from other US states submitted their numbers in the weeks and months to come.

It is clear that Beirut's imposed deadline led to population data that was incomplete and incoherent. But when compared against other sources of population data enumerating Lebanese in the United States, a mixed picture of the accuracy of his count emerges. For instance, the firmest numbers al-Khuri could present to the French Consulate in May 1921 concerned the Lebanese Maronites living in New York and Massachusetts, but in both states, his numbers prove unreliable. In 1921, the bishop reported that 7,500 Lebanese Maronites lived in New York and another 5,977 in Massachusetts.[43] The US census conducted just months earlier in 1920, however, enumerated the Syrian and Lebanese population of New York at only 7,760, all religions and sects combined.[44] This discrepancy is even more severe in Massachusetts: al-Khuri reported registering 5,977 Lebanese Maronites, but the US census only found 3,150 total Syrian and Lebanese immigrants state-wide a year earlier.[45] So large a discrepancy cannot be explained only by Lebanese aliens being left out of the US census nor by Lebanese migrants dodging the census takers. Indeed, Syrian and Lebanese immigrant groups encouraged the community to register for the US census; the Syrian American Club saw it as a means of documenting Syrian aliens in preparation for their naturalization.[46] Such inconsistencies between the bishop's numbers and those of the US census cast doubts over their accuracy.

On the other hand, a comparison between al-Khuri's data with rigorous attempts by historians to assess the size of the Syrian and Lebanese communities in the United States reveal that the bishop's numbers are actually quite conservative. With additional data coming into al-Khuri's office through August 1921, nearly all of his estimated 55,000 Maronites in the United States were accounted for. In terms of raw numbers, there were many Maronites who remained uncounted. The US General Commissioner had confirmed the arrival of 89,971 Syrians and Lebanese (of all sects) between 1899 and 1919.[47] Performing another community audit in 1924, Syrian American scholar Philip K. Hitti estimated around 200,000 Syrians, Lebanese, and Palestinian immigrants lived in the United States (a figure drawn from 1880–1919 US immigration figures).[48] Historians now estimate that around 105,000 Syrians and Lebanese (of all religious and sects) lived in the United States by 1924.[49] Despite the sizable variance in these figures, it is clear that al-Khuri's estimates trended conservative.[50] Pressed for time and unable to tender precise head-of-household data to Beirut, al-Khuri seems to have relied on estimates sent by minor clergy working in the mahjar's peripheries. His data reveals, then, not an attempt to inaccurately portray the Church's share of Lebanese emigrants, but the extent to which the Patriarchate had yet to firmly centralize its own infrastructure in the diaspora.

Accompanying his figures to the French consulate, al-Khuri enclosed an appeal to the High Commissioner to recognize that in his opinion, the Maronites abroad made "more contact with Europe . . . establishing a moral rapport in the name of civilization" than any other Lebanese sect. The bishop continued that in Greater Lebanon, Christians "fear the fanaticism of Islam" and that "France's supporters (among the Lebanese) come from villages and towns with a Christian majority."[51] As shepherd to his flock, he hoped that France would include the diasporic Maronites in the Lebanese body politic more fully because, he concluded, they had the most to lose by surrendering a demographic majority in their own country. In response, the French General Consul of New York reassured al-Khuri that "with respect to this question that concerns you, I have just received specific reassurances regarding the legitimate apprehensions on the part of the Lebanese."[52] When the High Commissioner of Beirut released the findings of their census later that year, they concluded that 42,637 Lebanese lived in the United States, 25,000 of whom were Maronite and lived (as al-Khuri had written) in the northeast.[53] The heads of household al-Khuri counted were offered receipts that served as legal registration.[54]

Collecting population data from each of Lebanon's six municipal districts and from the diaspora, the High Commissioner's office set about amalgamating the data, a task completed in December 1921. That same month, Beirut announced Lebanon's first general elections to elect members for a new Representative Council in 1922.[55] According to Arrêté 1307, the Representative Council would advise the Mandate in administrative affairs; its representatives would be elected by universal male suffrage, but a registration receipt from the 1921 census was required to be eligible to vote.[56] Although the High Commissioner had insisted in 1921 that the census was an administrative (not a political) tool, the Mandate excluded Lebanese who had evaded census takers from the vote.[57] In both Lebanon and its diaspora, Sunni organizations and Arab nationalists had boycotted the census, protesting against recognition of the Lebanese state.[58] In the mahjar, eligible Christian migrants sought out voluntary registration in larger numbers, whereas Muslim and Druze migrants were more likely to evade census takers. In addition to determining who had access to suffrage, the Mandate grafted the census's confessional ratios onto seats in the Representative Council: with a clear majority at 55 percent, the council reserved six seats for Lebanese Christians for every five Muslim ones (6:5).[59]

This 6:5 electoral ratio depended on inclusion of emigrants in the census, in 1921 and preserved in 1932. To reach it, the Mandatory government paired the numbers of resident Lebanese with tax-paying emigrants.[60] These were grouped into Christian (Maronite, Greek Orthodox, Greek Catholic, and Protestant numbers) and Muslim (Sunni, Shiʿi, and Druze) categories: 327,267 and 273,366, respectively, creating the enduring 6:5 ratio. The exclusion of the Lebanese diaspora, by contrast, would have produced a strikingly different result: Christians would comprise an exceptionally slim majority at 51.9 percent of the resident population, and Muslims at 48.08 percent. Even without taking the largely Muslim boycott into account, the gap between "majority" and "minority" closes when emigrant numbers are excluded. Although the inclusion of emigrants does not appear to have upset the demographic outcomes of any single electoral district, it clearly ensured that Christian representatives safely outnumbered Muslim ones. Furthermore, with even representative districts of 20,000, the Representative Council's Muslim constituencies were not only fewer but more broadly drawn.[61] Muslim representatives likely had greater difficulty in asserting an agenda and attracting the loyalty of their constituencies in a confessional system that was already difficult to navigate.

The same law that governed voting eligibility for resident Lebanese voters, Arrêté 1307, also included provisions in article 28 that theoretically allowed tax-paying Lebanese emigrants to vote.[62] Although the Mandate and its consulates abroad made significant efforts to register emigrants for the census, the state did not pursue the issue of emigrant voting rights. Rather, Lebanese emigrants who registered with the census could freely vote in Lebanon's 1922 council election only if they returned to their village of origin to cast the ballot (and only if the returnees had paid Lebanese taxes).[63] Despite appeals by prominent Lebanese emigrants for absentee balloting, the French Mandate never made such accommodations. The reason was certainly not a lack of consular infrastructure to undertake absentee balloting, because the French invested considerable resources into Syrian and Lebanese consulates in the Americas dedicated to engaging, administering, and policing Arab migrants through the 1920s. Rather, the High Commissioner's haste in registering emigrants for the census and subsequent reticence to extend them the suffrage reveals a Mandate-era posture toward the mahjar. The Lebanese abroad were, to the Mandate, a convenient national constituency, to be counted for demographic purposes but not closely consulted in matters of Lebanese politics. If Lebanese emigrants could be compelled to repatriate to exercise the vote, this was all to the good for a Mandate government concerned with maintaining a state in which Christians enjoyed permanent demographic and political preeminence.

The Church's Use of the 1921 Census

As a high-profile census taker, Bishop Shukrallah al-Khuri was placed suddenly at the center of Greater Lebanon's most pressing political questions. Back home, the Maronite Church under Patriarch Ilyas Huwayyik had entered French mandatory politics as a formal representative for Lebanon's Maronites, a confessional constituency that Huwayyik sought to refashion as a national community. The counting of Maronites in the diaspora in 1921 bolstered the Patriarchate's authority in Lebanese national politics, but it also placed the Church under immense pressure to standardize its presence abroad and shepherd Maronite migrants in a more centralized way. Toward those ends, one of al-Khuri's goals was to collect information about Maronite religious practice, make contact with roving priests and clergy, and oversee the Church's reorganization in the Americas.[64] Decades of emigration had spread Maronite faithful outward from the major urban colonies into progressively smaller communities across Latin and North America.[65] With itinerant Lebanese peddlers, traders, textile workers, and smugglers travelled itinerant priests; they saw to the spiritual needs of these migrants but maintained extremely limited contact with Bkerke. Where major Maronite churches had existed before the First World War, the war years precipitated the crises of famine and epidemic; as the Patriarchate strove to provide humanitarian assistance, matters of Church administration fell by the wayside.[66] Emerging from the maelstrom after 1918, Maronite believers (and often clergy) abroad were deeply divided over political questions; the Patriarchate's support for the French Mandate was an especially fraught issue.[67]

The Maronite Patriarchate's goals in the Lebanese mahjar, then, closely resembled those of the Mandate: to embrace emigrants abroad and so bolster the Church's claims in Lebanon; to stanch the ongoing emigration of Maronites abroad; and to refract Bkerke's central authority into the diaspora after a period of lapses contact. Patriarch Huwayyik, furthermore, wished to reinvest the emigrant faithful in their place of origin, and this desire meant that al-Khuri's own position as intermediary between the mother church and the divided diasporic parishes was as significant as his relationship with Beirut. al-Khuri worked in an ambiguous space between secular and clerical powers: a Church laying claim to political preeminence; the French Mandate building a confessional republic; and an array of émigré political parties, nationalists, and rogue clerics looking to advance their own agendas. Each of these groups influenced how the census was conducted, who it reached, and how its data impacted emigrant lives.

The most obvious ecclesiastic impact of al-Khuri's work was the church's reorganization and the development of new Maronite missions, particularly in Latin America. These missions would remedy the problems brought on by the war: the devolution and decentralization of church authority under the weight of conflict; infighting and accusations of corruptions (both financial and liturgical) among clergy; and the pervasive fear that Maronite believers would leave the fold for other Latin Catholic denominations. The bishop's original 1921 questionnaire does not appear in the Bkerke letters, but the responses of the mahjar's priests reveal a focus on ritual adherence, spiritual practices, and doctrinal conformity in addition to more routine data on numbers of parishioners.[68] Most of the respondents eagerly demonstrated their passion for orthodoxy. Writing from Saint George Maronite Church in New York City (one of America's oldest), Father Jirjis Baʿalani drafted a particularly thorough response letter describing the church's philanthropic societies, tight accounting of finances, and questions of ritual: "there has not been and there shall be no relics of saints in this church."[69]Baʿalani then outlined a system of payments given to needy parishioners, and he appealed to Shukrallah al-Khuri for an extra priest for his growing congregation. Father Baʿalani's letter also shows evidence that his congregation understood al-Khuri's census to be about expanding the Maronite Church's authority abroad, but registered their dissent. Along with the names of heads-of-household required, Baʿalani admits that "the parishioners [raʿiyya] of this diocese are of two minds regarding the census."[70] In New York, as elsewhere in the mahjar, the Maronite community remained divided over the issue of the Church's role in politics. Even as it stresses conformity with Bkerke, Father

Ba'alani's response letter nevertheless includes an attendant image of a congregation ambivalent about the Patriarchate's role as census taker.

Meanwhile, another letter from Mexico City reveals that some saw opportunity in the bishop's audit. By 1921, sizable groups of Maronites worked in Mexico, particularly in Mexico City and Mérida, but perhaps because these communities were among the youngest in the diaspora, Mexico boasted few official Maronite institutions.[71] In August 1921, an itinerant priest in Mexico City submitted his response to the Bishop al-Khuri. Part of a network of clerics who followed Lebanese peddlers into the Latin American interior, the priest embraced this chance to ask the Patriarchate to build a church for the local immigrant community. He asked Bishop al-Khuri to prevail on Patriarch Huwayyik for more direct communication between Bkerke and the Lebanese of Mexico, and he attached a petition bearing signatures and seals of two dozen of merchants, nearly all of them textile traders.[72] Bishop al-Khuri saw requests like this one from Mexico as exceptional and, forwarding the documents directly to the Patriarch, he opined that "although the clergy has been sufficient in ensuring the representation of Lebanese Maronites in the United States and Canada," places south of the border lacked formal spiritual guidance, raising the specter of a émigré flock lost in the wilderness.[73]

Shukrallah al-Khuri was deeply concerned about the lack of Maronite infrastructure in the Latin American mahjar and fearful that this would precipitate a departure of Maronite émigrés to rival Catholic rites.[74] Patriarch Huwayyik and Maronite clergy expressed dismay at the prospect of "losing" Maronite believers, especially through the assimilation of Lebanese emigrants to their host societies.[75] The political preeminence of secular nationalist and anti-clerical parties in the Lebanese mahjar further bolstered these fears, especially in Latin America where the Patriarchate saw an unguarded flank. Through the early 1920s, for instance, the Alliance Libanaise (Hizb al-Ittihad al-Lubnani) operated widely across Latin Americas. Although its Cairo headquarters acquiesced to the Maronite Church's role in Lebanese politics after initially opposing it, the party's satellites in Argentina, Brazil, Mexico, Chile, and Cuba splintered into factions over the issue.[76] In most of these places, criticism of the Patriarchate's relationship with the French High Commissioner fed a pro-Independence Lebanese politics in Maronite circles underserved by Bkerke's central authority. Writing of these matters to Patriarch Huwayyik, Bishop al-Khuri stressed that the Church needed to enhance its presence in Latin America, especially given that Maronite emigrants represented both a temporal and spiritual constituency for Lebanon.[77]

Reading the bishop's reports from Bkerke, Patriarch Ilyas Huwayyik issued an August 1921 proclamation to tackle these problems on three fronts. First, existing Church infrastructure would be centralized and placed under Bkerke's direct authority. Second, locales with sizable Maronite communities would be provided with new priests, missions, and churches to ensure the faith's continuation abroad. Finally, through these new missions, Bkerke would pursue a public relations project aimed at improving the image of Lebanese Maronites in the Americas. Huwayyik believed that through the provision of Maronite schools, charities, and social clubs, the faith's public profile could be enhanced, stemming the pressures Maronite emigrants felt to assimilate into rival Catholic rites. Patriarch Huwayyik's declaration authorized the establishment of new Maronite missions in Rio de Janeiro, Mendoza, and Tucuman "to extend a helping hand to our sons in the *mahjar* for the purpose of returning glory to them, and to raise the name of our dear sect in the eyes of the Brazilians (etc.) through the works of our honorable Lebanese sons."[78]

Both the Maronite Patriarchate and the French Mandate saw the 1921 census as a means of establishing authority within Lebanon and, where possible, of reinvesting emigrants in their homeland, but the project also piqued the expectations of the emigrants they courted. In the early 1920s, Lebanese emigrants petitioned for citizenship rights, citing their inclusion in the 1921 census as proof of these entitlements. Societies such as the Lebanon League of Progress (Jam'iyyat al-Nahda al-Lubnaniyya) invoked the census within larger claims on the right to travel under French protection, to trade in Lebanon, to obtain Lebanese nationality (or give it to dependents in the Americas), and to participate in the Maronite Church's reformation. Some of these Lebanese claimants held receipts of registration; others carried tax receipts or French sauf conduit passports documenting their relationship with French Lebanon. Many others had no formal claim beyond the legal assurances that as former Ottoman subjects, they would eventually be granted the nationality option. Even for emigrants had already naturalized as citizens of the United States, Brazil, Argentina, or elsewhere, the formalities of their nationality mattered little to them; from the perspective of Lebanese activists, their politics of citizenship and claims-making was based not on the presence (or absence) of documentation, but on substantive claims of partnership with the French Mandate. They invoked the census as a living social contract between two Lebanons: the emigrant and the resident.

In response to these pressures, both the Mandate state and the Patriarchate created new forums for emigrant representation and engagement. For Bkerke, this meant the construction of lay Maronite organizations in places boasting larger numbers of emigrants and few Maronite churches. The largest of these organizations was the United Maronite Society (Jam'iyyat al-Ittihad al-Maruni), established in 1921 and headquartered in New York City. The United Maronite Society opened chapters in each of Bkerke's new missions; it also claimed a formal relationship with the Lebanon League of Progress to capitalize on its extensive diasporic networks and periodical press. Naʿum Mukarzil also served on the United Maronite Society's executive board along with Bishop Shukrallah al-Khuri, Khayrallah Istafan, Francis Wakim, and various Lebanese nationalists.[79] The organization's president was Naʿum Hatem, a journalist for *al-Huda* descended from Mount Lebanese notables from the Ottoman mutasarrifate, who had recruited for the United States army during the war alongside his nephew, Albert Hatem.[80]

With headquarters offices in New York and Buenos Aires, the United Maronite Society's principal objective was "to gather Maronite opinion in the diaspora in service to progress in matters of morality, patriotism, and social values."[81] The organization presented itself as a representative chamber linking emigrant Maronites to the mother Church, offering the Patriarch a pathway toward centralizing, unifying, and representing the diaspora's interests in Lebanon's politics. In a 1924 letter to Patriarch Huwayyik, Hatem and New York office secretary, Alex Habib, described the group as a place for Maronite emigrants to assert themselves more directly as partners in building Lebanon's confessional democracy while also serving as a lay forum for political action.[82] The ubiquity of Maronite priests among the organization's trustees, however, underscores that this forum had its own internal hierarchy and was funded primarily by the Church. Although a lay organization, it was not the place for criticism of the clergy or Church politics.

For a Patriarchate seeking to exert new authority in the diaspora, the United Maronite Society served an important intermediary role in bringing Maronites and secular activists back into the fold.[83] The society's mandate "to serve the interests of the Maronite faithful [al-taʾifa] in the mahjar and the homeland" including "any political trend that calls for progress in matters of the nation, its politics, and the preservation of its independence," empowered it to represent Lebanese Maronites in matters beyond Church business.[84] In the early 1920s, for example, the society launched a petition campaign to convince the French consulates in New York and Buenos Aires to liberalize regulations at Lebanese ports to allow goods from Lebanese traders in the mahjar to enter the marketplace. The campaign specifically focused on the impact that Maronite commerce from abroad could have on the port of Jounieh, a new and growing entrepot to the Matn district where many of the mahjar's business establishments had originated. The United Maronite Society argued that if emigrant commerce were allowed to flow through Jounieh more freely, the influx would revitalize Mount Lebanon's economy, driving new investment abroad, and more firmly plugging Lebanon into mahjari trades in bulk cloth, ready-wear clothing, laces, and shipping.[85] Such petitions illustrate that although the Church initially envisioned the United Maronite Society as an arm of its own mission, the society quickly became something like an émigré chamber of commerce.[86]

The other major site where Lebanese émigrés practiced a politics of citizenship was the French consulate. Like Bkerke, Beirut developed new infrastructure designed to claim emigrants in the Americas. The French High Commissioner's office attempted to manage Lebanese emigrants as a national constituency through travel policies and laws that extended Lebanese nationality to emigrants on a highly selective basis. Aware of the diaspora's wartime legacy of involvement with homeland politics, Mandate authorities managed the mahjar carefully, checking against the citizenship claims of emigrants with unsavory political ties while opening the door to those supportive of French rule. A great sorting system emerged from the foundations of the 1921 census. French policies through the 1920s display a goal to mandate the mahjar while tackling new waves of emigration.

Taming the Lebanese Diaspora through Migration Policy

The findings of the 1921 Lebanese census formed the basis for Lebanon's first legislative structures, setting the precedent for the confessional representation that ultimately continued through independence. Despite these enduring legacies, however, the census captured a discrete moment in time, immortalizing French assumptions about the Lebanese mahjar, its fealties to the homeland, and the likelihood that Lebanese emigrants would permanently return home. Structurally, the inclusion of emigrants secured the 6:5 demographic ratio that Mandate officials desired, but its preservation depended on both the diaspora's continuing investment in Lebanese politics and a French expectation that new emigration would cease altogether. When Lebanon's ports reopened after the end of the war, however, Lebanese emigration to the Americas immediately resumed. Annual departure numbers quickly surpassed even those of the late Ottoman period, draining Mount Lebanon in particular of its Maronite and Greek Orthodox laborers.[87]

The French Mandate introduced new travel policies designed to stymie new emigration of Lebanese abroad, situating such policies within a broader rhetoric of protecting and maintaining a Christian majority for Lebanon. These policies employed both carrot and stick. On one hand, Beirut encouraged repatriation of emigrants to Lebanon through a liberal—but selective—travel regime and, in 1925, through the provision of Lebanese nationality to select emigrants abroad. On the other hand, the state also introduced measures to explicitly curtail the mobility of Lebanese at home, and to facilitate the deportation of clandestine migrants back to Lebanon.

Renewed emigration from Lebanon constituted a major governance problem for the Mandate, and French officials cited the departure of Christians from historical Mount Lebanon, in particular, as challenging the demographic balance they were attempting to maintain there.[88] High Commissioner Gouraud was not the first official to point out the emigration problem: Ottoman officials had described emigration as an impediment to progress before the war, but the mutasarrifate had made only limited attempts to minimize departures through Beirut's port.[89] The French Mandate confronted this obstacle by steadily introducing travel restrictions. Between 1921 and 1924, the French issued passports, standardized port controls, and introduced surveillance over consulates in cities abroad hosting Lebanese communities; taken collectively, the measures sought to limit access to legal departure from Lebanon while also regulating return migration.

These policies were not fully implemented until 1924, and even then, the system was not watertight. One major complication lay in the absence of coherent nationality laws. Many Lebanese in the mahjar carried census receipts as proof of national belongings, but there was no internationally agreed upon basis for either Syrian or Lebanese nationality before the 1923 Treaty of Lausanne. That treaty, furthermore, entitled individuals to exercise a nationality *option*; it did not grant them a formal nationality. In August 1924, the French Mandate drafted Arrêté 2825, the first in a series of laws that would create a Lebanese nationality code. Arrêté 2825 naturalized all Lebanese living in Lebanese territory and extinguished all claims upon Turkish citizenship. Lebanese emigrants, by contrast, were given two years to opt for Lebanese nationality or else seek naturalization in their domiciles abroad. Notably, the law did not include provisions for dual citizenship. The goal was to encourage repatriation of Lebanese emigrants as well as to issue a standard set of Lebanese passports, facilitating the closer regulation of travelers to and from Beirut. Arrêté 2825 later formed the basis for Lebanon's 1925 Nationality Law, which offered Lebanese citizenship to native residents of Lebanese territory, emigrants registered with the 1921 census, and any patrilineal descendent of a Lebanese citizen.[90]

In addition to laws governing Lebanese nationality and access to French and, later, to Lebanese passports, the French High Commissioner's office under Maxime Weygand also targeted passenger traffic through Lebanese ports with stiffer regulations. French efforts were furthered by changing attitudes about Mediterranean migrants in the major receiving states of the Americas. In the United States, for instance, the Johnson-Reed Act of 1924 introduced strict national origins quotas for new immigration; only 100 Syrians and Lebanese could be legally admitted, and shipping companies bringing more Arabs would be turned around at the port and held responsible for returning them to their point of origin.[91]

In theory, the Johnson-Reed Act effectively ended new Syrian and Lebanese immigration into the United States. In practice, steamships turned away from the port in New York carried Syrian migrants instead to ports in Brazil and Argentina. The Syrian and Lebanese colonies in South America grew rapidly and outpaced the communities in the United States by the mid-1920s.[92] Clandestine migration presented another option for migrants. Smuggling networks emerged in Mexico, Cuba, and South America to meet the demands of Syrians and Lebanese stranded by US laws barring their entry.[93] Back in Lebanon, accusations of smuggling and extortion of travelers provided the Mandate with a pretext for cracking down on the passenger trade entirely. Beirut's High Commissioner prosecuted shipping companies involved in passenger traffic aggressively in the mid-1920s, but with mixed success.[94]

The Mandate also pursued Lebanese emigrants into the mahjar. In 1924, new consular offices opened in Buenos Aires, Rio de Janeiro, São Paulo, Santos (Mexico), and New York City to cater to émigré Syrians and Lebanese. These consulates were staffed with local dragomans hired from among the Mandate's mahjari partners.[95] Typically, the Mandate's dragomans came from the Syrian colony and were long-time informal collaborators. The High Commissioner described the new consul clerks as carrying out the Mandate's responsibility for "maintaining and ensuring the rights and contacts (of emigrants) with their place of origin."[96] Assigned a desk in the French consulate, these men engaged the local community, issued passports, and arbitrated disputes among emigrants. But surveillance was the dragoman's most important task; such officials sent regular reports to Paris and Beirut about political happenings among the Syrian and Lebanese communities in the Americas.

The French Mandate was eager to engage with and embrace Lebanese emigrants, but they were also highly aware of anticolonial and pro-independence movements headquartered in this diaspora. The consulates in these communities particularly targeted Arab nationalist activities. In 1924, for instance, a New York City dragoman named Rashid Takieddine reported on 'Abd al-Rahman Shahbandar's plans to tour the Americas fundraising and seeking signatures for petitions against the French Mandate in Syria.[97] His counterpart in Buenos Aires, Shukri Abi Sa'ab, was tasked with promoting French actions in Syria among the migrant community, daunting work that made him extremely unpopular following France's bombardment of Damascus during the Great Syrian Revolt in 1925.[98]

Through restricting emigration from Lebanon, facilitating repatriation, and surveilling Lebanese in the diaspora, the French Mandate clearly envisioned sound migration policy as the touchstone for maintaining Lebanon's demographic balance. At the same time, the Beirut High Commissioner's office also encouraged the resettlement of Christian refugees from elsewhere in the post-Ottoman world. Following the Turkish War of Independence in 1923, for instance, High Commissioner Weygand proposed that Armenians expelled from Turkish territories could be quickly assimilated into existing Armenian communities in Beirut and elsewhere in Lebanon. Of a wave of refugees 96,000 strong, 35,000 Armenians entered Lebanon in 1924.[99] Armenians resettled in Lebanon as a result of such programs were, crucially, granted access to Lebanese citizenship under regulation 15 of the 1925 Nationality Law.[100] In practical terms, this community became more easily naturalized as citizens than Lebanese Muslims who had evaded census-takers just four years earlier.[101]

French Mandate authorities linked the issue of emigration from Lebanon's Christian districts directly to the influx of Anatolian refugees.[102] In a 1924 report to the League of Nations, the High Commissioner even described Christian refugees as a replacement population, writing that, "the question of Anatolian Christian expulsion from Turkey has taken an even greater significance than the continued emigration of Syrians and especially the Lebanese, who depart in large numbers for the Americas."[103] The newcomers would help to revive Lebanese industries impacted by emigration: "they will contribute a necessary artisan class to Syria and Lebanon, skilled in the trades, and by default they will compensate for the rarefaction of labor, itself a consequence of the traditional emigration of Lebanese to the Americas."[104] The French also valued them as potential partners in the Mandate and wished to integrate them into a new "respectable lower middle class" of tradesmen and professionals.[105]

Conclusion

Both the French Mandate and the Maronite Patriarchate approached the mahjar with new vigor in the early 1920s. The census was an administrative entry point that institutionalized a new relationship between church, state, and a newly defined Lebanese citizenry. In its undertaking, the Lebanese census was simultaneously local and transnational in scope. Determined to claim the mahjar for Lebanon, the Mandate included emigrants in the census, putting their numbers to work for Lebanese state-building but also setting an extraterritorial precedent that impacted Lebanese politics through independence. Examining the census as an undertaking—surveying its methodology, conduct, and immediate implications for the interwar mahjar—reveals a remarkable irony. In iterating Greater Lebanon's territorial framework, French officials not only depended on emigrants abroad but also relied on Lebanese clergy to reach them. Like the passports and petitions that preceded the Mandate's creation, data collection for this census depended on the High Commissioner's ability to tap into informal conduits of power, non-state actors with extraterritorial reach who nevertheless acted as agents of sovereign authority. Census data gathered from Lebanese communities in the Americas facilitated the construction of Lebanon's earliest post-Ottoman republican structures. At the same time, the Maronite Patriarchate was more than mere census-taker, embracing the opportunity for a spiritual reclamation of the Maronite faithful from rival Catholic rites.

The census, then, allowed both the Mandate and the Church to domesticate the diaspora, but in doing so, it also offered Lebanese emigrants new opportunities to make political claims. Emigrant census registrants understood themselves to be a fundamental part of the Lebanese body politic; holding up their receipts, they petitioned the French for travel rights, formal nationality papers, consular representation, and the absentee voting rights in Lebanese elections. The Mandate frequently failed to deliver on these expectations, tipping off emigrant grievances, inspiring debate in the mahjari press, and sometimes, gatherings outside the French consulates abroad.

Acutely aware of the Maronite Patriarchate's mediating role in mandatory Lebanon, emigrants also appealed to the clergy to prevail on French officials on their behalf. When the French consulate began to restrict visas to Lebanon for emigrants domiciled permanently abroad, for instance, grievance letters flooded into the Maronite Patriarchate. Writing from Buenos Aires in 1928, textile merchant Butrus Kairuz asked Patriarch Huwayyik for help in appealing his visa denial. As a member of the United Maronite Society of Buenos Aires, Kairuz protested his disagreeable treatment at the hands of the city's French consul, who had rejected his application for a round-trip visa to Mount Lebanon to visit family. He explained he and several other Lebanese were stranded abroad by the whims of petty French bureaucrats, and "having been unable to secure our own rights and liberties, we appeal to you, your Excellency, to prevail on the French Consulates to restore our rights to us."[106] In closing, Kairuz requested the Patriarch bring the matter of emigrant travel rights to the Lebanese parliament. He appended stamps and seals from several dozen Maronite leaders in Buenos Aires to the bottom, revealing that for these emigrants, the power to petition did not stop with the state.

In including emigrants in the census, the French fulfilled its obligations within the League of Nations mandate system and secured a desired demographic outcome, but they also walked the Mandate into a contradictory set of impulses toward the mahjar. Initially touted as an evidence of the Mandate's new politics of embrace, the establishment of new consular offices representing French Syria and Lebanon illustrates a desire to refract state authority into migrant communities across the Americas. These offices collected intelligence from the migrant community, surveilled nationalist politics, and regulated the mobility, migration, and employment patterns of Syrian and Lebanese migrants. Progressively through the mid-1920s, the consulates engaged in migration restriction, transforming the consulates into a focal point for anticolonial activists eager to confront the Mandate. If the census had once allowed Lebanese emigrants a chance to be counted for nation-building purposes, the regulatory regimes built on its data sought to discourage Lebanese migration. For neighboring Syrians living in the mahjar, they felt the effects of these regulatory regimes more acutely. Uncounted by a French Mandate that ruled their own homeland not through legislation but by force, Syrian migrants experienced the Mandate's consulates abroad as engaged in diasporic partition, a wholesale marooning of migrants abroad.

Conclusion

It had been ten years since Talaat Pasha fired him for insubordination. An empire fell, and another rose in its footprint. No longer an Ottoman subject, Amin Arslan mourned Syria as it stumbled from war to war. Writing President Woodrow Wilson in 1918, he had lamented, "Sir, my parents are dead, my ancestral home has fallen to ruin. My political career is over."[1] But as the French occupied and partitioned his home, Arslan obtained Argentinian citizenship, later explaining that "rather than being the subject of a colony, [I] preferred to be a citizen in a respected state."[2] In October 1925, he stood defiantly outside the French consulate in Buenos Aires, joined by the Syrian Union and nearly one thousand Syrians from the neighborhood. The exiled emir again led the charge against disguised colonialism, this time against the French Mandate.[3]

Like many nationalists in the mahjar, Arslan initially appealed to the great powers as the guarantors of Syria's liberation. He recruited men for the French Légion d'Orient and had initially endorsed the prospect of a limited French Mandate over a unified greater Syria.[4] He had hoped France would help Syrians rebuild their country and expressed his belief that "independence for Syria and Lebanon under the aegis of France" would turn on the principles of technical assistance and military protection.[5] But like Shukri Ghanim, Georges Samné, Naʿimi Jafet, and other Syrianists in the mahjar, Amin Arslan was shocked and dismayed by France's 1919 support for a plan to partition Syria from Lebanon. Revoking his support for the Mandate, Arslan threw his lot in with Hashemite Arab nationalism, attended Argentina's General Syrian Congress in 1919, and established himself as one of the mahjar's most outspoken critics of French rule.[6]

Amin Arslan opposed the creation of greater Lebanon for several reasons. First, he described the partition as unsanctioned by the national aspirations of the Syrian people, including his own Druze community that found itself scattered on both sides of Lebanon's eastern border. More important, Arslan argued that the creation of ethnic and confessional states in former Ottoman Syria bred sectarian conflict and hampered economic growth; France was grooming Lebanon to be a new French colony, not an independently functioning nation-state.[7]

France's imperial ambitions were particularly evident in its harsh treatment of Druze rebels during the early weeks of the Great Syrian Revolt of 1925. France's bombardment of Damascus in October 1925 was the shocking crescendo of a deepening French colonialism in Syria.[8] Fearing a general strike in Syria, High Commissioner General Maurice Sarrail ordered the city's bombardment with no advance warning.[9] Not even foreign diplomats, including key French allies, were informed of the plan. Civilian casualties were heavy: 1,200 Damascene civilians perished, and the bombing earned Sarrail widespread international condemnation. In Buenos Aires, Amin Arslan led the march to the French consulate to condemn the bombardment and visually demonstrate that the Mandate did not represent the will of the Syrians. Alongside him were Syrian anticolonial revolutionaries Dr. Jurj Sawaya (once a doctor in Boston and former correspondent for *Fatat Boston*) and Ta'au "Felipe" Homad. Together, the three men noted the League of Nations' refusal to rescue Syrians trapped under military occupation. All three went on to raise funds for Druze rebels in Hawran Province and found themselves subject to ongoing French surveillance.[10]

The bombardment shattered perceptions of the legitimacy of French rule in Syria among migrants living in the mahjar. Contrary to French propaganda "ceaselessly repeated . . . by Poincaré, Briand, and the majority of the French newspapers that the Syrians themselves wanted and solicited the French Mandate," Amin Arslan denounced the Mandate in speeches and the press as a dehumanizing and ugly "system of disguised colonialism."[11] The former Ottoman diplomat went on a Latin American speaking tour to raise funds for victims of the French bombing; he then published a booklet entitled *La Revolución Siria Contra el Mandato Francés* that he sent to policymakers in hopes that it would spur South-South anticolonial solidarities. The volume contextualized the Syrian revolt as a people's revolution against a brutal imperial regime. In particular, Arslan confronted French claims that Syrians had assented to the division of their lands:

> In an instant, they traced over a map, carving a zone A and a zone B, this zone Blue and the other Red, and then Great Britain said to France, "let us part!" just as they had done with the German colonies in Africa. The division was made, without painful haggling. BUT THOSE PEOPLE WHO WERE DIVIDED, WERE THEY CONSULTED? NO, IN NO FORM AT ALL.[12]

Not only did Syrians vehemently oppose French rule, but they also found the Mandates to be a thinly veiled colonial project, both in intention and execution. Syria was a dumping ground for French officials, Arslan argued, including 80,000 French troops and an expanding civilian staff. The state's economic policies were designed to extract Syrian commodities, particularly tobacco.[13]

Quoting liberally from French newspapers, Arslan determined that the pre-occupation of French educated society with Syria's potential as a consumer market revealed the Mandate as an exploitive imperial project on par with African colonization.[14]

But the Mashriq was not the only place the French instituted the logic of partition. Arslan also condemned French policies toward Syrian and Lebanese migrants in Latin America, arguing they showed an impulse to divide and po-lice the migrant community, and to prohibit migrant political work focused on the homeland. Arslan focused his protest on the consulate itself; after 1921, the French established special consular offices in several cities hosting large num-bers of Syrian and Lebanese migrants. Although France promised the League of Nations that these offices operated independently of their French masters, "the diplomatic and consular representation provided to Syrians and Lebanese abroad are entirely controlled by the larger French Consulate and the Ministry of Foreign Affairs." As arms of French imperial power, the Syria/Lebanon consulates in the Americas focused primarily on policing political crimes, espe-cially those associated with the press:

> As the local press was muzzled by preventative censorship, only the free émigré periodicals became the venue for venting anger, dissent, and indignation against [the Mandate's] violent acts. But at the mere mention of independence, the French prohibit all periodicals from abroad.[15]

The French consulate in Buenos Aires had Amin Arslan under strict surveillance and appointed a local dragoman, Shukri Abi Saʿab, with the unenviable task of monitoring his movements, countering his public statements, and begging Argentinian newspapers and statesmen to ignore his entreaties.[16] Abi Saʿab also cancelled Arslan's passport in an effort to clip his wings. As the Syrian commu-nity grew more restive over the Mandate's handling of the revolt back home, the consulate threatened to deny Syrian nationality to the entire community of 110,000 eligible Arabs in Argentina.[17]

The Mandate's threat to effectively denationalize an entire emigrant commu-nity reveals how thoroughly the French had embraced partition as the catch-all solution for Syria and its mahjar. The forceful imposition of new borders in the post-Ottoman Middle East had created a system of nation-states, but it also challenged Mandate authorities with policing border-crossings and with settling complex nationality and citizenship claims by indigenous communities, both settled and nomadic. Labor migrants, expatriates, and self-styled exiles living abroad presented the Mandate with an interminable series of legal quandaries, especially when they appeared at the consulate to request repatriation rights while others disputed France's right to rule entirely. The emigrant's right to a nationality, manifested through the stamping of passports, was the central dispute between the French Mandate and the mahjar. Over 90 percent of Syrian and Lebanese emigrants still carried Ottoman documents; depriving them of new passports would maroon them permanently.[18]

The French Mandate's consular offices emerged in the Americas following the 1923 Treaty of Lausanne, an internationalist promise to grant migrant communities access to the nationality option. In theory, articles 34 and 36 gave Syrians and Lebanese living abroad a three-year window to opt into a post-Ottoman nationality. In practice, the Mandate's consulates embraced nationality provisions in ways that bolstered French rule in the Middle East, filtering claimants through close political vetting.[19] Opponents identified a serious disjuncture, for instance, in how easily Lebanese migrants received passports and access to nationality compared to Syrians. Having counted emigrant Lebanese in that country's 1921 census, the High Commissioner of Beirut honored census registration receipts for passport applications. When Lebanon got its first nationality law in 1925, census registration could be used by migrants to assert Lebanese nationality.

Syrian migrants, by contrast, were not as demographically useful to the French Mandate, and there was no comparable attempt to draw in Syrians from abroad. In Damascus, Mandate authorities were primarily concerned with keeping order and suppressing ongoing nationalist rebellions, and migrants abroad protested French rule in their homeland.[20] To these Syrian migrants, Lebanon's nationality law looked like the provision of rights to pro-French partners.[21] Although bound by Lausanne and the League of Nations to create nationality provisions for Syrian migrants, Mandate officials continuously delayed them and instead, subjected these migrants to a politicized vetting process.[22]

Mandate officials routinely blamed nationalist agitation for passport delays in the mahjar, but the Buenos Aires consulate's threat refuse nationality to all 110,000 Syrians in Argentina was unprecedented. With Lausanne set to expire in 1926, the consequence of this French reprisal would have been the cancellation of their Ottoman passports and, by default, the entire community's legal transformation into citizens of the Turkish Republic. Both Turkey and Argentina protested the Mandate's policy, arguing it would leave this population effectively stateless. In an interesting twist, the Argentinian diplomat who confronted the French was Jurj Sawaya, a naturalized Arab Argentinian, a friend of Amin Arslan's, and a local figure in Arab nationalist politics.[23] Sawaya had recently been appointed as Argentina's ambassador to the French Mandate in Beirut, but the French protested his appointment and Sawaya was forced to step down. Before he did so, he transformed the Syrian nationality question into a major diplomatic controversy.[24]

Had it cancelled the passports and nationality claims of Argentina's entire Syrian community, the Mandate would have succeeded in permanently severing the ties—political networks, migration circuits, and economic lifelines—that emigrants maintained with friends and relatives in the Middle East. In a walled world with paper borders, the deprivation of documents would relinquish Syrian migrants of any claims they had on their homeland. Under international pressure, however, the French consulate relented, and it resumed processing Syrian documents after a standoff of several weeks.

That said, Syrian migrants continued to report serious obstacles when applying for travel documents. Those seeking repatriation were vetted by officials such as Shukri Abi Sa'ab, who they complained routinely subjected them to political tests and summarily denied them travel rights.[25] The Mandate frequently offered migrants temporary permits and sometimes gave them identity cards, but Syrians believed to be sympathetic to Arab nationalism were deprived of these.[26] The Mandate, meanwhile, delayed the legislation of a full Syrian nationality law. When the Lausanne treaty's window for the nationality option closed in 1926, the overwhelming majority of Syrians in Argentina continued to operate in a semi-documented world. By 1928, fewer than 10 percent had achieved recognition of any kind by the French Mandate; of those remaining, fewer than 3 percent had naturalized as Argentinian citizens.[27]

Although Amin Arslan's confrontation with Argentina's French consulate throws these tensions into sharp relief, the larger problems faced by Arab migrants regards their nationality claims were global. Syrians and Lebanese across the entire mahjar reported encountering obstacles when petitioning for rights of Mandatory citizenship, and especially when seeking permission to travel to the Middle East.[28] French authorities in Syria and Lebanon, meanwhile, seemed more frustrated by renewed emigration to the Americas. In the early 1920s, French officials applied diplomatic pressure to allies abroad, promoting restrictionist immigration policies in the United States, Brazil, Argentina, and elsewhere. The French Mandate supported, for instance, immigration quota legislation in the United States. When the Immigration Act of 1924 established a restrictive quota of 100 persons per year from Syria, Beirut's French High Commissioner pledged his partnership in immigration enforcement, including deportations.[29]

Mandate officials also pursued bilateral diplomacy as a means of controlling Syrian and Lebanese emigration in Latin America. In 1928, Brazil's consulate in Beirut coordinated with the French consulates in Brazil to stem new permanent emigration from Lebanon. The joint effort yielded a system of tightly regulated passes for Lebanese guest workers that explicitly forbade permanent emigration of women participating in the "bride trade," drawing complaint from migrant activists in São Paulo who argued the program preempted family reunification.[30] But perhaps showing the limits of the Mandate's ability to police migration in the mahjar, the French consulate in Argentina delegated the processing of documents for new migrants to local Syrian clubs.[31] In Buenos Aires, fee-based processing of Syrian migration created an economy for migration agents (*simasir*) who vigorously competed for French contracts. Ironically, some of these groups, like the Syrian Union, processed French passports and were simultaneously suspected of funding revolutionaries in the Middle East.[32]

In the end, the early French Mandate saw in the Syrian and Lebanese mahjar the same blend of opportunities and political threats evident in the late Ottoman Empire after the Young Turk Revolution. Like the Committee of Union and Progress party (hereafter CUP), Mandate officials selectively reached out to migrants abroad, seeing their clubs and institutions as useful instruments for refracting colonial authority over diasporic populations. Like the CUP, the French groomed emigrants for economic benefit and possible repatriation. But the mahjar was simultaneously a dangerous place, and the Syrian clubs a source of threat precisely because they were capable of opposing the government from spaces the state had only limited repressive capacities over. It seems that for both polities, the identification of the mahjar as a threat—of migrants and their politics as a crisis—was closely correlated with the desire to impose and defend territorial borders. For the Ottomans, these boundaries were battlefields; for the French, they were the borders of new nation states.

The French were among the great powers that capitalized on Syrian migrants beyond the Ottoman domain, working with them to oppose Istanbul during the First World War. The Syrians, Lebanese, and Palestinians who collaborated with the Entente during the war did so because they believed that the armistice would yield the liberation and independence of the Arab Middle East. Smuggling information, raising humanitarian relief, stamping passports, and enlisting in allied armies all abetted the Entente's war effort; and in some essence, this means that the activists of the Syrian mahjar took part in the political transformation of their homeland. But these activists were not colonial middlemen; rather, it is more fruitful to think of them as migrants who capitalized on the unique blend of revolutionary opportunities available in any frontier zone. Carrying many passports and deftly navigating the legal ambiguities that existed between Ottoman subjecthood and post-Ottoman nationalities, the war work of Syrian émigrés impacted the Middle East's transition into the Mandate, with both intended and unintended consequences.

France used its connections with Syrian clubs abroad to press its claims in Syria and Mount Lebanon, and consequently, the image of a collaborationist mahjar was among the legal fictions that France produced at the Paris Peace Conference. Constructing a narrative that the mahjar had supported the Mandate, however, also required the French to enact policies to domesticate the diaspora after 1920, rewarding allies while shunning perceived troublemakers. Ultimately, France learned in 1925 what the Ottomans had in 1915: that the Syrian and Lebanese mahjar was a useful political frontier, but not one that could be wholly controlled by the state. Unlike the Ottomans, however, the Mandate operated in an interwar world defined by the fastidious keeping of national borders, an obsession with migration and travel regulation, and a rising faith in partition as the solution for modern political conflict.

The partition of former Ottoman lands necessitated the forced fixing of nationalities in conformity with lines drawn on a map, criminalizing long-standing patterns of mobility and undermining the political claims of nomads, refugees, and migrants living abroad.[33] A similar process is evident in historical archives, where the dramatic partitioning of the mahjar from the Mashriq presents as the migrants' effacement from history. The production of place-based history is not natural or inevitable; rather, it reflects (and often replicates) the regulatory aims of the bordered state. The late Ottoman Empire's disengagement from the diaspora during the First World War iterates as archival silence, one later bolstered by French Mandate policies that simultaneously claimed and discounted emigrants after 1920. For both polities, discovering, reclaiming, and then forgetting the diaspora was a part of the state-building process. Forgetting the diaspora has been, furthermore, the final step in a broader process of partition, border assertion, and legal exclusion of emigrants in service to states that are principally situated in place. It is a lasting legacy of French colonialism that continues to guide the way histories of the region are written today.

The thrust of area studies scholarship once reinforced the silences of place-based history, framing the mahjar as a collection of immigrant narratives while replicating a linear vision of migration that this work reveals as limited. The histories of people who move are often retrofitted into the territorial narratives, rather than situated within their own lived social geographies. But by scattering the lives of migrants, refugees, nomads, and the displaced across several national contexts at once, their histories are deprived of their coherence and explanatory power. Recalling a moment—perhaps the final such moment—when the Syrian mahjar functioned as a frontier zone reveals the diasporic partition process for what it was: a colonial renegotiation of migrant rights and a consequent vision of migrants abroad as threatening.

This history of Syrians and Lebanese in the Americas has worked, where possible, from the various sheets of paper that shaped migrant lives from the Young Turk Revolution through the early French Mandate. In that time, these half million migrants literally papered the world; their letters, diaries, periodicals, and petitions now constitute a rich informal archive scattered across four continents, where they entice with a radical opportunity to

retrieve the mahjar from the unnatural bifurcations of nationalist historiography.[34] By reclaiming them from the margins through the papers they
carried, we are served with a powerful reminder: migrants were not—and are
not—merely at the margins of other people's histories. They are at the center
of their very own.

NOTES

Introduction

1. "A Conflagração: Outras Informações: Na Argentina," *Estado de São Paulo* (São Paulo), April 14, 1915, 1.
2. "Una Tropelía Germania en la Argentina: un Insolente 'Ultimatum' al Cónsul Turquía, Digna Actitud de Emir Emin Arslan, La Colectividad Otoman se Opone Decisamente," *Crítica* (Buenos Aires), April 13, 1915, 1.
3. "La Guerra: El Consulado General de Turquia Actitud del Emir Arslan," *La Prensa* (Buenos Aires), June 5, 1915, 6.
4. "A Conflagração," 1.
5. ʿAjaj Nuwayhid and Khaldun Nuwayhid, *al-Amir Amin Arslan: Nashir Thaqafat al-ʿArab fi-l-Arjantin* (Beirut: Dar al-Istiqlal li-l-Disarat wa-l-Nashr, 2010), 73.
6. "La Guerra: El Consulado General de Turquia," 6.
7. "La Guerra: El Consulado General de Turquia," 6.
8. Nuwayhid and Nuwayhid, *al-Amir Amin Arslan*, 67, 74–75.
9. "Los Piratas Operando en la Argentina: Alemania se Adueña del Consulado Turco," *Crítica* (Buenos Aires), May 20, 1915, 1.
10. "A Conflagração," 1.
11. "La Guerra: El Consulado General de Turquia," 6.
12. Ministère des Affaires Etrangères, Paris, Guerre 1914–1918, Turquie, LeFevre-Pontalis to Briand, Cairo, April 12, 1916. In Antoine Hokayem, Daad Bou Malhab ʿAtallah, and Jean Charaf (eds.), *Documents Diplomatiques Français Relatifs àl'histoire du Liban et de la Syrie àl'époque du Mandat, Vol. 1: Le Démantèlement de l'Empire Ottoman et les Préludes du Mandat* (Paris: l'Harmattan, 2003), 132–133.
13. Ami Ayalon, *The Press in the Arab Middle East: A History* (New York: Oxford University Press, 1995), 71–73. For an examination of lynchings involving Syrians in the United States, see Sarah Gualtieri, "Strange Fruit? Syrian Immigrants, Extralegal Violence and Racial Formation in the Jim Crow South," in *Race and Arab Americans Before and After 9/11*, ed. Nadine Naber and Amaney Jamal (Syracuse, NY: Syracuse University Press, 2008).
14. Syrian governor Cemal Pasha justified the convictions and listed the condemned men in *La vérité sur la question syrienne* (Istanbul: Imprimerie Tanine, 1916).
15. Charles Issawi, "The Historical Background of Lebanese Emigration, 1800–1914," in *The Lebanese in the World: a Century of Emigration,* ed. Albert Hourani and Nadim Shehadi (London: Centre for Lebanese Studies, 1992), 31. Up to 45 percent of migrants who left Mount Lebanon before 1914 returned after 1920; Akram Fouad Khater, *Inventing Home: Emigration, Gender, and the Middle Class in Lebanon, 1870–1920* (Berkeley: University of California Press, 2001), 118–127.

16. Studies that explicitly link the experience of war with migration and displacement include Reşat Kasaba, *A Moveable Empire: Ottoman Nomads, Migrants, and Refugees* (Seattle: University of Washington Press, 2009); Mehmet Beşikçi. *The Ottoman Mobilization of Manpower in the First World War: Between Volunteerism and Resistance* (Leiden: Brill, 2012); Isa Blumi, *Ottoman Refugees 1878-1939: Migration in a Post-Imperial World* (London: Bloomsbury Academic, 2013); Dawn Chatty, *Displacement and Dispossession in the Modern Middle East* (Cambridge: Cambridge University Press, 2010).

17. On issues relating to categorizing "migrants" and "refugees" see Chatty, *Displacement and Dispossession*, 11-22. For a discussion of the contemporary stakes of this distinction, see "From the Editor," *Middle East Report* 46, no. 278 (Spring 2016), 1-2.

18. Mustafa Aksakal, *The Ottoman Road to War in 1914: The Ottoman Empire and the First World War* (Cambridge: Cambridge University Press, 2010); M. Talha Çiçek, *War and State Formation in Syria: Cemal Pasha's Governorate during World War I, 1914-1917* (New York: Routledge, 2014).

19. Ilham Khuri-Makdisi, *The Eastern Mediterranean and the Making of Global Radicalism, 1860-1914* (Berkeley: University of California Press, 2010); Khater, *Inventing Home*; Sarah M. A. Gualtieri, *Between Arab and White: Race and Ethnicity in the Early Syrian American Diaspora* (Berkeley: University of California Press, 2009).

20. Andrew Arsan, *Interlopers of Empire: the Lebanese Diaspora in Colonial French West Africa* (London: Oxford University Press, 2014).

21. Simon Jackson, "Mandatory Development: The Political Economy of the French Mandate in Syria and Lebanon, 1915-1939" (PhD diss., New York University, 2009).

22. Reem Bailony, "Transnational Rebellion: The Syrian Revolt of 1925-1927" (PhD diss., University of California, Los Angeles, 2015); Reem Bailony, "Transnationalism and the Syrian Migrant Public: the Case of the 1925 Syrian Revolt," *Mashriq & Mahjar: Journal of Middle East Migration Studies* 1 (2013): 8-29; Steven Hyland, "Arisen from Deep Slumber: Transnational Politics and Competing Nationalisms among Syrian Immigrants in Argentina, 1900-1922," *Journal of Latin American Studies* 43, no. 3 (2011): 547-74; Gildas Brégain, *Syriens et Libanais d'Amerique du Sud, 1918-1945* (Paris: l'Harmattan, 2008).

23. Adam McKeown, "Global Migration, 1846-1940," *Journal of World History* 15, no. 2 (2004): 155-189; James Gelvin and Nile Green, eds., *Global Muslims in Steam and Print* (Berkeley: University of California Press, 2014); Liat Kozma, Cyrus Schayegh, and Avner Wishnitzer, eds., *A Global Middle East: Mobility, Materiality, and Culture in the Modern Age, 1880-1940* (London: I.B. Tauris, 2015).

24. Issawi, "The Historical Background of Lebanese Emigration," 30-31; John Karam, *Another Arabesque: Syrian-Lebanese Ethnicity in Neoliberal Brazil* (Philadelphia: Temple University Press, 2007), 6-7; Brégain, *Syriens et Libanais d'Amerique du Sud*, et.

25. Ignacio Klich, "Criollos and Arabic Speakers in Argentina: An Uneasy *Pas de Deux*, 1888-1914," in *The Lebanese in the World* (London: Centre for Lebanese Studies, 1992), 247.

26. Benedict Anderson, *Imagined Communities: On the Origins and Spread of Nationalism* (London: Verso, 1993). Scholars who note the fluidity of mahjari nationalisms before 1920 include Kais Firro, *Inventing Lebanon: Nationalism and the State under the Mandate* (London: I.B. Tauris, 2003); Asher Kaufmann, *Reviving Phoenicia: The Search for Identity in Lebanon* (London: I.B. Tauris, 2014); Hani Bawardi, *The Making of Arab Americans: From Syrian Nationalism to U.S. Citizenship* (Austin, TX: University of Texas Press, 2014).

27. Carol Hakim, *The Origins of the Lebanese National Idea, 1820-1920* (Berkeley: University of California Press, 2013); Gualtieri, *Between Arab and White*, 82. On the pragmatic politics belying wartime nationalism, see Stacy Fahrenthold, "Transnational Modes and Media: The Syrian Press in the Mahjar and Emigrant Activism during World War I," *Mashriq & Mahjar: Journal of Middle East Migration Studies* 1, no. 1 (2013): 32-57.

28. Nina Glick Schiller and Georges Eugene Fouron, *Georges Woke Up Laughing: Long-Distance Nationalism and the Search for Home* (Durham, NC: Duke University Press, 2001), 10-12.

29. Henry Melki, *al-Sihafa al-'Arabiyya fi al-Mahjar: wa-'Alaqatuha bi-l-Adab al-Mahjari* (Beirut: Dar al-Sharq al-Awsat li-l-Tiba' wa-l-Nashr, 1998), 10-13. For a complete geography of the mahjar press, see Philip di Tarrazi, *Tarikh al-Sihafa al-'Arabiyya*, 3 vols. (Beirut: al-Matba'a al-Adabiyya, 1933); Joseph Ilyas, *al-Sihafat al-Lubnaniyya: al-Qamus al-Musawwar*

(Beirut: al-Matba'a Antoun Ruhanna al-Shamali, 1997); Ibrahim 'Abdalla al-Musallima, *al-Sihafat al-'Arabiyya fi-l-Mahjar* (Cairo: al-'Arabi li-l-Nashr wa-l-Tawzi', 1994), 35–50; 'Amr Ibrahim al-Qandalchi, *al-'Arab fi-l-Mahjar: Wujuduhum, Sihafatuhum, Jam'iyyatuhum* (Baghdad: Manshurat al-Wizarat al-A'alam, 1977), among others.

30. Women's newspapers multiplied in number after 1910 as well, in part because of the availability of the Merganthaler machine. See Jurj Kallas, *Tarikh al-Sihafa al-Nisawiyya: Nasha'tuha wa-Tatawwuruha, 1892–1932* (Beirut: Dar al-Jil, 1996).

31. Khuri-Makdisi, *The Eastern Mediterranean*, 97.

32. John Torpey, *The Invention of the Passport: Surveillance, Citizenship, and the State* (Cambridge: Cambridge University Press, 2000); Adam McKeown, *Melancholy Order: Asian Migration and the Globalization of Borders* (New York: Columbia University Press, 2008); Will Hanley, "Papers for Going, Papers for Staying: Identification and Subject Formation in the Eastern Mediterranean," in *A Global Middle Eas: Mobility, Materiality, and Culture in the Modern Age, 1880–1940*, ed. Liat Kozma, Cyrus Schayegh, and Avner Wishnitzer (London: I.B. Tauris, 2015),190–192.

33. Farhana Ibrahim, "Re-making a Region: Ritual Inversions and Border Transgressions in Kutch," *Journal of South Asian Studies* 34 (December 2011), 447.

Chapter 1

1. Mary Mokarzel, *al-Hoda 1898–1968: The Story of Lebanon and Its Emigrants as Taken from the Newspaper al-Hoda* (New York: al-Hoda Press, 1968), 1–5.

2. Ilham Khuri-Makdisi, *The Eastern Mediterranean and the Making of Global Radicalism, 1860–1914* (Berkeley: University of California Press, 2010), 35–60; Thomas Philipp, *Jurji Zaidan and the Foundations of Arab Nationalism* (Syracuse, NY: Syracuse University Press, 2014), 21–35.

3. Sallum Mukarzil, *al-Kitab al-Lubnani: li-tadhakar Yubil al-Nahda al-Lubnaniyya al-Fuddi* (New York: Matba'at al-Huda, 1937), 21–22.

4. Henry Melki, *al-Sihafa al-'Arabiyya fi al-Mahjar: wa-'Alaqatuha bi-l-Adab al-Mahjari* (Beirut: Dar al-Sharq al- Awsat li-l-Tiba' wa-l-Nashr, 1998), 46–49.

5. Kemal Karpat, "The Ottoman Emigration to America, 1860–1914," *International Journal of Middle East Studies* 17, no. 2 (1985): 182–183; see also Kohei Hashimoto, "Lebanese Population Movement 1920–1939: Towards a Study," in *The Lebanese in the World: A Century of Emigration*, ed. Albert Hourani and Nadim Shehadi (London: I.B. Tauris, 1992), 87.

6. Akram Fouad Khater, *Inventing Home: Emigration, Gender, and the Middle Class in Lebanon, 1870–1920* (Berkeley: University of California Press, 2001), 110.

7. On the terminology of Syrian mahjari settlements as "colonies," see Steven Hyland, *More Argentine than You: Arabic-Speaking Immigrants in Argentina* (Albequerque, NM: University of New Mexico Press, 2017), 1–9.

8. Alixa Naff, "New York: The Mother Colony," in *A Community of Many Worlds: Arab Americans in New York City*, ed. Philip Kayal and Kathleen Benson (New York: Syracuse University Press, 1994), 7–10.

9. Adam McKeown, "Global Migration, 1846–1940," *Journal of World History* 15, no. 2 (2004): 155–189.

10. James Gelvin and Nile Green, eds., *Global Muslims in the Age of Steam and Print* (Berkeley: University of California Press, 2015), 1–11.

11. Leslie Page Moch, *Moving Europeans: Migration in Western Europe since 1750* (Bloomington: University of Indian Press, 1992).

12. Isa Blumi, *Ottoman Refugees 1878–1939: Migration in a Post-Imperial World* (London: Bloomsbury Academic, 2013).

13. Roger Owen, *The Middle East in the World Economy, 1800–1914* (London: I.B. Tauris, 1993), 244–248; Karpat, "The Ottoman Emigration to America," 175–209; Akram Fouad Khater, "Becoming 'Syrian' in America: A Global Geography of Nation and Ethnicity," *Diaspora: A Journal of Transnational Studies* 14, no. 2/3 (2005), 299–331; Leila Tarazi Fawaz, *Merchants and Migrants in Nineteenth Century Beirut* (Lincoln: University of Nebraska Press, 1983).

14. Charles Tilly, "Trust Networks in Transnational Migration," *Sociological Forum* 22, no. 1 (2007), 3–24.

15. Alixa Naff, *Becoming American: The Early Arab Immigrant Experience* (Carbondale, IL: Southern Illinois University Press, 1993).

16. Ignacio Klich, "Criollos and Arabic Speakers in Argentina: An Uneasy *Pas de Deux*, 1888–1914," in *The Lebanese in the World: a Century of Emigration*, ed. Albert Hourani and Nadim Shehadi (London: Centre for Lebanese Studies, 1992), 248.

17. Sarah Gualtieri, "Gendering the Chain Migration Thesis: Women and Syrian Transatlantic Migration, 1878–1924," *Comparative Studies of South Asia, Africa, and the Middle East* 24, no. 1 (2004), 68; Donna Gabaccia, *From the Other Side: Women, Gender, and Immigrant Life in America* (Bloomington: University of Indiana Press, 1994), 28.

18. Thomas Philipp, *The Syrians of Egypt, 1725–1975* (Stuttgart: Berliner Islamstudien Bd., 1985), 11–12.

19. Melki, *al-Sihafat al-'Arabiyya*, 45–46; 65–66; Donald M. Reid, "The Syrian Christians and Early Socialism in the Arab World," *International Journal of Middle East Studies* 5, no. 2 (1974), 180–183.

20. Khuri-Makdisi, *The Eastern Mediterranean*, 35–39; Albert Hourani, *Arabic Thought in the Liberal Age, 1798–1939* (Cambridge: Cambridge University Press, 1983); Marwan Buheiry, ed., *Intellectual Life in the Arab East, 1890–1919* (Beirut: American University of Beirut, 1981).

21. Betty S. Anderson, *The American University of Beirut: Arab Nationalism and Liberal Education* (Austin: University of Texas Press, 2011).

22. Naff, "New York: The Mother Colony," 7–10.

23. Khater, *Inventing Home*, 56.

24. Roger Owen, "The Provinces of Greater Syria, 1850–1880," in *The Middle East in the World Economy, 1800–1914* (New York: I.B. Tauris, 1981), 158–161.

25. Akram Fouad Khater, "'House' to 'Goddess of the House': Gender, Class, and Silk in 19th Century Mount Lebanon." *International Journal of Middle East Studies* 28, no. 3 (1996), 329–331.

26. Leslie Page Moch, "Connecting Migration and World History, Demographic Patterns, Family Systems and Gender," *International Review of Social History* 52 (2007), 102–104; Gualtieri, "Gendering the Chain Migration Thesis," 71–74.

27. Evelyn Shakir, *Bint Arab: Arab and Arab American Women in the United States* (Westport: Praeger: 1997), 38–43; Gualtieri, "Gendering the Chain Migration Thesis," 71–74; Naff, *Becoming American*, 128–161; Khater, *Inventing Home*, 82–83.

28. Naff, *Becoming American*, 128–135.

29. Dirk Hoerder, *Cultures in Contact: World Migrations in the Second Millennium* (Durham: Duke University Press, 2002), 331–332.

30. Charles Issawi, "The Historical Background of Lebanese Emigration, 1800–1914," in *The Lebanese in the World*, ed. Albert Hourani and Nadim Shehadi (London: Centre for Lebanese Studies, 1992), 31.

31. Élie Safa, "L'émigration libanaise" (PhD diss., Université Saint Joseph, Beirut, 1960), 188–191; Karpat, "The Ottoman Emigration to America," 183–184; Issawi, "The Historical Background to Lebanese Emigration," 31.

32. David Gutman, "Travel Documents, Mobility Control, and the Ottoman State in an Age of Global Migration, 1880–1915," *Journal of Ottoman and Turkish Studies* 3, no. 2 (2016), 348–358.

33. Engin Denis Akarli, "Ottoman Attitudes towards Lebanese Emigration, 1885–1910," in *The Lebanese in the World*, 109–110.

34. Issawi, "The Historical Background to Lebanese Emigration," 31.

35. In 1926, estimates were that 200,000 Lebanese lived in the United States (29 percent of the diaspora), 177,000 in Brazil (25.7 percent), and 110,000 in Argentina (16 percent). Growth in the Syrian community in Egypt had slowed after 1920, and in 1926 it hosted 120,000 (17.4 percent). These colonies dwarfed Syrian and Lebanese communities elsewhere in the Americas: the community in Mexico, for instance, was 20,000 in 1926 and Cuba's Lebanese community was 16,000. See Hashimoto, "Lebanese Population Movement 1920–1939," 107.

36. Faour Brothers bank in New York provided start-up capital for the city's textile and garment industries. In Brazil, the Jafet Brothers used the Abdalla Bros. bank to fund its Ypiranga factory.

See Sallum Mukarzil, *Tarikh al-Tijara al-Suriyya fi-l-Muhajara al-Amrikiyya* (New York: al-Matbaʿa al-Suriyya al-Amrikiyya, 1921), 20–21.

37. A swift comparison: in 1900, £200,000 would be valued at $26.7 million (US) in 2018. In 1910, £800,000 would be valued at $107 million (US) in 2018, reflecting a quadrupling of remittances in 10 years; see Eric W. Nye, Pounds Sterling to Dollars: Historical Conversion of Currency, accessed Sunday, July 29, 2018, http://www.uwyo.edu/numimage/currency.htm.

38. A. A. Naccache, Inspector of Public Works and Agriculture, in A. Ruppin, *Syrien als Wirtschaftsgebeit* (Berlin, 1917), as cited by Issawi, "The Historical Background of Lebanese Emigration," 27.

39. On peddling see Naff, *Becoming American*, 128–133; John Tofik Karam, *Another Arabeque: Syrian-Lebanese Ethnicity in Neoliberal Brazil* (Philadelphia: Temple University Press, 2007), 12; Evelyn Shakir, *Bint Arab: Arab and Arab American Women in the United States* (Westview, CT: Praeger, 1997), 38.

40. Gualtieri, "Gendering the Chain Migration Thesis," 68; Akram Fouad Khater, "'House' to 'Goddess of the House:' Gender, Class, and Silk in 19th Century Mount Lebanon," *International Journal of Middle East Studies* 28, no. 3 (1996), 329–331. Anatolian migrants also engaged in textile work, particularly in leathers; see Işıl Acehan, "'Ottoman Street' in America: Turkish Leatherworkers in Peabody, Massachusetts," *International Review of Social History* 54 (2009), 16–44.

41. Mary Ann Haick DiNapoli, "The Syrian-Lebanese Community of South Ferry from Its Origin to 1977," in *A Community of Many Worlds*, 15.

42. Khater, "'House' to 'Goddess of the House,'" 33.

43. Karam, *Another Arabesque*, 10–12.

44. ʿIsa Asʿad, *Tarikh Homs*, vol. 2 (Homs: Mutraniyyat Homs al-Urthudoxiyya, 1983), 386–387.

45. Antunius Jafet, *Dhikriyyat: Nisf Qarn 1903–1953* (São Paulo: Dar al-Tibaʿa wa-l-Nashr al-ʿArabiyya, 1957), 12.

46. Jurj Atlas, "Shabibat Homs fi al-Mahjar," *al-Karma* (São Paulo), October 1914, 269.

47. Karam, *Another Arabesque*, 10–11.

48. Jeffrey Lesser, *Negotiating National Identity: Immigrants, Minorities, and the Struggle for Ethnicity in Brazil* (Durham, NC: Duke University Press, 1999), 54; Arthur Ruppin, "Migration from and to Syria," in *Syria: An Economic Survey* (New York: Provisional Zionist Committee, 1918), 271.

49. Naff, *Becoming American*, 7.

50. Philip K. Hitti, *The Syrians in America* (New York: Doran Company, 1924), 62.

51. Rania Maktabi, "The Lebanese Census of 1932 Revisited: Who Are the Lebanese?" *British Journal of Middle Eastern Studies* 26, no. 2 (1999), 224–252. For a copy of the 1921 census, see "Population du Grand Liban," *Correspondance d'Orient*, May 15–30, 1922, 270.

52. Karpat, "The Ottoman Emigration to America," 182–183.

53. Karam, *Another Arabesque*, 6; Khater, "Becoming 'Syrian' in America," 299.

54. Gualtieri, *Between Arab and White*, 47.

55. Mintaha Alcuri Campos, *Turco Pobre, Sírio Remediado, Libanês Rico: Trajectória do Imigrante Libanês no Espirito Santo* (Vitória: Instituto Jones dos Santos Neves, 1987), 21. Notable new work is beginning to recover the histories of Muslim immigration to the Americas; see Sally Howell, *Old Islam in Detroit: Rediscovering the Muslim American Past* (Oxford: Oxford University Press, 2014); María del Mar Logroño Narbona, Pauli G. Pinto, and John Tofik Karam, eds., *Crescent Over Another Horizon: Islam in Latin America, the Caribbean, and Latino USA* (Austin: University of Texas Press, 2015).

56. Philip M. Kayal and Joseph Kayal, *The Syrian-Lebanese in America: A Study in Religion and Assimilation* (Boston: Twayne Publishers, 1975), 107–108; Michael Suleiman, "Impressions of New York City by Early Arab Immigrants," in *A Community of Many Worlds*, 43, 46; Naff, *Becoming American*, 36–37.

57. ʿAli Hamiya, *al-ʿAllama wa-l-Duktur Khalil Saʿadeh: Siratuhu wa-aʿmaluh, 1857–1934* (Beirut: al-Furat li-l-Nashr wa-l-Tawziʿ, 2007), 170.

58. Antunius Jafet, *Dhikrayyat*, 10–11.

59. On peddling, see Naff, *Becoming American*, 128–133; Karam, *Another Arabesque*,12. Shakir argues peddling was in decline in 1914, and that the trade's centrality in historical narratives is

evidence of a pervasive "peddlers to proprietors" narrative in oral histories; Shakir, *Bint Arab*, 38. Sarah Gualtieri shows that in 1916, Ford Motor Company employed 555 Syrian men in their Dearborn, Michigan plant; in time, Henry Ford's promise of a "five dollars a day" wage drew so many workers that the city became the second largest settlement of Syrians in the United States by 1920; Sarah M. A. Gualtieri, *Between Arab and White: Race and Ethnicity in the Early Syrian American Diaspora* (Berkeley: University of California Press, 2009), 48–50; Naff, *Becoming American*, 119–120, 139–141.

60. Gualtieri, "Gendering the Chain Migration Thesis," 69.

61. Samuel L. Bayly, *Immigrants in the Lands of Promise: Italians in Buenos Aires and New York City, 1870–1914* (Ithaca: Cornell University Press, 1999), 71; figures from Bayly's table 15, US Department of Commerce and Labor, Bureau of Statistics, *Statistical Abstract of the United States, 1911* (Washington D.C., 1912); US Department of Commerce, Bureau of the Census, *Historical Statistics of the United States: Colonial Times to 1957* (Washington D.C.: Author, 1960).

62. Ronald M. Schneider, *"Order and Progress": A Political History of Brazil* (Boulder, CO: Westview Press, 1991), 69–70.

63. Bayly, *Immigrants in the Lands of Promise*, 70–71.

64. Edward Prince Hutchinson, *Legislative History of American Immigration Policy, 1798–1965* (Philadelphia: University of Pennsylvania Press, 1981), 48–49.

65. Jeffrey Lesser, *Immigration, Ethnicity, and National Identity in Brazil, 1808 to the Present* (Cambridge: University of Cambridge Press, 2013), 26.

66. Giralda Seyfirth, "German Immigration and Brazil's Colonization Policy," in Samuel L Bayly and Eduardo José Miguez, eds., *Mass Migration to Modern Latin America* (Wilmington: Scholarly Resources Inc., 2003), 231–233.

67. Reşat Kasaba, *A Moveable Empire: Ottoman Nomads, Migrants, and Refugees* (Seattle: University of Washington Press, 2009), 118–120; Dawn Chatty, *Displacement and Dispossession in the Modern Middle East* (Cambridge: Cambridge University Press, 2010), 108–127; Joel Beinin, *Workers and Peasants in the Modern Middle East* (Cambridge: University of Cambridge Press, 2001), 79.

68. Jeffrey Lesser, *Negotiating National Identity: Immigrants, Minorities, and the Struggle for Ethnicity in Brazil* (Durham: Duke University Press, 1999), 45.

69. Bayly, *Immigrants in the Lands of Promise*, 77.

70. Dirk Hoerder, "Migration in the Atlantic Economies: Regional European Origins and Worldwide Expansion," *European Migrants: Global and Local Perspectives* (Boston: Northeastern University Press, 1996), 34–35.

71. Klich, "Criollos and Arabic Speakers," 242–243. Indeed, Khalil Sa'adih ended up in Argentina in 1914 because his ship was turned away from New York due to fears about trachoma on board.

72. Bayly, *Immigrants in the Lands of Promise*, 79.

73. Donna Gabaccia, *Foreign Relations: American Immigration in Global Perspective* (Princeton: Princeton University Press, 2012), 76–77.

74. See, for example, "Maktabat Mirat al-Gharb," *Mirat al-Gharb*, January 3, 1919, 6; "Maktabat al-Huda," *al-Huda*, January 6, 1916, 6.

75. Sallum Mukarzil, "Jaridat al-Huda al-Yawmiyya wa-Matba'atiha," in Ya'qub Rufa'il, *al-Shawa'ir al-Sharifa* (New York: Matb'at al-Huda, 1924), 86–106.

76. Khuri-Makdisi, *The Eastern Mediterranean*, 99–102; Ami Ayalon, *Reading Palestine: Printing and Literacy, 1900–1948* (Austin: University of Texas Press, 2004), 87–92.

77. Ayalon, *Reading Palestine*, 93–102; Khuri-Makdisi, *The Eastern Mediterranean*, 49–57.

78. Comité Central Syrien, *La Syrie devant la conference* (Paris: s.p., 1919); Hizb al-Ittihad al-Lubnani, *Lubnan Ba'd al-Harb* (Cairo: Matba'at al-Ma'ruf, 1919).

79. For recent critiques of framing mahjari identity in confessional terms see Khater, *Inventing Home*, 87–91; Gualtieri, *Between Arab and White*, 82–87; Bawardi, *The Making of Arab Americans*, 44–49.

80. Gualtieri, "Gendering the Chain Migration Thesis," 68–70.

81. Jurj Kallas, *Tarikh al-Sihafa al-Nisawiyya: Nasha'tuha wa-Tatawwuruha, 1896–1932* (Beirut: Dar al-Jil, 1996), 34–38. See also Khater, *Inventing Home*, 154–157; Naff, *Becoming*

American, 276; Ellen Fleischmann, *The Nation and Its 'New' Women: The Palestinian Women's Movement, 1920-1948* (Berkeley: University of California Press, 2003), 83-91; Beth Baron, *Egypt as a Woman: Nationalism, Gender, and Politics* (Berkeley: University of California Press, 2005), 107-110; Lisa Pollard, *Nurturing the Nation: the Family Politics of Modernizing, Colonizing, and Liberating Egypt, 1805-1923* (Berkeley: University of California Press, 2005), 168-72.

82. Kallas, *Tarikh al-Sihafa al-Nisawiyya*, 12-14.
83. Klich, "*Criollos* and Arabic Speakers," 256.
84. María del Mar Logroño Narbona, "The Development of Nationalist Identities in French Syria and Lebanon: a Transnational Dialogue with Arab Immigrants to Argentina and Brazil, 1915-1929" (PhD diss., University of California, Santa Barbara, 2007), 137.

Chapter 2

1. "Akhbar Mahliyya: 'Id al-Dustur al-'Uthmani," *al-Wafa'* (Lawrence, MA), July 31, 1908, 7.
2. Najib Sawaya, translation of Mundj Bey speech, "al-Ihtifal bi-'Id al-Dustur al-'Uthmani," *al-Kawn* (New York, NY), August 6, 1908, 1.
3. Sawaya, "al-Ihtifal bi-'Id al-Dustur," 1-2.
4. Michelle Campos, *Ottoman Brothers: Muslims, Christians, and Jews in Early Twentieth Century Palestine* (Palo Alto, CA: Stanford University Press, 2011); Bedross Der Matossian, *Shattered Dreams of Revolution: From Liberty to Violence in the Late Ottoman Empire* (Palo Alto, CA: Stanford University Press, 2014), 24-32.
5. Birgis Faris Jumayyil, *Hizb al-Ittihad al-Lubnani wa-Lubnan al-Kabir* (Beirut: al-Markaz al-Istishari li-l-'Alam wa-l-Tawthiq al-Madrasi, 1996), 107.
6. Sawaya, "al-Ihtifal bi-'Id al-Dustur," 2-3.
7. Sawaya, "al-Ihtifal bi-'Id al-Dustur," 3.
8. "Satisfaction Among Exiles: Turks, Armenians, Syrians of This Country Approve Young Turk Victory," *New York Times* (New York, NY), April 25, 1909, 2.
9. Charles Issawi, "The Historical Background of Lebanese Emigration, 1800-1914," in *The Lebanese in the World: A Century of Emigration*, ed.. Albert Hourani and Nadim Shehadi (London: I.B. Tauris, 1992), 26-27.
10. Campos, *Ottoman Brothers*, 20-58; Matossian, *Shattered Dreams*, 49-73; Hasan Kayalı, *Arabs and Young Turks: Ottomanism, Arabism, and Islamism in the Second Constitutional Period of the Ottoman Empire, 1908-1918* (Berkeley: University of California Press, 1997), 52-71.
11. On substantive citizenship, see Rainer Baubock, "Towards a Political Theory of Migrant Transnationalism," *International Migration Review* 37, no. 3 (2003), 704; Nina Glick Schiller and Georges Eugene Fouron, *Georges Woke Up Laughing: Long-Distance Nationalism and the Search for Home* (Durham: Duke University Press, 2001), 20-25.
12. Pauline Lewis, "A Sociotechnical History of the Telegraph in the Ottoman Empire, 1855-1908" (PhD diss., University of California, Los Angeles, 2018).
13. "al-Mudar'a al-Suriyya al-'Uthmaniyya," *al-Kawn* (New York, NY), August 13, 1908, 3.
14. Aykut Kansu, *The Revolution in 1908 in Turkey* (Leiden: Brill, 1997), 134-135.
15. Kansu, *The Revolution in 1908 in Turkey*, 135.
16. "Foes Face to Face: Mehmed Ali and Mundji Bey Pass Angry Words," *Washington Post* (Washington, DC), August 13, 1908, 1.
17. "Foes Face to Face," 1. Mundji Bey's spite at Mehmed Ali Bey extended beyond political differences. Mundji Bey was himself Ottoman Ambassador until 1900 when he was reassigned to New York because of his constitutionalist sympathies; see "Tale of Turkish Guile: One Version of Consul General Mundji Bey's Recall from Washington," *Saint Paul Globe* (St Paul, MN), December 16, 1900, 24.
18. "Akhbar Mahliyya: Mudih al-Sihafa al-Amrikiyya li-l-Safir al-'Uthmani," *al-Kawn* (New York, NY), August 13, 1908, 3.
19. "Police Guard Mehmed: Former Turkish Envoy Takes Death Threats Seriously," *Washington Post* (Washington, DC), August 14, 1908, 1; "Mehmed Had Big Sum: Turkish Government May Arrest Deposed Minister," *Washington Post* (Washington, DC), August 23, 1908, 1.
20. Kansu, *The Revolution in 1908 in Turkey*, 144-145.

21. "The Turkish Legation in Washington," *London Times* (London), August 17, 1908, 5.
22. Nader Sohrabi, *Revolution and Constitutionalism in the Ottoman Empire and Iran* (New York: Cambridge University Press, 2011), 176.
23. "Sultan in Danger of Losing the Throne," *New York Times* (New York, NY), July 31, 1908, 3.
24. "Sultan in Danger," 3.
25. "Akhbar Mahliyya: Mundji Bey wa-baʿd al-Armin," *al-Kawn* (New York, NY), September 3, 1908, 2.
26. "Sultan Calls Exiles: Amnesty for All Political Refugees Proclaimed," *Washington Post* (Washington, DC), July 31, 1908, 4. See also Işıl Acehan, "Reconstructing the Boundaries of Belonging: Transnationalization among Middle Eastern Immigrants in the United States," paper delivered at the Middle East Studies Association Annual Meeting, New Orleans, October 12, 2013.
27. Mundji Bey, "The Regenerated Ottoman Empire," *The North American Review* 188, no. 634 (September 1908), 401.
28. Mundji Bey, "The Regenerated Ottoman Empire," 402.
29. Mundji Bey, "The Regenerated Ottoman Empire," 402.
30. Mundji Bey, "The Regenerated Ottoman Empire," 403.
31. Campos, *Ottoman Brothers*, 21–50.
32. Alixa Naff, *Becoming American: The Early Arab Immigrant Experience* (Carbondale, IL: University of Illinois Press, 1987), 128–135.
33. Kansu, *The Revolution in 1908 in Turkey*, 180; see also "Syrians Express Indignation," *Washington Post* (Washington, DC), August 11, 1908, 2.
34. Nakhle Mutran, "Jamʿiyyat at-Ittihad al-Suriyya al-ʿUthmaniyya," *al-Kawn* (New York, NY), August 13, 1908, 2.
35. Sawaya was then editor in chief of *al-Kawn* newspaper. Najib Sawaya and Mundji Bey, "Jamʿiyyat al-Ittihad al-Suri al-ʿUthmaniyya," *al-Kawn* (New York, NY), August 13, 1908, 2–3.
36. "Hurriyat al-Sihafa al-ʿUthmaniyya, al-Kawn fi-Surya," *al-Kawn* (New York, NY), August 20, 1908, 7.
37. Sawaya and Mundji Bey, "Jamʿiyyat al-Ittihad al-Suri al-ʿUthmaniyya," 2.
38. Najib Sawaya, "Kayfa Naʿish wa-Kayfa Yaʿishun: al-Firq bayna al-Haya al-Mazluma wa-l-Haya al-Nirriyya," *al-Kawn* (New York, NY), October 15, 1908, 8.
39. Sawaya, "Kayfa Naʿish wa-Kayfa Yaʿishun," 8.
40. Sawaya, "Kayfa Naʿish wa-Kayfa Yaʿishun," 8.
41. Sawaya and Bey, "al-Jamʿiyya al-ʿUmumiyya," 1–2; Sawaya, "Qaʾimat al-Iktitab li-Binaʾ al-Madrasa al-Suriyya al-ʿUthmaniyya," *al-Kawn* (New York, NY), August 13, 1908, 3–4.
42. Nijmeh Hajjar, *The Politics and Poetics of Ameen Rihani: The Humanist Ideology of an Arab American Intellectual* (London: Tauris Academic Studies, 2010), 47; the cited exchanges reproduced in Amin al-Rihani, *al-Qawmiyyat* (Beirut: Dar al-Jil, 1989).
43. "Syrian Bishop Kisses Supporters in Court: There to Press a Libel Charge Against His Countrymen," *New York Times* (New York, NY), September 27, 1905, 5; Bishop Raphael Hawaweeny, "Syrian Bishop Says That Base Slanders Against Him," *New York Times* (New York, NY), October 26, 1905, 5; "Syrian Bishop Cleared in Court," *New York Times* (New York, NY), December 5, 1905, 5.
44. "Ila al-Amam, ya Jamʿiyyat al-Ittihad al-Suri al-Umumiyya!" *al-Kawn* (New York, NY), October 22, 1908, 2.
45. David Nicholls, "Lebanese of the Antilles: Haiti, Dominican Republic, Jamaica, and Trinidad," in *Lebanese in the World*, 339–378; Karpat, "The Ottoman Emigration," 181–184.
46. "Ila al-Amam, ya Jamʿiyyat al-Ittihad al-Suri al-Umumiyya!" 2.
47. Brenda Plummer, "Race, Nationality, and Trade in the Caribbean: The Syrians in Haiti, 1903–1934," *International History Review* 3, no. 4 (1981), 517–539. Haiti's immigration laws continued to be a sore point in the relationship between the CUP and Syrian advocacy networks in New York, see Samuel Dolbee, "Ottomans of the Caribbean (and New York)," *Tovsuz Emrak* August 2012. Accessed March 1, 2017 at http://www.docblog.ottomanhistorypodcast.com/2012/08/ottomans-of-caribbean-and-new-york.html?q=caribbean

48. Juliet Davis, "The New World and the 'New Turks': The American-Turkish Claims Commission an Armenian Americans' Contested Citizenship in the Interwar Period," *Journal of Genocide Research* 19, no. 3 (2017), 299–317.

49. Sarah Gualtieri, *Between Arab and White: Race and Ethnicity in the Early Syrian American Diaspora* (Berkeley: University of California, 2009), 64–67; see also "Syrians Are Declared Free White Persons," *Atlanta Constitution* (Atlanta, GA), September 16, 1915, 7.

50. Gualtieri, *Between Arab and White*, 60–61; Jurj Khayrallah (later the chairman of the New Syrian National League) was another SAA petitioner backed. He received citizenship by volunteering with the US Army; Record of Naturalization, Elias George Khairallah, Boston, September 20, 1918; Petitions and Records of Naturalization, US District and Circuit Courts of the District of Massachusetts (National Archives Microfilm Publication M1366, roll 93); Records of District Courts, Record Group 21, National Archives and Records Administration. (Hereafter NARA/RG21/M1366/R-93).

51. "al-Qanun al-ʾAsasi: Jamʿiyyat al-Ittihad al-Suri," *al-Kawn* (New York, NY), October 15, 1908, 4. The name was typically rendered as "United Syria Society" in English, but it also is referred to as the Syrian Union Society or Syrian American Association of New York; see Louise Seymour Houghton, "Syrians in the United States IV," *The Survey: Social, Charitable, Civic: A Journal of Constructive* 27 (1911), 957–962.

52. "Court News: The Turkish Consul General of London," *Times of London* (London), April 1, 1910, 13.

53. Ignacio Klich, "Argentine-Ottoman Relations and Their Impact on Immigrants from the Middle East," *The Americas* 50, no. 2 (1993), 180–185.

54. Liliana Cazorla, *Presencia de inmigrantes sirios y libanese en el desarrollo industrial argentina, primera parte* (Buenos Aires: Fundación los Cedros, 2000), 40–41. Alejandro Schamún, *La Siria Nueva: Obra Histórica, Estadística y Comercial de la Colectividad Sirio-Otomana en las Repúblicas Argentina y Uruguay* (Buenos Aires: Empresa Assalam, 1917), 37; María del Mar Logroño Narbona, "The Development of Nationalist Identities in French Syria and Lebanon: A Transnational Dialogue with Arab Immigrants to Argentina and Brazil" (PhD diss., University of California, Santa Barbara, 2007), 116–117.

55. ʿAjaj Nuwayhid and Khaldun Nuwayhid, *al-Amir Amin Arslan: Nashir Thiqafiyya al-ʿArab fi al-Arjintin* (Beirut: Dar al-Istiqlal li-l-Dirasat wa-l-Nashr, 2010), 89–94.

56. Amin Arslan, *Mudhakkirat* (Buenos Aires: al-Matbaʿa al-Tijariyya, 1934), 64–65; Klich, "Argentine-Ottoman Relations," 178–180.

57. Stephen Hyland, "'Arisen from Deep Slumber': Transnational Politics and Competing Nationalisms among Syrian Immigrants in Argentina, 1900–1922," *Journal of Latin American Studies* 43, no. 3 (2011), 548.

58. Schamún, *La Siria Nueva*, 31; by 1921 this number appreciated to 110,000; see Gildas Brégain, *Syriens et Libanais d'Amérique du Sud, 1918–1945* (Paris: l'Harmattan, 2008), 59.

59. Hyland, "Arisen from Deep Slumber," 566.

60. On this use of "turco," see Christina Civantos, *Between Arabs and Argentines: Argentine Orientalism, Arab Immigrants, and the Writing of Identity* (Albany, NY: State University of New York Press, 2006), 88–99.

61. Alejandro Schámun in *La Nacion* (Buenos Aires), May 7, 1907, 8.

62. Klich, "Argentine-Ottoman Relations," 194–195; *Assalam* (Buenos Aires), December 12, 1969.

63. Akram Fouad Khater, "'House' to 'Goddess of the House': Gender, Class, and Silk in 19th Century Mount Lebanon," *International Journal of Middle East Studies* 28, no. 3 (1996), 325–348.

64. Schámun, *La Siria nueva*, 29; Klich, "Argentine-Ottoman Relations," 200.

65. Civantos, *Between Arabs and Argentines*, 115–118.

66. Nuwayhid and Nuwayhid, *al-Amir Amin Arslan*, 28–29.

67. Jamʿiyyat al-Rabita al-Adabiyya, *ʿAmal Jamʿiyyat al-Rabita al-Adabiyya wa-Maytamiha al-Urthudoksiyya fi-Homs* (Homs: Matbaʿat al-Salama, 1948), 3.

68. Nami Jafet, "A Constituição Otomana: Discurso Proferido em 23 de Julho de 1912," in *Ensaios e Discursos*, trans. Taufik Daúd Kurban (São Paulo: SP Editura, 1947), 238.

69. Jafet, "A Constituição Otomana," 246–247.

70. The image of a mahjar in rebellion is of a later vintage, constructed first through the memoirs of Ottoman statesmen and by Arab American chroniclers after 1920. Cemal Pasha, for instance, deployed the vision of a subversive mahjar in *La vérité sur la question syrienne* (Istanbul: Imprimerie Tanine, 1916). See also Akram Fouad Khater, *Inventing Home: Emigration, Gender, and the Middle Class in Lebanon, 1870–1920* (Berkeley: University of California Press, 2001),, 49–52.

71. Jafet, "A Constituição Otomana," 247.

72. Ibrahim Farah, "'Id al-Dustur," *al-Fara'id* (São Paulo), July 23, 1914, 1.

73. Sohrabi, *Revolution and Constitutionalism*,72.

74. Engin Deniz Akarlı, *The Long Peace: Ottoman Lebanon, 1861–1920* (Berkeley: University of California Press, 1993); Carol Hakim, *The Origins of the Lebanese National Idea, 1840–1920* (Berkeley: University of California Press, 2013), 60–64; Jumayyil, *Hizb al-Ittihad al-Lubnani*, 111.

75. Kayalı, *Arabs and Young Turks*, 183.

76. Hakim, *The Origins of the Lebanese National Idea*, 211–212.

77. Abdulrahim Abuhusayn, "An Ottoman against the Constitution: the Maronites of Mount Lebanon and the Questions of Representation in the Ottoman Parliament," in *Religion, Ethnicity, and Contested Nationhood in the Former Ottoman Space*, edited by Jørgen Nielsen (Leiden: Brill, 2012), 95–6.

78. Pamphlet, *al-Ittihad al-Lubnani fi-l-Qatr al-Masri* (Cairo: s.d. circa 1919), 5l; Asher Kaufmann, *Reviving Phoenicia: in Search of Identity in Lebanon* (London: I.B. Tauris, 2004); 57.

79. Sallum Mukarzil, "Jaridat al-Huda al-yawmiyya wa-matba'atiha," in Ya'cub Rufa'il, *al-Shawa'ir al-Sharifa: Majmu'at al-Khutab wa-l-Qasa'id allati Tuliyat fi-l-Ma'adaba al-Wataniyya allati Aqamatha al-Jaliyya al-Suriyya al-Lubnaniyya fi-Niyu Yurk* (New York City: al-Huda Press, 1924), 86–106.

80. Na'um Mukarzil, "Bayan al-Qasad: Jam'iyyat al-Nahda al-Lubnaniyya," *al-Huda* (New York, NY), August 14, 1913, 3.

81. Sallum Mukarzil, *al-Kitab al-Lubnani: li-tadhakar Yubil al-Nahda al-Lubnaniyya al-Fuddi* (New York: Matba'at al-Huda, 1937), 47.

82. Cemal Pasha, *La vérite sur la question syrienne*, 41. Mukarzil was tried in absentia, but his Beirut collaborators, the Khazin brothers, were executed in May 1916, "al-Nahda al-Lubnaniyya," *al-Tahalluf al-Lubnani* (Buenos Aires), January 23, 1920, 21–23.

83. María Narbona identifies the São Paulo branch's co-founders as As'ad Bishara, Antun Jabbara, As'ad Bitar, and Shukri al-Khuri; "The Development of Nationalist Ideologies," 109.

84. Mukarzil, *al-Kitab al-Lubnani*, 44–45.

85. Mukarzil, *al-Kitab al-Lubnani*, 45–46.

86. Mukarzil, *al-Kitab al-Lubnani*, 55.

87. *Watha'iq al-Mu'tamar al-'Arabi al-Awwal 1913: Kitab al-Mu'tamar wa-l-Murasilat al-Diblumasiyya al-Faransiyya al-Muta'alaqa biha* (Beirut: Dar al-Hadatha, 1980), 46.

88. *Watha'iq al-Mu'tamar al-'Arabi al-Awwal*, 113–4.

89. Eliezer Tauber, *The Emergence of the Arab Movements* (London: Routledge, 2013), 186–91.

90. Najib Diyab, "Amani al-Suriyyin al-Muhajirin," *Watha'iq al-Mu'tamar al-'Arabi al-Awwal*, 66–7. His deployment of backwardness or under-development reflects a larger depiction of the Syrian mahjar uplifting its homeland though humanitarian, educational, and political works.

91. Diyab, "Amani al-Suriyyin al-Muhajirin," *Watha'iq al-Mu'tamar al-'Arabi al-Awwal*, 67–68.

92. For a discussion of Diyab's use of revolutionary rhetoric after 1918 see Bailony, "Transnationalism and the Syrian Migrant Public," 14–5.

93. Charlotte Karem Albrecht, "An Archive of Difference: Syrian Women, the Peddling Economy, and U.S. Social Welfare," *Gender and History* 28, no. 1 (2016), 127–149. Gualtieri, *Between Arab and White*, 88–92.

94. Diyab, "Amani al-Suriyyin al-Muhajirin," *Watha'iq al-Mu'tamar al-'Arabi al-Awwal*, 68.

95. "Qararat al-Mu'tamar al-'Arabi al-Awwal," *Watha'iq al-Mu'tamar al-'Arabi al-Awwal*, 113.

96. Hakim, *The Origins of the Lebanese National Idea*, 212.

97. "Qararat al-Mu'tamar al-'Arabi al-Awwal," *Watha'iq al-Mu'tamar al-'Arabi al-Awwal*, 113.

98. "Fi Nizara Kharijiyya Fransa," *Watha'iq al-Mu'tamar al-'Arabi al-Awwal*, 149.

99. Mustafa Aksakal, *The Ottoman Road to War in 1914: The Ottoman Empire and the First World War* (New York: Cambridge University Press, 2008).

100. M. Talha Çiçek, *War and State Formation in Syria: Cemal Pasha's Governorate during World War I, 1914–1917* (New York: Routledge, 2014), 24.

101. On universal conscription see State Department translation of Ottoman Interior Ministry Notice No. 57574, "Proclamation of High Council Board of Ulemas," Constantinople, November 29, 1914, (National Archives Microfilm Publication M367, roll 19); Records of the Department of State, Record Group 21, National Archives and Records Administration (hereafter NARA/RG59/M367/R-19), 14–5.

102. Melanie Tanielian, "Feeding the City: the Beirut Municipality and the Politics of Food During World War I," *International Journal of Middle East Studies* 46, no. 4 (2014), 737–758; Elizabeth Williams, "Economy, Environment, and Famine: World War I from the Perspective of the Syrian Interior," in *Syria in World War I: Politics, Economy, and Society*, ed. M. Talha Çiçek (New York: Routledge, 2014), 150–168; Zachary Foster, "The 1915 Locust Attack in Syria and Palestine and Its Role in the Famine During the First World War," *Middle Eastern Studies* 51, no. 3 (2015), 370–391; Elizabeth Thompson, *Colonial Citizens: Republican Rights, Paternal Privilege, and Gender in French Syria and Lebanon* (New York: Columbia University Press, 2000), 19–37; Çiçek, *War and State Formation*, 43–56; Kayalı, *Arabs and Young Turks*, 192–196.

103. Issawi, "The Historical Background to Lebanese Emigration," 31; Thompson, *Colonial Citizens*, 21–22.

104. State Department translation of Ottoman Interior Ministry Notice No. 57574, "Proclamation of High Council Board of Ulemas," Constantinople, November 29, 1914 (NARA/RG59/M367/R-19/763.72/1357), 9–12.

105. Çiçek, *War and State Formation in Syria*, 94–95.

106. Archives Diplomatiques, Nantes, Syrie-Liban (hereafter AD, SL), Report on l'Alliance Libanaise, Cairo, January 21, 1919. In Antoine Hokayem, D. Bou Malhab ʿAtallah, and J. Charaf, eds., *Documents diplomatiques français relatifs à l'histoire du Liban et de la Syrie à l'époque du mandat: Le démantèlement de l'Empire ottoman et les préludes du mandat: 1914–1919* (Paris: l'Hamattan, 2003), 462.

107. Ministère des Affaires Etrangères, Paris (hereafter MAE), Guerre 1914–1918, Turquie, Defrance to Briand, "Syrie," Cairo, April 21, 1916. In Hokayem, ʿAtallah, and Charaf, *Documents diplomatiques français*, 133.

108. Jurj Atlas, *al-Kalimat al-Khalida* (São Paulo: Dar al-Tibaʿa wa-l-Nashr al-ʿArabiyya, s.d. 193-), 4–12.

109. Historians researching the origins of Middle Eastern nationalisms often raise the question about when, precisely, Arabist societies in Syria shifted from to separatist and nationalist ideologies. The consensus is that nationalism was a creation of the First World War and more specifically, of the post-1918 moment. On this debate, see Rashid Khalidi, Lisa Anderson, Muhammad Muslih, and Reeva Simon, eds., *The Origins of Arab Nationalism* (New York: Columbia University Press, 1993); James Jankowski and Israel Gershoni, eds., *Rethinking Nationalism in the Arab Middle East* (New York: Cornell University Press, 1992); Gelvin, *Divided Loyalties*; Kayalı, *Arabs and Young Turks*; Hakim, *The Origins of the Lebanese National Idea*; Kaufmann, *Reviving Phoenicia*; among others.

110. Shukri al-Khuri, "Lubnan wa-l-Harb al-Haliyya," *al-Nahda al-Lubnaniyya* (São Paulo), September 29, 1914, 1.

111. On Mukarzil, see Andrew Arsan, *Interlopers of Empire: The Lebanese Diaspora in French West Africa* (Oxford: Oxford University Press, 2014), 203–204; Kais Firro, *Inventing Lebanon: Nationalism and the State under the Mandate* (London: I.B. Tauris, 2003), 18; Hajjar, *The Politics and Poetics of Ameen Rihani*, 61–68.

112. Y. Stimson to Secretary of State William Philips, Buenos Aires, November 4, 1918 (NARA/RG59/M367/R-389/763.72119/3033), 1–2.

113. "A Conflagração: Outras Informações: Na Argentina," *Estado de São Paulo* (São Paulo), April 14, 1915, 1.

114. "Una Tropelía Germania en la Argentina: un Insolente 'Ultimatum' al Cónsul Turquía, Digna Actitud de Emir Emin Arslan, La Colectividad Otoman se Opone Decisamente," *Crítica* (Buenos Aires), April 13, 1915, 1.

115. "La Guerra: El Consulado General de Turquia Actitud del Emir Arslan," *La Prensa* (Buenos Aires), June 5, 1915, 6.

116. Howard Elkins to Secretary of State, "Rupture of Diplomatic Relations with Turkey," Paris, June 10, 1917, (NARA/RG59/M367/R-44/763.72/5598), 2–3.

117. "Los Piratas Operando en la Argentina: Alemania se Adueña del Consulado Turco," *Crítica* (Buenos Aires), May 20, 1915, 1.

118. MAE, Guerre 1914–1918, Turquie, Defrance to Briand, "Syrie," Cairo, April 21, 1916. In Hokayem, ʿAtallah, and Charaf, *Documents diplomatiques français*, 133. Çiçek, *War and State Formation in Syria*, 49. Among those hanged: Shukri al-ʿAsali (editor, *al-Qabas*); ʿAbd al-Ghani al-ʿUraisi (*al-Mufid*); Ahmad Tabbarra (*al-Ittihad al-ʿUthmani* and *al-Islah*); ʿAbd al-Hamid al-Zahrawi (*al-Hadara*); Philipe and Farid al-Khazin (*al-Arz*); Saʿid al-ʿAql (*al-Ahwal*). Others were convicted in absentia, having already fled abroad to the mahjar. They remained beyond the grasp of Ottoman authorities: including Rashid Rida, Faris Nimr, Shibli Shumayyil, Rafiq al-ʿAzm, Naʿum Mukarzil; Ayalon, *The Press in the Arab Middle East*, 71. For a complete list of indictments and the executed see Cemal Pasha, *La Vérité sur la question syrienne* (Istanbul: Impr. Tanine, 1916).

119. Narbona, "The Development of Nationalist Ideologies," 100. On Arslan's involvement in the Légion d'Orient recruitment campaign, see Brégain, *Syriens et Libanais d'Amérique du Sud*, 144.

120. *La Vanguardia* announces the first issue of Arslan's newspaper on July 14, 1915; "Periodismo," *La Vanguardia* (Buenos Aires), July 15, 1915, 5. *La Nota* ran from 1915 through 1921, although Arslan passed ownership of the title on to Carlos Alberto Leumann; Verónica Delgado, "Reconfiguraciones de Debates y Posiciones del Campo Literario Argentino en el Seminario *La Nota*, 1915–1920," *Anciajes* VIII (Universidad de la Plata, 2004), 81–99; Pablo Tornielli, "Hombre de tres mundos: Para una biografía política e intelectual del emir Emín Arslán," *Dirasat Hispanicas: Revista Tunecina de Estudios Hispanicos* 2 (2015), 157–181.

121. Cemal Pasha, *La Vérité sur la question syrienne*, 39–42.

122. Stacy Fahrenthold, "Transnational Modes and Media: The Syrian Press in the Mahjar and Emigrant Activism during World War I," *Mashriq & Mahjar: Journal of Middle East Migration Studies* 1, no. 1 (2013), 32–57.

123. Keith David Watenpaugh, *Bread from Stone: The Middle East and the Making of Modern Humanitarianism* (Berkeley: University of California Press, 2015), 30–58.

124. Jurj Atlas, "Shabibat Homs fi-l-Mahjar," *al-Karma* (São Paulo), December 1914, 17; ʿAbd al-Massih Haddad, "Suriya wa-Jamʿiyyatuna," *al-Saʾih* (New York, NY), May 4, 1916, 1–2.

125. Faris Najm, "al-Sihafa al-Suriyya fi-l-Barazil: min-Jamʿiyyat al-Sihafa al-Baraziliyya," *al-Karma* (São Paulo), March 1922, 91. According to Atlas's memoirs, he also published a serial called *al-Ittihad al-ʿArabi* which carried the same tagline. It is possible the two publications were one and the same, although neither has been independently located; Jurj Atlas, "Falsafa al-Haqiqa wa-l-Khiyal," *al-Kalimat al-Khalida*, 18.

126. *A Social Survey of the Washington Street District of New York City* (New York: Trinity Church Men's Committee, 1914), 40–41.

127. "Qatil fi-Chile," *al-Murshid* (Santiago, Chile), April 2, 1916.

128. "Hadith Makdar," *al-Murshid* (Santiago, Chile), April 2, 1916.

129. "Qatil Suri," *al-ʿAdl* (Buenos Aires), April 4, 1916, reproduced in "al-Suriyyin fi-Amrika al-Janubiyya," *al-Huda* (New York, NY), April 5, 1916, 2. See also Steven Hyland, *More Argentine Than You: Arabic-Speaking Immigrants in Argentina* (Albequergue, NM: University of New Mexico Press, 2017), 85-94.

130. "Porte Gets Demand: Must Heed Appeal for Syrians or Strain U.S. Friendship," *Washington Post* (Washington, DC), July 7, 1916, 1; "Ask $5,000,000 Relief: Nation-Wide Campaign Launched for Syrians and Armenians," *Washington Post* (Washington, DC), October 4, 1916, 3. In New York City and Boston, relief workers from the United Syria Society (Jamʿiyyat al-Ittihad al-Suri); the Lebanon League of Progress (Jamʿiyyat al-Nahda al-Lubnaniyya), the

Syrian Mount Lebanon Liberation League, the Syrian American Club (al-Muntada al-Suri al-Amriki), the New Syria National League (Hizb al-Suriya al-Jadida al-Wataniyya), the Mount Lebanon Club (al-Muntada al-Lubnani), the Syrian Ladies Aid Societies of New York and Boston, and village relief networks each participated in ACASR and Red Cross drives.

131. Bureau of Investigation case number 8000-15656, "Neutrality Matter: Various," Cleveland, May 1, 1917 (National Archives Microfilm Publication M1085); Investigative Reports of the Bureau of Investigation, Record Group 65.2.2.2, National Archives and Records Administration (hereafter NARA/RG 62.2.2/M1085/8000-15656), 1–2.

132. "Neutrality Matter: Various," Cleveland, NARA/RG 62.2.2/M1085/8000-15656, 2.

133. Watenpaugh, *Bread from Stones*, 97–100; Karine V. Walther, *Sacred Interests: The United States and the Islamic World, 1821–1921* (Durham, NC: Duke University Press, 2015), 271–318.

134. Trad was editor of Buenos Aires' *al-Jadid* newspaper, along with Mikha'il al-Samra, Najib Samra, and Chemal 'Abd al-Malik. The publication was founded in 1905, and it became a twice-weekly in 1908 and a daily newspaper in 1912. Centre des Archives Nationales Libanaise, Beirut, De Tarrazi Collection, Mikha'il al-Samra to Philippe de Tarrazi, São Paulo, May 26, 1913. De Tarrazi's collection of mahjari newspapers formed the basis of his multivolume encyclopedia, *Tarikh al-Sihafa al-'Arabiyya*, 2 vols. (Beirut: al-Matba'a al-Adabiyya, 1933).

135. Na'um Mukarzil, "Bayna al-Suriyin: bi-Ism al-Massih wa-l-Muhammad," April 5, 1916, 6.

136. 'Abd al-Massih Haddad, "Qatil bayna al-Suriyin," *al-Sa'ih* (New York, NY), April 6, 1916, 1.

137. Trad and Atlas had an enduring friendship despite that Trad was a Francophile Lebanist and Atlas a Hashimite Arabist. Atlas hosted Trad at his clubhouse to speak on the need for Syrians to "break the Turkish yoke" hoisted upon their back, one of hundreds of microstories illustrating the fluidity of nationalist politics in the wartime mahjar. See Atlas, "Falsafa al-Haqiqa wa-l-Khiyal," *al-Kalimat al-Khalida*, 21.

138. Hafiz Khizam al-Homsi, "Barid min Mutataw'i al-Homsi al-Suri fi-l-Jaysh al-Fransi," *al-Sa'ih* (New York, NY), April 10, 1916, 1. See also Khizam, "Fi-Sahat al-Qital," *al-Sa'ih* (New York, NY), July 20, 1916, 1; on Trad see also 'Ali Hamiya, *al-'Allama wa-l-Duktur Khalil Sa'adeh: Siratuhu wa-a'maluh, 1857-1934* (Beirut: al-Furat li-l-Nashr wa-l-Tawzi', 2007), 114–115.

139. Simon Jackson, "Global Recruitment: The Wartime Origins of French Mandate Syria," in Alison Carol and Ludivine Brock, eds., *France in an Era of Global War, 1914–1945: Occupation, Politics, Empire* (Basingstoke: Palgrave MacMillan, 2014), 137; N.E. Bou Nackhlie, "Les Troupes Spéciales: Religious and Ethnic Recruitment, 1916–46," *International Journal of Middle East Studies* 25, no. 4 (1993), 647–648.

Chapter 3

1. Library and Archives Canada, Personnel Record of the First World War, RG 150 Canadian Expeditionary Force, Box 754–747, item 44977, "Bishara, Gabriel regimental number 67160," 9–10.

2. Jibra'il Ilyas Ward, *Kitab al-Jundi al-Suri fi-Thalatha Hurub* (New York: al-Matba'a al-Tijariyya al-Suriyya al-Amrikiyya, 1919), 10.

3. Ward published these words, attributed to Bishara, in both *al-Huda* and *al-Sha'b* alongside a query regarding next of kin and repatriation of his remains. Ward, *Kitab al-Jundi al-Suri*, 122.

4. Bishara's terminology concerning Genghis Khan (al-dawla al-jankiziyya) invokes the belief among Syrian supporters of the Entente was that Germany had transformed the Ottoman Empire into a Teutonic colony. It also captured derisive notions about the Ottomans as Turks. Ward, *Kitab al-Jundi al-Suri*, 122.

5. Gabriel Ward to Syrian American Club of Boston, 23 November 1918, box 1, folder 5, Evelyn Shakir Collection, Arab American National Museum, Dearborn, MI (henceforth AANM/ES/1/5), 1–2.

6. "Ahad Jabarat al-Suriyyun," *Abu al-Hawl* (São Paulo), s.d. May 1917, and "Jundi Yada'u al-Suriyyin wa-l-Lubnaniyyin ila-l-Tatawwu'," *al-Huda* (New York, NY), s.d. May 1917, in Ward, *Kitab al-Jundi al-Suri*, 125–129.

7. Precise numbers of Syrian enlistments are difficult to come by. Contemporary sources report that between 12,000 and 15,000 Syrians served in the US army, a figure that is almost certainly too high. See John Moroso, "Fall of Damascus Thrills Our Syrians," *New York Times* (New York, NY), October 6, 1918, 48; George Khairallah to Frank Polk, New York, January 15, 1919 (National Archives Microfilm Publication M367, roll 392); Records of the Department of State, Record Group 59, National Archives and Records Administration (henceforth NARA/RG59/M367/R-392/763.72119/3456), 2. See also Hampson Gary to Robert Lansing, "Transmitting a memorandum called 'America and Syria,'" Cairo, February 27, 1919, NARA/RG 59/M367/R-392/763.72119/4555, 5–6. In 1924, Philip Hitti enumerated 13,965 enlistments in *The Syrians in America* (New York: G.H. Doran, 1924), 102. Sarah Gualtieri points out differences between Hitti's figure and rates as high as 15,000 described by the Syrian American Club (in writings by one of its members, Jurj Khayrallah). Comparisons with Selective Service records, the Naturalization Index, and Army cards suggest closer to 10,000 Syrian migrants served at least one enlistment term. Sarah Gualtieri, *Between Arab and White: Race and Ethnicity in the Early Syrian American Diaspora* (Berkeley, CA: University of California Press, 2009), 210 n.18.
8. James Renton, "Changing Languages of Empire and the Orient: Britain and the Invention of the Middle East, 1917–18," *Historical Journal* 50, no. 3 (2007), 645–670.
9. Nina Glick Schiller and Georges Fouron, *Georges Woke Up Laughing: Long-Distance Nationalism and the Search for Home* (Durham, NC: Duke University Press, 2001), 20; Isa Blumi, *Ottoman Refugees 1878–1939: Migration in a Post-Imperial World* (London: Bloomsbury, 2013), 79–82.
10. New Syria National League/Syrian American Club joint telegram to Robert Lansing, Secretary of State, Washington D.C., February 23, 1919, NARA/RG59/M367/R-394/763.72119/3841, 1; Benedict Anderson, *Imagined Communities: Reflections on the Origins and Spread of Nationalism* (London: Verso, 1992).
11. Na'um Mukarzil, "Fi Kull Yawm Khitab," *al-Huda* (New York, NY), June 7, 1917, 2.
12. Eliezer Tauber, "La Légion d'Orient et la Légion arabe," *Revue française d'histoire d'outre-mer* 81, no. 303 (1994), 172.
13. Shukri al-Bakhash, "Bayna al-Midhwad wa-l-Khandaq," *al-Fatat* (New York, NY), December 22, 1917, 1. See also Tauber, "La Légion d'Orient," 172–174.
14. Gregory Mann, *Native Sons: West African Veterans and France in the Twentieth Century* (Durham, NC: Duke University Press, 2006).
15. Simon Jackson, "Global Recruitment: the Wartime Origins of French Mandate Syria," in Alison Carrol and Ludivine Brock, eds., *France in the Era of Global War, 1914–1945: Occupation, Politics, Empire* (Basingstoke: Palgrave MacMillan, 2014), 137; Tauber, "Légion d'Orient," 174; N. E. Bou-Nacklie, "Les Troupes Spéciales: Religious and Ethnic Recruitment, 1916–46," *International Journal of Middle East Studies* 25, no. 4 (1993), 648–649.
16. Shukri al-Bakhash, "Nahu Suriya," *al-Fatat* (New York, NY), December 19, 1917, 1.
17. Andrew Arsan, "'This Age Is the Age of Associations': Committees, Petitions, and the Roots of Interwar Middle Eastern Internationalism," *Journal of Global History* 7, no. 2 (2012), 186–187; Simon Jackson, "Diaspora Politics and Developmental Empire: The Syro-Lebanese at the League of Nations," *Arab Studies Journal* 21, no. 1 (2013), 169–171.
18. This terminology borrowed from Carol Hakim, *The Origins of the Lebanese National Idea, 1840–1920* (Berkeley, CA: University of California Press, 2013), 217–220.
19. Eliezer Tauber, *The Arab Movements in World War I* (London: Frank Cass, 1993), 197–199.
20. Jam'iyyat al-Nahda al-Lubnaniyya, "Ila al-Watan Yahama al-Watan," *al-Huda* (New York, NY), May 1, 1917, 4.
21. The French funded the CCS in Paris at similar levels: see Tauber, *Arab Movements*, 209.
22. Jam'iyyat al-Nahda al-Lubnaniyya, "Ila al-Watan," 4. The LLP kept two doctors on retainer: Rashid Baddur and Najib Barbur in New York.
23. Hugh Cleveland to Bainbridge Colby, Secretary of State, "Reason for Creation of Eastern Legion," Paris, December 26, 1919, NARA/RG59/M367/R-475/763.72119/9557, 4–5.
24. Jam'iyyat al-Nahda al-Lubnaniyya, "Ila al-Watan," 4.
25. Shukri al-Bakhash, "al-Wizarat al-Harbiyya al-Fransawiyya wa-l-Firq al-Sharqiyya," *al-Fatat* (New York, NY), December 19, 1917, 2; Jackson, "Global Recruitment," 143.
26. Jam'iyyat al-Nahda al-Lubnaniyya, "Ila al-Watan," 4.

27. Tauber, *Arab Movements*, 200–201.
28. Gabriel Ilyas Ward, "'ar an la-Tasil Dama'una illa 'ala Khanja al-Saffah," *al-Huda* (New York, NY), June 2, 1917, 3.
29. Tauber, *Arab Movements*, 211.
30. Ilyas Yusuf and Shakir Karam, "al-Suriyyun wa-l-khidma al-'askariyya fi-Kanada," *al-Nasr* (New York, NY), January 18, 1918, 3, translation of November 3, 1917 public address.
31. Ward, *Kitab al-Jundi al-Suri*, 61–64.
32. Yusuf and Karam, "al-Suriyyun wa-l-khidma al-'askariyya," 3.
33. "al-Tajnid al-Inklizi Huna," *al-Bayan* (New York, NY), June 2, 1917, 1.
34. Yusuf and Karam, "al-Suriyyun wa-l-khidma al-'askariyya," 3.
35. "al-Khawatir: Bayna al-Harb wa-l-Tard wa-l-Sajn," *al-Huda* (New York, NY), May 3, 1917, 5.
36. E. (Ayyub) Tabet, Mikhail Naimy, Syria-Mount Lebanon League of Liberation to Woodrow Wilson, New York City, 10 May 1918, NARA/RG59/M367/R-381/763.72119/1686, 1–2.
37. Ward, *Kitab al-Jundi al-Suri*, 73; Erez Manela, *The Wilsonian Moment: Self-Determination and the Origins of Anticolonial Nationalism* (Oxford: Oxford University Press, 2007), 23–55.
38. *Second Report of the Provost Marshal General to the Secretary of War on the Operations of the Selective Service System to December 20, 1918* (Washington, D.C.: Government Printing Office, 1919), 86–88.
39. Nancy Gentile Ford, *Americans All! Foreign-born Soldiers in World War I* (College Station, TX: Texas A&M University Press, 2001), 60–61.
40. Na'um Mukarzil, "al-Lubnaniyyun wa-l-Suriyyun tujaha al-Khidma al-'Askariyya," *al-Huda* (New York, NY), June 1, 1917, 3.
41. Mukarzil, "al-Lubnaniyyun wa-l-Suriyyun," 3.
42. Gualtieri, *Between Arab and White*, 58–61, 84.
43. Mukarzil, "al-Lubnaniyyun wa-l-Suriyyun," 3.
44. "Syrians Loyal to United States," *Christian Science Monitor* (Boston, MA), May 28, 1917, 9.
45. "Syrians Loyal," 9; Massachusetts Census of Populations, Suffolk County, Boston City, District 13–514, Ward 20, page 9b, line 81, Elias Shannon (National Archives and Records Administration Publication T626, Fifteenth Census of the United States, 1930, Roll 957), Records of the Bureau of the Census, Record Group 29, National Archives and Records Administration.
46. Bilingual Liberty Loan advertisement, "La Tathabbat Marra Wahida innaka Amriki bal Mi'a Marra/Prove you are 100% American," *al-Nasr* (New York, NY), September 30, 1918, 5.
47. Moroso, "Fall of Damascus"; Syrian American Club of Boston Records, AANM/ES/1/5.
48. Mukarzil, "Fi kull yawm khitab," 2.
49. "Asas manh al-sh'ub huquq taqrir mustaqbaliha," *al-Huda* June 2, 1917, 2. See also Manela, *Wilsonian Moment*, 28–30.
50. Ward, *Kitab al-Jundi al-Suri*, 11.
51. On Costa Najour, see Gualtieri, *Between Arab and White*, 60–62.
52. Yusuf Jirjis 'Abdu, "Murasilat: Atlanta Jurjya, 1 Disimbir," *al-Fatat* (New York, NY), December 13, 1917, 5.
53. Basilius Kherbawi, "Hal yajuz li-l-Masihiyi an yatajannad?" *al-Sa'ih* (New York, NY), s.d. June 1917, reprinted in Ward, *Kitab al-Jundi al-Suri*, 116.
54. Ward, *Kitab al-Jundi al-Suri*, 118.
55. Na'um Mukarzil, "Bayna al-Suriyyin: bi-ism al-Massih wa-l-Muhammad," *al-Huda* (New York, NY), April 5, 1916, 6; 'Abd al-Massih Haddad, "Qatil bayna al-Suriyyin," *al-Sa'ih* (New York, NY), April 6, 1916, 1–2.
56. Hakim, *Origins*, 1–13.
57. al-Bakhash, "Nahu Suriya," 1.
58. E. (Ayyub) Tabet, Mikhail Naimy, Syria-Mount Lebanon League of Liberation to Woodrow Wilson, New York City, May 10, 1918, NARA/RG59/M367/R-381/763.72119/1686, 1–2. See also Makdisi, *Faith Misplaced*, 136–146.
59. Tannus Yusuf Doumit and Shukri al-Bakhash, "al-Bakhash wa-l-mudafi'in salafan," *al-Huda* (New York, NY), May 1, 1917, 2.
60. Christopher Capozzola, *Uncle Sam Wants You: World War I and the Making of the Modern American Citizen* (New York, NY: Oxford University Press, 2008), 152–159.

61. Naʿum Mukarzil, "Akhbar Mahliyya: Tajrim Sihafiyyun," *al-Huda* (New York, NY), May 4, 1917, 2.

62. Ambassador Jean Jusserand to Robert Lansing, Secretary of State, "Memo 5267, on behalf of A. Tabet," Washington, D.C., October 24, 1917, NARA/RG59/M367/R-217/763.72112/ 5267, 1–4.

63. al-Bakhash, "Nahu Suriya," 1.

64. al-Bakhash, "Nahu Suriya," 1.

65. Bureau of Investigation case no. 84061, Perkins, "Naoum Mokarzel—French Consul— Spanish Consul, alleged interference of Spanish Consul with Selective Draft of Syrians in the United States," New York, January 28, 1918 (National Archives Publication M1085, Investigative Records Relating to German Aliens), Investigative Reports of the Bureau of Investigation, Record Group 65.2.2, National Archives and Record Administration (henceforth NARA/RG65.2.2/M1085/84061), 16–17.

66. Busha, "Alli Muharem, alleged representing himself as Turkish consul," Philadelphia, November 19, 1918. NARA/RG65.2.2/M1085/R-751/329549, 1–2. See also "Gross Frauds on Draft Suspected: Follows Arrest of Joseph Solomon and Said Joseph," *Boston Daily Globe*, January 15, 1918.

67. Ford, *Americans All*, 56.

68. See "Alien Slackers May Not Escape Service," *New York Times* (New York, NY), April 22, 1917, 3; "Deportation of Alien Slackers," *Christian Science Monitor* (Boston, MA), August 1, 1917, 1.

69. War Department organizational records, 77th Division records, Office of the Chief of Staff, memorandum no. 79, 21 May 1918, cited in Ford, *Americans All*, 63.

70. Ford, *Americans All*, 64.

71. Shukry Yusuf, "Syrian American Association bylaws," October 10, 1914, AANM/ES/1/6. See also Gualtieri, *Between Arab and White*, 85.

72. War Department, "Rates of monthly pay for enlisted men," *Official Army Register December 1, 1918* (Washington, D.C.: Government Printing Office, 1918), 1138–1139. Donald Cole, *Immigrant City: Lawrence, Massachusetts 1845–1921* (Chapel Hill, NC: University of North Carolina Press, 1963), 183.

73. AANM/ES/1/6, 1918.

74. See, for instance, Peter Arthur Abraham, Boston, May 9, 1919, NARA/RG 21/M1368/ R-99, 1.

75. Saʿab, "Hawl harakat al-tatawwuʿ al-wataniyya," *al-Huda* (New York, NY), May 5, 1917, 5.

76. Ford, *Americans All*, 37–39.

77. Tauber, *Arab Movements*, 201. Such was the case of Melham George, investigated for draft evasion in 1918 but subsequently cleared because he was "fighting the Turks in Palestine" with the French; Dunn, "Visa investigation, Melham Maroum George," Bangor, August 30, 1918, NARA/RG65.2.2/M1085/R-692/277009, 1–2.

78. "Organize "Foreign Legions" at Devens: War Office Experiments with New Scheme," *Daily Boston Globe* (Boston, MA), August 17, 1918.

79. Laurence Winship, "Camp Devens Foreign Legion presents a Babel of Tongues: Slav and Italian and Greek and Armenian, but all Americans at Heart," *Daily Boston Globe* (Boston, MA), August 25, 1918, 32.

80. Katharine Bartlett, "Real Men without a Country," *Boston Daily Globe* (Boston, MA), January 13, 1918, 41.

81. New York State Archives, Records of National Guard Service Man Serving in World War I from New York. WWI Army Cards. Service no. 1929681, Alex Assa. September 25, 1917.

82. New York State Archives, Records of National Guard Service Man Serving in World War I from New York. WWI Army Cards. Service no. 4105624, Azeez Boulous.

83. New York State Archives, Records of National Guard Service Man Serving in World War I from New York. WWI Army Cards. Service no. 2673038, Halim Azar.

84. New York State Archives, Records of National Guard Service Man Serving in World War I from New York. WWI Army Cards. Service no. 2672508, Dickran Azarian.

85. New York State Archives, Records of National Guard Service Man Serving in World War I from New York. WWI Army Cards. Service no. sans number, Awaid Azeezah.

86. Perkins, Special Agent interview with Mukarzil, "Naoum Mokarzel—French Consul—Spanish Consul, Alleged Interference of Spanish Consul with Selective Draft of Syrians in the United States," New York, February 20, 1918 report, NARA/RG65.2.2/ 83061, 18–19.

87. Perkins, "Naoum Mokarzel: Alleged Interference of Spanish Consul," New York, April 4, 1918, NARA/RG65.2.2/ 83061, 16–17.

88. "Gross Frauds on Draft Suspected: Follows Arrest of Joseph Solomon and Said Joseph," *Boston Daily Globe* (Boston, MA), January 15, 1918.

89. Spanish passports were particularly suspicious to immigration officials in Texas, but in a few cases men with French passports were also detained. Van V. Curtis, "Syrian Suspect: Bahid Karaham," Nogales, December 3, 1917, NARA/RG65.2.2/M1085/96779, 1–7.

90. Perkins, "Naoum Mokarzel: Alleged Interference of Spanish Consul," New York, April 4, 1918, NARA/RG65.2.2/M1085/83061, 17.

91. "Mr. Zaloom" is the only name given in this report. Perkinsidentifies him as "club secretary," but his identity is otherwise obscured; I have not identified anyone by this name on the club's executive board, during or after the war.

92. Perkins, Special Agent interview with Zaloom, New York, April 4, 1918, NARA/RG65.2.2/ M1085/83061, 17.

93. Perkins, "Naceep Mallouf," New York, January 30, 1918, NARA/RG 65.2.2/M1085/ 8000-130577, 4–5.

94. Naʿum Mukarzel, "al-Lubnaniyyun wa-l-Suriyyun tujaha al-Khidma al-ʿAskariyya," *al-Huda* (New York, NY), June 1, 1917, 3.

95. Naceep Mallouf was not the only Lebanese migrant to use this reasoning. Another declarant named Khalil Jurj also successfully pled his case on this basis during the same investigation.

96. Perkins, "Naceep Mallouf," New York, January 30, 1918, NARA/RG 65.2.2/M1085/ 8000-130577, 1–5.

97. Harrison and Bielaski to Charles DeWoody and Perkins, "Loyalty of Syiran: N. A. Mokarzel," New York, April 14, 1918, NARA/RG 65.2.2/M1085/8000-130577, 32–35.

98. Testimony of M. Gadol to Perkins, "Loyalty of Syrian: N. A. Mokarzel," New York, sans date, NARA/RG 65.2.2/M1085/8000-130577, 16.

99. Testimony of Mokarzel to Perkins, "Loyalty of Syrian: N. A. Mokarzel," New York, February 20, 1918, NARA/RG 65.2.2/M1085/8000-130577, 18–19.

100. Shakir Khuri, the owner of a Cleveland boarding house for Druze laborers, testimony to Perkins, "Loyalty of Syrian: N. A. Mokarzel," New York, February 20, 1918, NARA/RG 65.2.2/M1085/8000-130577.

101. A. Bielaski, Bureau Chief, to Charles DeWoody, Esq., "Mohammed Hajjar," New York, September 20, 1918, NARA/RG65.2.2/M1085/R-700/283862, 1–3.

102. Ayyub Tabet, "Khiyana Wataniyya," *al-Shaʿb* (New York, NY), August 26, 1918, 4; Tabet's translation in Bielaski, "Mohammed Hajjar," New York, September 20, 1918, NARA/ RG65.2.2/M1085/R-700/283862, 2–3.

103. The Bureau investigated the Spanish Consulate for its role in Ottoman passport fraud. Though they found no evidence of collusion with Muhammad Hajjar, Syrians relied on functionaries in Spain's consular network to obtain documents to depart the United States through New York's port or across the Mexican border. French Consul Joseph Flamand testimony to Robert Valkenburgh, "James MG Fay—Turkish, Syrian and French Passports," Boston, July 30, 1919, NARA/RG 65.2.2/M1085/R-811/369154, 3.

104. Ayyub Tabet to Post Office Solicitor, Perkins, "Loyalty of Syrian: N. A. Mokarzel," New York, February 20, 1918, NARA/RG 65.2.2/M1085/8000-130577, 1. See also E. Tabet, "Alleged Extortion in Passport Charges," New York, October 10, 1919, NARA/RG65.2.2/M1075/ R-622/374306, 1–3.

105. *Al-Huda* (New York, NY), March 11, 1918, 1.

106. Spanish Consul General Francisco Javier de Salas Sicher to N.A. Mokarzel, New York, March 20, 1918. Reprinted in *al-Fatat*, March 26, 1918, 1.

107. Ironically, one of the witnesses interviewed about Mukarzil in June 1918 was Ayyub Tabet, who admitted that they were "traditional old enemies." Tabet called Mukarzil "rabid" but also certified that his loyalties to the Entente were unquestionable. Perkins, "Loyalty of Syrian: N. A. Mokarzel," New York, NARA/RG 65.2.2/M1085/8000-130577, 42–45.

108. Ward, *Kitab al-Jundi al-Suri*, 112.
109. Ward, *Kitab al-Jundi al-Suri*, 101.
110. Beşikçi, *Ottoman Mobilization*, 259.
111. William Yale to Leland Harrison, Department of State, "Report #2 dealing with Arabia and Hedjaz situation," Cairo, November 5, 1917, NARA/RG59/M367/R-381/763.72119/ 1707, 18–19. See also Beşikçi, *Ottoman Mobilization*, 257–264; Eugene Rogan, *The Fall of the Ottomans: The Great War in the Middle East* (New York: Basic Books, 2015), 302–305.
112. Gabriel Ward to Syrian American Club of Boston, November 23, 1918, AANM/ES/1/5; Ward, *Kitab al-Jundi al-Suri*, 70.
113. Jibra'il Ilyas Ward, "Hadith al-Muslim," *al-Huda* (New York, NY), May 11, 1917, 5.
114. Kayalı, *Arabs and Young Turks*, 174–202; Çiçek, *War and State Formation*, 39–63.
115. Ward, "Hadith al-Muslim," 5.
116. Jibra'il Ilyas Ward, "'Ar an la-tasil Dama'una illa 'ala Khanja al-Saffah," *al-Huda* (New York, NY), June 2, 1917, 3.
117. Fourth Registration of George A. Matook, 1942, Selective Service Registration Card, NARA/RG147/M2097/R-185/1753.
118. Wadi' Shakir and Jurj Ma'tuq, "Risala jundi Suri," *Fatat Boston* (Boston, MA), March 3, 1918, 1.
119. Wadi' Shakir, "al-Suri al-mutajannad," *Fatat Boston* (Boston, MA), March 3, 1918, 2.
120. Shakir and Ma'tuq, "Risala jundi Suri," 1–2.
121. Jurj Ma'tuq to Syrian American Club of Boston, June 4, 1918, AANM/ES/1/5, 1–3.
122. Jurj Ma'tuq to Syrian American Club of Boston, June 4, 1918, AANM/ES/1/5, 1–3.
123. Lily Pearl Balloffet, "From the Pampa to the Mashriq: Arab-Argentine Philanthropy Networks," *Mashriq & Mahjar* 4, no. 1 (2017), 4–28; Stacy Fahrenthold, "Sound Minds in Sound Bodies: Transnational Philanthropy and Patriotic Masculinity in *al-Nadi al-Homsi* and Syrian Brazil, 1920–32," *International Journal of Middle East Studies* 46, no. 2 (2014), 259–283.

Chapter 4

1. Among the books of Rev. Abraham Mitrie Rihbany are *A Far Journey* (New York: Houghton Mifflin, 1914); *The Syrian Christ* (Boston: Houghton Mifflin, 1916); *Militant America and Jesus Christ* (New York: Houghton Mifflin, 1917); *The Hidden Treasure of Rasmola* (New York: Houghton Mifflin, 1920), *Wise Men from East and West* (New York: Houghton Mifflin, 1922); *The Christ Story for Boys and Girls* (New York: Houghton Mifflin, 1923); *Seven Days with God* (New York: Houghton Mifflin, 1926); *The Five Interpretations of Jesus* (New York: Houghton Mifflin, 1940). He was also a founding member of the Syrian American Club of Boston and the Syrian Educational Society (an organization he ran with Dr. Philip K. Hitti). His Arabic editorials appeared in *al-Majalla al-'Arabiyya* (New York), *Fatat Boston* (Boston), and *al-Akhlaq* (New York).
2. "Khulasat al-Akhbar: 'ala al-Ta'ir al-Maymun," *Fatat Boston* (Boston, MA), January 25, 1919, 1.
3. "Ila Mu'tamar al-Sulh," *Mirat al-Gharb* (New York, NY), January 13, 1919, 3.
4. Susan Pedersen, *The Guardians: The League of Nations and the Crisis of Empire* (New York: Oxford University Press, 2015).
5. Erez Manela, *The Wilsonian Moment: Self-Determination and the International Origins of Anticolonial Nationalism* (New York: Oxford University Press, 2003).
6. Carol Hakim, *The Origins of the Lebanese National Idea* (Berkeley: University of California Press, 2013).
7. On petitions, see Pederson, *The Guardians*, 84–87; Hakim, *Origins*, 213–260; Andrew Arsan, "'This Age Is the Age of Associations': Committees, Petitions, and the Roots of Interwar Middle Eastern Internationalism," *Journal of Global History* 7, no. 2 (2012), 168-188; Simon Jackson, "Diaspora Politics and Developmental Empire: The Syro-Lebanese at the League of Nations," *Arab Studies Journal* 21, no. 1 (2013), 166–190; Reem Bailony, "Transnationalism and the Syrian Migrant Public: the Case of the 1925 Syrian Revolt," *Mashriq & Mahjar: Journal of Middle East Migrations* 1, no. 1 (2013), 21–24; Natasha

Wheatley, "Mandatory Interpretation: Legal Hermeneutics and the New International Order in Arab and Jewish Petitions to the League of Nations," *Past & Present* 227 (2015), 205–248.

8. On this important work, see Hakim, *Origins,* 214–23; Asher Kaufman, *Reviving Phoenicia: The Search for Identity in Lebanon* (New York: I.B. Tauris, 2004), 70–79.

9. Pedersen, *The Guardians,* 77–82; Manela, *The Wilsonian Moment,* 55–62; Andrew Patrick, *America's Forgotten Middle East Initiative: The King-Crane Commission of 1919* (London: I.B. Tauris, 2015), 9–27.

10. William Yale to Leland Harrison, "The Syrian Question Report #12," Cairo, January 28, 1918 (National Archives Microfilm Publication M367, roll 381); Records of the Department of State, Record Group 59, National Archives and Records Administration (henceforth NARA/ RG59/M367/R-381/763.72119/1717), 13–4. See also Gildas Brégain, *Syriens et Libanais d'Amerique du Sud, 1918–1945* (Paris: l'Harmattan, 2008), 140–45; María del Mar Logrono Narbona, "The Development of Nationalist Identities in French Syria and Lebanon: A Transnational Dialogue with Arab Immigrants to Argentina and Brazil" (PhD diss., University of California, Santa Barbara, 2007), 37–43, 67–70. For an example of French-subsidized propaganda in the mahjar, see the trilingual periodical *Fransa wa-l-Sharq/Franco Libano Sirio/ La Francia y El Orient* (Havana, Cuba), 1919.

11. Andrew Arsan, *Interlopers of Empire: The Lebanese Diaspora in Colonial French West Africa* (Oxford: Oxford University Press, 2014).

12. M.A.E./S.L. Brillion to Pichon, in Antoine Hokayem, Daad Bou Malhab 'Atallah, and Jean Charaf (eds.), *Documents diplomatiques Français relatifs à l'histoire du Liban et de la Syrie à l'époque du mandat, Vol. 1: Le Démantèlement de l'Empire Ottoman et les préludes du mandat* (Paris: l'Harmattan, 2003), 623.

13. Stephen Porter, *Benevolent Empire: U.S. Power, Humanitarianism, and the World's Dispossessed* (Philadelphia: University of Pennsylvania Press, 2016), 13–50.

14. Betty S. Anderson, *The American University of Beirut: Arab Nationalism and Liberal Education* (Austin: University of Texas Press, 2011), 119–150.

15. Jibra'il Ilyas Ward, *Kitab al-Jundi al-Suri fi Thalath Hurub* (New York: al-Matba'a al-Tijariyya al-Suriyya al-Amrikiyya, 1919), 17–26..

16. Timothy Marr, "Diasporic Intelligences in the American Phillipine Empire: the Transnational Career of Dr. Najeeb Mitrie Saleeby," *Mashriq & Mahjar* 2, no. 1 (2014), 78–106. Saleeby published his experiences in the American-occupied Philippines in Najeeb M. Saleeby, *The Moro Problem: An Academic Discussion of the History and Solution of the Problem of the Government in the Moros of the Phillipine Islands* (Manila: P.I. Press of E.C. McCullough & Co, 1913).

17. Rihbany, *America Save the Near East,* vii–x.

18. Rihbany, *America Save the Near East,* 28. Emphasis in the original.

19. Rihbany, *America Save the Near East,* 28.

20. Nader Sohrabi, *Revolution and Constitutionalism in the Ottoman Empire and Iran* (New York: Cambridge University Press, 2011), 39–40, 88–89.

21. Rihbany, *America Save the Near East,* 20–21. Italics in original.

22. Rihbany, *America Save the Near East,* 26. Quotation marks, capitalization, and italics in the original.

23. Rihbany, *America Save the Near East,* 33–34.

24. Rihbany, *America Save the Near East,* 78–81.

25. On lynching, see Sarah Gualtieri, *Between Arab and White: Race and Ethnicity in the Early Syrian American Diaspora* (Berkeley: University of California Press, 2009), 116–134.

26. Rihbany, *America Save the Near East,* 41–42.

27. Philip Hitti handwritten speech to the Syrian Educational Society of New York, June 1919. Philip K. Hitti Papers, box 1, folder 2, Immigration History Research Center Archives, University of Minnesota, Minneapolis.

28. Arab American National Museum, Dearborn, MI. Evelyn Shakir Collection (hereafter AANM/ES), New Syria National League Records (Boston), box 1, folder 6, Boston, December 16, 1918, Faris Malouf to Abraham Rihbany, 1–2.

29. Samuel Zwomer to Robert Lansing, Secretary of State, "Pamphlet called 'the Future of Syria,'" Cairo, July 12, 1918, NARA/RG59/M367/R-382/763.72119/1819, 7–8.

30. James Renton, "Changing Languages of Empire and the Orient: Britain and the Invention of the Middle East, 1917–18," *Historical Journal* 50, no. 3 (2007), 645–670.

31. Zwomer to Lansing, July 12, 1918, NARA/RG59/M367/R-382/763.72119/1819, 9.

32. Zwomer to Lansing, July 12, 1918, NARA/RG59/M367/R-382/763.72119/1819, 5–7. The pamphlet also cites the Syrian American Club of New York (the New Syria National League's clearest predecessor) for this figure. It also claimed 35,000 Syrians were eligible to vote in Canada and describes a possible US oil concession to Standard Oil as leverage for those negotiating a possible US Mandate in Syria.

33. Philip K. Hitti telegram to Secretary of State, New York, November 22 1918, NARA/RG59/M367/R-387/763.72119/2740, 1; Hani Bawardi, *The Making of Arab Americans: From Syrian Nationalism to U.S. Citizenship* (Austin: University of Texas Press, 2014), 115.

34. Abraham Rihbany, "Amirka fi-Suriya," *Mirat al-Gharb* (New York, NY), February 19, 1919, 2.

35. New Syria National League Executive Committee Open Letter, New York, April 7, 1919, New Syria National League Records, box 1, folder 5, Evelyn Shakir Collection, AANM/ES/1/5, 1.

36. Habib Ibrahim Katibah, *Syria for the Syrians, Under American Guardianship* (Boston: Syrian National Society, February 1919), 15.

37. Abraham Rihbany, "Khulasat al-Akhbar: ʿala al-Taʾir al-Maymun," *Fatat Boston* (Boston, MA), January 25, 1919, 1.

38. Rihbany, *America Save the Near East*, 62.

39. George Khairallah to Ibrahim al-Khuri, Syrian American Club of Boston, New York City, February 11, 1919, AANM/ES/1/5.

40. George Khairallah and New Syria National League to Frank Lyon Polk, New York, January 15, 1919, NARA/M367/R-382/763.72119/3456, 1–3.

41. Narbona, *The Development of Nationalist Ideologies*, 37–43; Brégain, *Syriens et Libanais d'Amerique du Sud*, 152–3. These petition drives did not always go well; a French effort to win Syrian signatures in Chile utterly backfired as Syrian clubs refused to cooperate and instead submitted heavily revised petitions with terms contrary to those drafted by the French consulate. M.A.E., S.L., Valparaiso, February 2, 1919, Gilbert to Pichon. In Hokayem, ʿAtallah, and Charaf, *Documents diplomatiques*, 474–475.

42. M.A.E., S.L., Paris, October 12, 1918, Jean Gout to Stephen Pichon. In Hokayem, ʿAtallah, and Charaf, *Documents diplomatiques*, 387–388.

43. The Alliance Libanaise broke from its pro-French position after the first Lebanese delegation (which it sponsored) in 1919 as France invoked a Christian identity for the new Lebanese state. By the time France sponsored the second Lebanese delegation under Maronite Patriarch Ilyas Huwayyik, the Lebanese Alliance was no longer among France's allies in the mahjar.

44. Statement by al-Jamaʿa al-Suriyya, "Hal Tatawahhad Surya," *Fatat Boston* (Boston, MA), January 21, 1919, 3.

45. Representing the LLP, Mukarzil arrived in Paris but was unable to gain entry in the early weeks of the meeting. He later gained admittance after writing the French Foreign Ministry in May 1919. M.A.E., S.L., Paris, May 30, 1919, Cambon to Georges-Picot, telegram introduction of Naoum Mokarzel. In Hokayem, ʿAtallah, and Charaf, *Documents diplomatiques*, 593–594.

46. "Raʾihum fi-Ghanim wa-Jamʿiyyatihi," *Mirat al-Gharb* (New York, NY), February 1, 1919, 5.

47. Najib Diyab, "Muʾtamar Marseilles Aydan," *Mirat al-Gharb* (New York, NY), January 11, 1919, 2.

48. Faris Nimr to Paris Peace Conference, Cairo, s.d. January 1919, NARA/RG59/M367/R-399/763.72119/4302, 50.

49. Faris Nimr to Paris Peace Conference, Cairo, s.d. January 1919, NARA/RG59/M367/R-399/763.72119/4302, 52–53. A. D. Nantes, S. L., Papiers Georges-Picot. LeFevre to Georges-Picot, "Le parti modéré syrien." Cairo, February 26, 1919. In Hokayem, ʿAtallah, and Charaf, *Documents diplomatiques*, 486. This letter included the names of the organizing committee: Faris Nimr, Suleiman Nasif, Saʿid Shukair Pasha, Naʿum Shukair, Yaʿqub Sarruf, Amin Mirshaq, and Greek Orthodox Bishop of Aleppo (exiled to Cairo during the war) Mgr. Rufaʾil.

50. Faris Nimr to Paris Peace Conference, Cairo, s.d. January 1919, NARA/RG59/M367/R-399/763.72119/4302, 53.

51. Eliezer Tauber, *The Formation of Iraq and Syria* (London: Routledge, 1995), 159–161.

52. Paul Knabenshue to Secretary of State, "The Situation in Syria," Beirut, July 31, 1919, NARA/RG59/M367/R-430/763.72119/6602, 8–9.

53. M.A.E., S.L., Paris, March 18, 1919, Shukri Ghanim to Clemenceau. In Hokayem, ʿAtallah, and Charaf, *Documents diplomatiques*, 498–499.

54. Arch. Diplom. Nantes, Mandat, Syrie-Liban, 1er Versement, Secretariat General, Report of the Bureau B of O.E.T.A. (Ouest), "l'Alliance Libanaise," January 12, 1919. In Hokayem, ʿAtallah, and Charaf, *Documents diplomatiques*, 462–7.

55. Hakim, *Origins*, 211.

56. Birgis Faris Jumayyil, *Hizb al-Ittihad al-Lubnani* (Beirut: al-Markaz al-Istishari li-l-ʿAlam wa-l-Tawthiq al-Madrasi, 1996), 111–113.

57. M.A.E., S. L., Paris, March 18, 1919. In Hokayem, ʿAtallah, and Charaf, *Documents diplomatiques*, 498–499.

58. Auguste Adib Pacha, *Le Liban après la guerre* (Paris: E. Léroux, 1918). Also produced in Arabic as *Lubnan baʿd al-Harb* (Cairo: Matbaʿat al-Maʿarif, 1919). See M.A.E., S.L., Paris, February 25, 1919, Daoud Ammoun, "Note about the borders of the Grand Liban presented to the Conference de la Paix." In Hokayem, ʿAtallah, and Charaf, *Documents diplomatiques*, 492–493.

59. Hakim, *Origins*, 245–250; Kais M. Firro, *Inventing Lebanon: Nationalism and the State Under the Mandate* (New York: I.B. Tauris, 2002), 17–19; Kaufmann, *Reviving Phoenicia*, 85–86; Raghid el-Sulh, *Lebanon and Arabism, 1936–1945* (London: I.B. Tauris), 14–16.

60. The threat, Ghanim opined, was of France's own making: the revelations of the terms of Sykes-Picot seriously damaged the ability of Francophile Syrian nationalists to command the popular voice of the Syrian people. M.A.E., S.L. Ghanim to Clemenceau, Paris, March 18, 1919. In Hokayem, ʿAtallah, and Charaf, *Documents diplomatiques*, 498–499.

61. Ayyub Tabet, "Suriyya fi-l-Muʾtamar al-Silmi," *al-Saʾih* (New York, NY), February 12, 1919, 1.

62. AD, Mandat, SL, 1er Versement, Papiers Georges-Picot, LeFevre-Pontalis to Georges-Picot, Paris, February 26, 1919. Hokayem, ʿAtallah, and Charaf, *Documents diplomatiques*, 485–486. Tabet's decision to back a US Mandate in Syria was probably a surprise to the French Foreign Ministry. In February 1919, days before the first Lebanese delegation, Tabet proclaimed his support for a French Mandate over united Syria. He reversed his position on after the first Lebanese delegation endorsed the *Grand Liban*. "Department of State Weekly Report, February 7, 1920," Washington, DC, NARA/RG59/M367/R-92/763.72/10175, 86.

63. Rihbany's other major focus was the preservation of Palestine and its immediate independence on an anti-Zionist model. The group he met in Paris, the Palestine Anti-Zionism Society, was also based in New York, and the society shared several board members with the New Syria National League including Dr. Philip Hitti and Dr. Fuʾad Shatara. Najib Diyab, "Amirka fi-Suriyya (Rihbany's letter reprinted letter)," *Mirat al-Gharb* (New York, NY), February 19, 1919, 3. Dr. Shatara later went on to establish the New Syria Party in Michigan in the 1920s; Bawardi, *The Making of Arab Americans,*104–158.

64. Abraham Mitrie Rihbany, "The East at the Peace Conference," *Wise Men from the East and from the West* (Boston: Houghton Mifflin Company, 1922), 212–213.

65. Ibrahim al-Khuri, "ila Ahrar al-Watan," *Fatat Boston* (Boston, MA), March 3, 1919, 3.

66. al-Khuri, "ila Ahrar al-Watan," 3.

67. Jibrail Mansur, "Huquq al-Talab wa-l-Ihtijaj," *Fatat Boston* (Boston, MA), April 12, 1919, 1–2.

68. Mansur, "Huquq al-Talab wa-l-Ihtijaj," 2.

69. ʿAli Hamiya, *al-ʿAllama wa-l-Duktur Khalil Saʿadih: Siratuhu wa-Aʿmaluhu* (Beirut: al-Furat li-l-Nashr, 2007), 87–92.

70. Hamiya, *Khalil Saʿadih*, 128; ʿAbd al-Massih Haddad, "ʾAkhbar Mahaliya," *al-Saʾih* (New York, NY), August 24, 1916, 2.

71. Hamiya, *Khalil Saʿadih*, 131.

72. Badr el-Hage, *Khalil Saʿadih: Silsilat al-ʾAʿmal al-Majhula* (London: Riad el-Rayyes, 1987), 18–20.

73. Khalil Saʿadih, "Kitab Maftuḥ ʾila al-Suriyyin wa-l-Lubnaniyyin wa-l-Filistiniyyin," *al-Majalla* (Buenos Aires), November 15, 1918.
74. Hamiya, *Khalil Saʿadih*, 133.
75. American Commissioner Wallace and US Consul Paul Knabenshue to Secretary of State, Paris, October 9, 1919, NARA RG 59, M367, roll 440, 763.72119/72321, 1.
76. Nami Jafet, *Ensaios e Discursos, Traduzido do Arabe por Taufik Daud Kurban* (São Paulo: São Paulo Editora, 1947), 116; Antunius Jafet, *Dhikrayyat: Nisf Qarn 1903–1953* (São Paulo: Dar al-Tibʾa wa-l-Nashr al-ʿArabiyya, 1957), 12.
77. Jafet, *Ensaios e Discursos*, 106.
78. Jafet, *Ensaios e Discursos*, 113.
79. Jafet, *Ensaios e Discursos*, 116.
80. El-Hage, *Khalil Saʿadih*, 20.
81. Hani Bawardi, *The Making of Arab Americans: From Syrian Nationalism to U.S. Citizenship* (Austin: University of Texas Press, 2014).
82. Maronite Patriarchal Archive, Bkerke, Lebanon, Ilyas Huwayyik Correspondence (hereafter Bkerke-Huwayyik), folder 87, document 193. Sociedade Sirio-Libanense to Patriarch Huwayyik, Mérida, Mexico, October 13, 1919.
83. M.A.E., S.L., Brillouin to Stephen Pichon, Santiago de Cuba, July 3, 1919. In Hokayem, ʿAtallah, and Charaf, *Documents diplomatiques*, 622–623.
84. M.A.E, S.L. Brillion to Pichon, Santiago de Cuba, July 3, 1919. In Hokayem, ʿAtallah, and Charaf, *Documents diplomatiques*, 623.
85. Makdisi, *Faith Misplaced*, 137. Bliss's support for the US Mandate and the prevalence of SPC alumni in the New Syria parties convinced French officials that British and US intelligence agencies influenced them (likely erroneously); see A.D., S.L., LeFevre-Pontalis to Georges-Picot, Cairo, February 26, 1919. In Hokayem, ʿAtallah, and Charaf, *Documents diplomatiques*, 485–486.
86. AANM/ES, New Syria National League Records (New York City), box 1, folder 5. Faris Nimr and Yacub Sarruf to Jurj Khayrallah, Cairo, April 1, 1919, 1–2.
87. American Consul Hampton Gary to Robert Lansing, Secretary of State, Cairo, April 11, 1919, NARA/RG59/M367/R-403/763.72119/4555, 11.
88. George Khairallah open letter to New Syria National League, New York City, April 7, 1919, AANM/ES/1/5, 1.
89. Khairallah open letter to New Syria National League, AANM/ES/1/5, 1, 3–5.
90. Makdisi, *Faith Misplaced*, 140–141; Patrick, *America's Forgotten Middle East Initiative*.
91. "Near East Mandates: Local Opinion Favors Americans," *London Times* (London), July 30, 1919, 37.
92. Paul Knabenshue to Secretary of State, American Peace Mission, "Syrian Political Situation," Beirut, July 31, 1919, NARA/RG59/M367/R-430/763.72119/6602, 7–8.
93. Knabenshue to the American Peace Mission, July 31, 1919, 8.
94. Knabenshue to the American Peace Mission, July 31, 1919, 9.
95. "Mr. Wilson's Refusal of Paris Documents," *London Times* (London), August 12, 1919, 9.
96. M.A.E., S.L., "Les Revendications du Liban: Memoire de la delegation Libanaise a la Conference de la Paix," Paris, October 25, 1919. In Hokayem, ʿAtallah, and Charaf, *Documents diplomatiques*, 715–720.
97. Bkerke-Huwayyik, folder 87, document 193, Sociedade Sirio-Libanense to Huwayyik, Mérida, Mexico, October 13, 1919.
98. American Commissioner Wallace and American Consul in Beirut Knabenshue to US Secretary of State, Beirut, October 9, 1919, NARA/RG59/M367/R-440/763.72119/7232, 1–2.
99. Najib Saleeby, Central Committee of the United Syrian American Societies to Robert Lansing, US Secretary of State, Washington, DC, December 31, 1919, NARA/RG59/M367/R-440/763.72119/8574, 1–2.
100. Saleeby et al. to Lansing, December 31, 1919, 2.
101. Laura Robson, *States of Separation: Transfer, Partition, and the Making of the Modern Middle East* (Berkeley: University of California Press, 2017); Charlie Laderman, "Sharing the Burden? The American Solution to the Armenian Question, 1918–1920," *Diplomatic*

History 40, no. 1 (2016), 664–694; Juliet Davis, "The New World and the 'New Turks': The American-Turkish Claims Commission and Armenian-Americans' Contested Citizenship in the Interwar Period," *Journal of Genocide Research* 19, no. 3 (2017), 299–317.

102. Keith David Watenpaugh, *Bread from Stones: the Middle East and the Making of Modern Humanitarianism* (Berkeley: University of California Press, 2015), 96–97.

103. Lewis Heck to Secretary of State, Constantinople, March 24, 1919, NARA/RG59/M367/R-404/763.72119/4683, 1–2. "Turquie et Etats-Unis," *Le Courier de Turquie,* March 21, 1919, 1.

104. Report of the American Section of the International Commission on Mandates in Turkey, Paris, August, 28 1919, NARA/RG59/M367/R-439/763.72119/7161, 115.

105. Report of the American Section of the International Commission on Mandates in Turkey, 116.

106. Frank Polk to Woodrow Wilson, Washington, D.C., March 3, 1919, NARA/RG 59/M367/R-401/763.72119/4433, 2.

107. William Phillips to Miran Sevasly, Armenian National Delegation, Boston, April 2, 1919, NARA/RG59/M367/R-401/763.72119/4433, 1.

108. Rihbany, *Wise Men from the East and from the West,* 208, 211.

Chapter 5

1. Ya'cub Rufa'il also established the New York City serial, *al-Akhlaq,* editing it from 1920 until 1925.

2. Joseph Flamand testimony to Agent Robert Valkenburgh, Bureau of Investigation case number 369154, "James MG Fay- Turkish, Syrian and French Passports," Boston, July 30, 1919 (National Archives Microfilm Publication M1085, roll 811, Investigative Case Files of the Bureau of Investigation) Record Group 65.2.2.2, National Archives and Records Administration (hereafter NARA/RG 62.2.2/M1085/R-811/369154), 3.

3. Valkenburgh, "Fraudulent Passport Matter," Boston, July 30, 1919, NARA/RG 62.2.2/M1085/R-811/369154, 3.

4. Valkenburgh, "Re: Fraudulent Passport Matter," Boston, December 16, 1919, NARA/RG 62.2.2/M1085/R-811/369154, 158.

5. V. J. Valjavee, "Foaud Mehmed, Intimidation by Supposed Turkish Propaganda," November 23, 1918, NARA/RG 65.2.2/M1085/R-6/306290, 14.

6. Andrew Arsan, "'This age is the age of associations': Committees, petitions, and the roots of interwar Middle Eastern internationalism," *Journal of Global History* 7, no. 2 (2012), 181.

7. William Yale to Leland Harrison, "The Syrian Question Report #12," Cairo, January 28, 1918, NARA/RG59/M367/R-381/763.72119/1717, 13–14. For an example of French-subsidized propaganda in the *mahjar,* see the trilingual periodical *Fransa wa-l-Sharq/Franco Libano Sirio/La Francia y El Orient* (Havana: 1919).

8. Hakim, *The Origins of Lebanese National Idea,* 241–246.

9. Lauren Banko, "Claiming Identities in Palestine: Migration and Nationality under the Mandate," *Journal of Palestine Studies* 46, no. 2 (2017), 26–43; Benjamin Thomas White, "Refugees and the Definition of Syria, 1920-1939," *Past and Present* 235 (2017), 141–178.

10. John Torpey, "The Great War and the Birth of the Modern Passport System," *Documenting Individual Identity: the Development of State Practices in the Modern World,* ed. Jane Caplan and John Torpey (Princeton: Princeton University Press, 2001), 256; Leo Lucassan, "A Many-Headed Monster: the Evolution of the Passport System in the Nederlands and Germany in the Long Nineteenth Century," *Documenting Individual Identity,* 236–7.

11. David Gutman, "Travel Documents, Mobility Control, and the Ottoman State in an Age of Global Migration, 1880–1915," *Journal of Ottoman and Turkish Studies* 3, no. 2 (2016), 348–58.

12. Kemal Karpat, "The Ottoman Emigration to America, 1860-1914," *International Journal of Middle East Studies* 17, no. 2 (1985), 181–2; Engin Akarli, "Ottoman Attitudes Towards Emigration," *Lebanese in the World: a Century of Emigration,* ed. Albert Hourani and Nadim Shehadi (London: I.B. Tauris and Centre for Lebanese Studies, 1992), 130–1l; Engin

Akarli, *The Long Peace: Ottoman Lebanon, 1861-1920* (Berkeley: University of California Press, 1993), 61–3.

13. Caplan and Torpey, eds., *Documenting Individual Identity: The Development of State Practices in the Modern World*; Adam M. McKeown, *Melancholy Order: Asian Migration and the Globalization of Borders* (New York: Columbia University Press, 2008); May Ngai, *Impossible Subjects: Illegal Aliens and the Making of Modern America* (Princeton: Princeton University Press, 2004); Donna R. Gabaccia, *Foreign Relations: American Immigration in Global Perspective* (Princeton: Princeton University Press, 2014); Will Hanley, *Identifying with Nationality: Europeans, Ottomans, and Egyptians in Alexandria* (New York: Columbia University Press, 2017); Laura Robson, *States of Separation: Transfer, Partition, and the Making of the Modern Middle East* (Berkeley: University of California Press, 2017); Banko, "Claiming Identities in Palestine," 26–43; Theresa Alfaro-Velcamp, *So Far From Allah, So Close to Mexico: Middle Eastern Immigrants in Modern Mexico* (Austin: University of Texas Press, 2007), 25–44.

14. Torpey, "The Great War," 269.

15. Torpey, "The Great War," 264. The order responded to similar measures by America's European allies and was issued to mutually regulate travelers across the Atlantic.

16. Craig Robertson, *The Passport in America: The History of a Document* (New York: Oxford University Press, 2010), 189–90. The act was also called the Wartime Measure Act, Passport Control Act, and the Entries and Departures Control Act of 1918.

17. Robertson, *The Passport in America*, 190.

18. These were obtained by establishing "proof of necessity" to travel; a doctor's certification satisfied the requirement but applicants were often rejected by the State Department. Robertson, *The Passport in America*, 194.

19. *US Statutes at Large*, vol. 40, part 1: 559; Executive Order No. 2932, August 8, 1918. See also Robertson, *The Passport in America*, 191; Torpey, "The Great War," 265. Congress dropped the language governing the exit of foreign nationals from US soil in late 1919 but kept the rest of the regulations in force. The Fay case thus hinged on a passport law only weeks from revision.

20. On Armenians, see Gutman, "Travel Documents," 347–68; Juliet Davis, "The New World and the 'New Turks': The American-Turkish Claims Commission and Armenian-Americans' Contested Citizenship in the Interwar Period," *Journal of Genocide Research* 19, no. 3 (2017), 299–317.299–317. In an interesting counterpoint, Salonican Jews seeking passports to travel to the United States encountered difficulties because of their nationality in 1917; Devin Naar, "From the 'Jerusalem of the Balkans' to the *Goldene Medina*: Jewish Immigration from Salonika to the United States," *American Jewish History* 93, no. 4 (2007), 460–1.

21. See, for instance, copy of Italian Foreign Service letter to US Secretary of State, Rome, July 9, 1915, NARA/RG59/M367/R-196/763.72112/1410, 1–4.

22. A. Michael, US Consul letter to Secretary of State, Rio de Janeiro, January 22, 1919, NARA/RG59/M367/R-223/763.72112/7011, 1–2.

23. Gus Jones, "Syrian Activities: Order Refusing Permission to Depart for Mexico," El Paso, March 15, 1918, NARA/RG/65.2.2/M1085/111694, 5; "Emile J. Couri," New York, July 20, 1918, NARA/RG65.2.2/M1085/R-6/241285, 1–2.

24. Carol Hakim, *The Origins of the Lebanese National Idea* (Berkeley: University of California Press, 2013), 207–210.

25. Argentina similarly allowed Syrians and Lebanese to opt into French diplomatic protection via passports; Ignacio Klich, "Argentine-Ottoman Relations and their Impact on Immigrants from the Middle East," *The Americas* 50, no. 2 (1993), 180.

26. Robertson, *The Passport in America*, 185–186.

27. Christopher Gratien, "The Mountains Are Ours: Ecology and Settlement in Late Ottoman and Early Republican Cilicia (PhD diss., Georgetown University, 2015), 433–463.

28. John Torpey, *Invention of the Passport: Surveillance, Citizenship, and the State* (Cambridge: Cambridge University Press, 2000), 20.

29. Robertson, *The Passport in America*, 194.

30. Davis, "The New World," 311–313.

31. Akram Fouad Khater, *Inventing Home: Emigration, Gender, and the Middle Class in Lebanon, 1870–1920* (Berkeley: University of California Press, 2001), 53.

32. The English version of this ad explicitly describes Europe as the recipient of this assistance, but in the Arabic translation "Europe" is changed to "the devastated countries" (al-buldan al-mankuba) referencing relief work in Syria and Mount Lebanon. "Stay in America! For the Good of All Humanity," *al-Nasr* (New York, NY), March 29, 1919, 7. The ad's translator, Shukri al-Bakhash, repatriated to Zahle in 1920.

33. American Commission to Sec. of State Phillips, Paris, March 22, 1919, NARA/RG59/M367/R-398/763.72119/4248, 1, capitalization in original, emphasis mine.

34. American Commission to Sec. of State Phillips, Paris, March 22, 1919, 1.

35. Valkenburgh, Affidavit of Fateh Abbas, Boston, July 29, 1919, NARA/RG65.2.2/M1085/R-811/369154, 4–5.

36. George Kelleher briefing to Frank Burke, Bureau Chief, Washington, October 2, 1919, NARA/RG65.2.2/M1085/R-811/369154, 3–4.

37. Kelleher briefing to Burke, October 2, 1919, 4.

38. Valkenburgh briefing, Boston, October 29, 1919, NARA/RG65.2.2/M1085/R-811/369154, 2.

39. Valkenburgh briefing, October 29, 1919, 3.

40. The State Department informed Chief Frank Burke that there had been additional departures of Turkish men with names suspiciously close to those listed as witnesses in the Fay case under Serbian, Croatian, and Slovenian passports. L. Winslow, Counsel for State Department to Frank Burke, Bureau of Investigation, Washington, October 27, 1919, NARA/RG65.2.2/M1085/R-811/369154, 1. The State Department issued a notice banning the departure of those men left on Valkenburgh's list; briefing, November 1, 1919, NARA/RG/65.2.2/M1085/R-811/369154, 2.

41. Valkenburgh briefing, October 29, 1919, 2–3.

42. Refers to Agent Perkins, "Naoum Mokarzel—French Consul—Spanish Consul, Alleged Interference of Spanish Consul with Selective Draft of Syrians in the United States," New York, January 28, 1918, NARA/RG65.2.2/M1085/103577, 16–17.

43. Valkenburgh briefing, October 29, 1919, 2–3.

44. M. L. Newman, "Jas. M. G. Fay, Turkish, Syrian, and French Passports," New York City, October 20, 1919, NARA/RG 65.2.2/M1085/R-811/369154, 3.

45. Valkenburgh interview with informant Louis Thomas, Cambridge, October 10, 1919, NARA/RG65.2.2/M1085/R-811/369154, 2. The doctor charged clients $10 for this service.

46. Valkenburgh, Boston, August 5, 1919, NARA/RG65.2.2/M1085/R-811/369154, 4.

47. Agent Valkenburgh was interviewing Spiros Kaliris, one of Fay's conspirators, when James Fay called his office to surrender. Valkenburgh, Boston, August 5, 1919, 4.

48. Valkenburgh, Boston, August 5, 1919, 4.

49. Valkenburgh, Boston, August 5, 1919, 4.

50. Lewis Heck, American Commissioner to William Philips, Secretary of State, Constantinople, March 31, 1919, NARA/RG59/M367/R-398/763.72119/4762, 1–2, 15. See also M. Vital Cuinit, *La Turquie d'Asie: Géographie administrative statistique descriptive et raisonée de l'Asie-Mineure* (Paris: Ernest Leroux, 1894).

51. Ronald Gregor Suny, *"They Can Live in the Desert but Nowhere Else": A History of the Armenian Genocide* (Princeton: Princeton University Press, 2015); Taner Akçam, *A Shameful Act: The Armenian Genocide and the Question of Turkish Responsibility* (New York: Holt, 2007).

52. Vahid Cardashian to William Philips, Department of State, "The Armenian Question Before the Peace Conference," transcript of Armenian National Delegation's February 26, 1919 presentation, Paris April 26, 1919, NARA/RG59/M367/R-405/763.72119/4760, 25–6.

53. Cardashian to Philips, "The Armenian Question Before the Peace Conference," 26.

54. Kurdish League to American Commissioner G. Richards, Constantinople, August 11, 1919, NARA/RG59/M367/R-429/763.72119/6496, 1–2.

55. Karine V. Walther, *Sacred Interests: The United States and the Islamic World, 1821–1921* (Chapel Hill, NC: University of North Carolina Press, 2015), 304–313.

56. John McHugo, *Syria: A History of the Last Hundred Years* (London: Saqi Books, 2014).

57. According to Joseph Flamand, the Lebanon League of Progress, the Syrian Mount Lebanon League of Liberation, the Mount Lebanon Club, and Maronite priest Francis Wakim were all authorized to issue *sauf conduits* in New York. Flamand to Valkenburgh, Boston, July 30, 1919, NARA/RG65.2.2/M1085/R-811/369154, 3.

58. Valkenburgh, Boston, October 29, 1919, NARA/RG65.2.2/M1085/R-811/369154, 2-3.

59. F. F. Weise, Boston, October 16, 1919, NARA/RG65.2.2/M1085/R-811/369154, 2. Weise reported the conversation was in French and he believed both men did not know he could understand it.

60. Bureau Chief Burke to Agent Kelleher, New York City, October 15, 1919, NARA/RG65.2.2/M1085/R-811/369154, 1. Short-hand in original. See also Bureau Chief Burke to L. Winslow, State Department, Washington, October 17, 1919, NARA/RG65.2.2/M1085/R-811/369154, 1.

61. Undated handwritten memo on Department of Justice letterhead, NARA/RG65.2.2/M1085/R-811/369154, 1.

62. Robertson, *The Passport in America*, 189–190.

63. Some witnesses departed after being declared medically incompetent, and others purchased fake passports declaring them Serbian subjects. Winslow to Burke, Washington DC, October 27, 1919, NARA/RG65.2.2/M1085/R-811/369154, 1.

64. Rufa'il's claims flew in the face of his own role in determining Turks from Syrians through language testing eight weeks before this interview, a fact not lost on his interlocutor. J. F. Timoney interview with J. G. Raphael, "William Fay," New York City, September 15, 1919, NARA/RG65.2.2/M1085/R-811/369154, 4.

65. Joseph Baker interview with M. Khouri, "James M. G. Fay," New York City, September 19, 1919, NARA/RG65.2.2/M1085/R-811/369154, 3.

66. Timoney interview with J. G. Raphael, "William Fay," New York City, September 15, 1919, 4.

67. Joseph Flamand testimony, Boston, July, 30 1919, 3. Capitalization in original.

68. Valkenburgh interview with J. G. Raphael, New York City, October 27, 1919, NARA/RG65.2.2/M1085/R-811/369154, 3-4.

69. Valkenburgh interview with J. G. Raphael, New York City, October 27, 1919, 3-4.

70. Timoney interview with Raphael, New York City, October 6, 1919, 3.

71. Valkenburgh, Boston, August 5, 1919, NARA/RG65.2.2/M1085/R-811/369154, 4.

72. Valkenburgh interview with Joseph Yazbek, Boston, September 15, 1919, 4.

73. Robson, *States of Separation*, 141–69; Laura Robson, "Introduction," *Minorities in the Modern Middle East*, ed. Laura Robson (Syracuse: Syracuse University Press, 2015), 3–7.

74. The doctor was probably Rashid Baddur, who offered medical testing for Syrian army volunteers. It is not clear whether Weise's distinction between "Syrian" and "Arabic" refers to two distinct languages (e.g., Arabic and Syriac), two Arabic dialects, or simply reveals Weise's misunderstanding of the language tests administered. Weise, New York City, July 22, 1919, NARA/RG65.2.2/M1085/R-811/369154, 3.

75. Chief Frank Burke to Winslow, Department of State, Washington, August 9, 1919, NARA/RG65.2.2/M1085/R-811/369154, 1.

76. Sarah Gualtieri, *Between Arab and White: Race and Ethnicity in the Early Syrian American Diaspora* (Berkeley: University of California Press, 2009), 55–61.

77. Valkenburgh, Boston, October 17, 1919, 2.

78. Valkenburgh, Boston, October 10, 1919, 1.

79. Valkenburgh summary, Boston, December 15, 1919, NARA/RG65.2.2/M1085/R-811/369154, 1.

Chapter 6

1. Alexander D. M. Henley, "Remaking the Mosaic: Religious Leaders and Secular Borders in the Colonial Levant," *Religion and Society: Advances in Research* 6 (2015), 157.

2. MAE-Nantes, Box 1SL/1/V/1362, Recensement 1921, "Projet d'Arrete N° 336," September 6, 1920, 5.

3. See Asher Kaufmann, "Phoenicianism: the Formation of an Identity in Lebanon in 1920," *Middle Eastern Studies* 37, no. 1 (2001), 185.

4. MAE-Nantes, Box 1SL/1/V/1362, Recensement 1921, "Projet d'Arrete N° 336," September 6, 1920, 5.
5. Auguste Adib Pacha, *Liban après la guerre* (Paris: E. Leroux, 1918); Shaykh Farid Hubaysh, *Lubnan ba'd al-Harb* (Cairo: Matba'at al-Ma'rif, 1919), 4.
6. M.A.E., *E-Levant 1918–1940, Syrie-Liban*. February 13, 1919. Statement of the First Lebanese Delegation to the Conférence de la Paix. In Antoine Hokayem, Daad Bou Malhab 'Atallah, and Jean Charaf, *Documents Diplomatiques Français relatifs à l'histoire du Liban et de la Syrie à l'époque du Mandat, Vol. 1: Le Démantèlement de l'Empire Ottoman et les préludes du mandat* (Paris: l'Harmattan, 2003), 479–481.
7. Carol Hakim, *The Origins of the Lebanese National Idea, 1860–1920* (Berkeley: University of California Press, 2013), 241–253; Asher Kaufman, *Reviving Phoenicia: the Search for Identity in Lebanon* (New York: I.B. Tauris, 2004), 84–86; Kais M. Firro, *Inventing Lebanon: Nationalism and the State Under the Mandate* (New York: I.B. Tauris, 2003), 18–26; Lyne Lohéac, *Daoud Ammoun et la creation de l'état libanais* (Paris: Klincksieck, 1978).
8. Charles Issawi, "The Historical Background of Lebanese Emigration, 1800–1914," in *Lebanese in the World: A Century of Emigration*, ed. Albert Hourani and Nadim Shehadi (London: I.B. Tauris, 1992), 31.
9. On the 1932 census, see Rania Maktabi, "The Lebanese Census of 1932 Revisited: Who Are the Lebanese?" *British Journal of Middle Eastern Studies* 26, no. 2 (1999), 224–252.
10. Nina Glick Schiller and Georges Fouron, *Georges Woke Up Laughing: Long-Distance Nationalism in the Search for Home* (Durham, NC: Duke University Dress, 2001), 110–112.
11. Maktabi, "The Lebanese Census of 1932," 250–252.
12. Stephen Longrigg, *Syria and Lebanon under French Mandate* (New York: Oxford University Press, 1958), 127–128.
13. "Les élections municipales au Grand Liban," *Correspondance d'Orient* (Paris), vols. 287–288, June 15–30, 1922, 337; Elizabeth Thompson, *Colonial Citizens: Republican Rights, Paternal Privilege, and Gender in French Syria and Lebanon* (New York: Columbia University Press, 2000), 44; Longrigg, *Syria and Lebanon under French Mandate*, 127; Firro, *Inventing Lebanon*, 77–78; Denise Ammoun, *Histoire du Liban Contemporain* (Paris: Fayard, 1997), 268.
14. MAE-Nantes, Box 1SL/1/V/1362, Recensement 1921, "Article 20–21, Recensement Etat du Grand Liban," 9.
15. Peter Sluglett, "From Millet to Minority: Another Look at the Non-Muslim Communities in the Late Nineteenth and Early Twentieth Centuries," in *Minorities and the Modern Arab World*, ed. Laura Robson (Syracuse: Syracuse University Press, 2016), 19–38; Stanford Shaw, "The Ottoman Census System and Population, 1831–1914," *International Journal of Middle East Studies* 9 (1978), 327–328.
16. Edmund Burke III, "A Comprehensive View of French Native Policy in Morocco and Syria 1912–1925," *Middle Eastern Studies* 9, no. 3 (1973), 175–186; Khoury, *Syria and the French Mandate*, 55–57; Benjamin Thomas White, *The Emergence of Minorities in the Middle East: The Politics of Community in French Mandate Syria* (Edinburgh: Edinburgh University Press, 2011), 47–49.
17. White, *The Emergence of Minorities*, 45–46.
18. Article 6 of the Mandate for Syria and Lebanon, "Annexe II: Société des Nations, Mandat pour la Syrie et le Liban," in Ministère des Affaires Étrangères, *Rapport sur la situation de la Syrie et du Liban, Juillet 1922–Juillet 1923* (Paris: Imprimerie Nationale, 1923) 58.
19. White, *The Emergence of Minorities*, 53.
20. MAE-Nantes, Box 1SL/1/V/1362, Recensement 1921, "L no. 375, 6, CL," February 14, 1921, 1–2. Rania Maktabi argues that Gouraud's assumption was that tax-paying emigrants were likely to return to Lebanon, temporarily or permanently, and that emigrants in arrears were not likely to return. Rania Maktabi, "State Formation and Citizenship in Lebanon: The Politics of Membership and Exclusion in a Sectarian State," in *Citizenship and the State in the Middle East: Approaches and Applications*, ed. Nils August Butenschon, Uri Davis, and Manuel Sarkis Hassassian (Syracuse, NY: Syracuse University Press, 2000), 148.
21. MAE-Nantes, Box 1SL/1/V/1362, Recensement 1921, "Recensement, Etat du Grand Liban," 11.

22. MAE-Nantes, Box 1SL/1/V/1362, Recensement 1921, "Article 24, Recensement Etat du Grand Liban," 10–11.

23. Meir Zamir, *The Formation of Modern Lebanon* (Ithaca: Cornell University Press, 1988), 100; Longrigg, *Syria and Lebanon under French Mandate*, 127.

24. M.A.E., E-Levant 1918–1929, Syrie-Liban, Vol. 130, ff. 81bis-83bis. Telegram Circulaire du Président du Conseil aux Agents Diplomatiques et Consulaires de la République Fraçaise en Amérique, Beirut, February 9, 1921. Reproduced in Eliane Fersan, "L'Émigration Libanaise aux États-Unis: d'Aprés les Archives du Ministère de Affaires Étrangères de France" (MA thesis, Université Saint-Espirit de Kaslik, 2006), 163–164.

25. MAE-Nantes, Box 1SL/1/V/1362, Recensement 1921, "Article 17, Recensement, Etat du Grand Liban," 7.

26. M.A.E., SL, Vol. 130, ff. 81bis-83bis; Télégramme Circulaire du Président du Conseil aux Agents Diplomatiques et Consulaires de la République Fraçaise en Amérique, Beirut, February 9, 1921. Fersan, "L'Émigration Libanaise aux États-Unis," 163.

27. MAE-Nantes, Box 1SL/1/V/1362, Recensement 1921, "L no. 375, 6, CL," February 14, 1921, 3.

28. M.A.E., SL, Copy of French Foreign Ministry to French Consulates in the Americas, Paris, February 19, 1921, Vol. 130, 81–83.

29. Georges Labaki, *The Maronites in the United States* (Zouk Musbih, Lebanon: Notre Dame University of Louaize Press, 1993), 88–89.

30. Maronite Patriarchal Archives, Bkerke, Lebanon, Huwayyik Correspondence (hereafter Bkerke, Huwayyik), folder 96, document 16, French Consul of New York to Father Joseph Wakim and Bishop Shukrallah al-Khuri, Brooklyn, April 6, 1921.

31. Bkerke, Huwayyik, folder 96, documents 16–2/16–3, Appendix to French Consul of New York to Father Joseph Wakim and Bishop Shukrallah al-Khuri, Brooklyn, April 6, 1921.

32. Bkerke, Huwayyik, folder 96, document 16, French Consul of New York to Father Joseph Wakim and Bishop Shukrallah al-Khuri, Brooklyn, April 6, 1921.

33. Bkerke, Huwayyik, folder 96, document 163, Bishop Shukrallah al-Khuri to French Consul of New York, New York City, May 1, 1921.

34. Bkerke, Huwayyik, folder 96, document 164, Bishop Shukrallah al-Khuri to French Consul of New York, New York City, May 1, 1921.

35. Philip Hitti's 1924 estimates for each of these rites were Maronites: 90,000; Greek Orthodox: 85,000; and Melkites: 10,000; rendering a ratio of 9:8:1. Philip K. Hitti, *The Syrians in America* (New York: George H. Doran Company, 1924), 62.

36. 'Amr Ibrahim al-Qandilchi, *al-'Arab fi-l-Mahjar: Wujuduhum, Sihafatuhum, Jam'iyyatuhum* (Baghdad: Manshurat Wizarat al-A'lam, 1977), 11–18.

37. Henry Melki, *al-Sihafa al-'Arabiyya fi al-Mahjar: wa-'Alaqatuha bi-l-Adab al-Mahjari* (Beirut: Dar al-Sharq al-Awsat li-l-Tiba' wa-l-Nashr, 1998), 101.

38. In 1919, *al-Bayan*'s tagline was "No Protection except for American Protection," for instance. Melki, *al-Sihafa al-'Arabiyya fi-l-Mahjar*, 104.

39. Reem Bailony, "Transnationalism and the Syrian Migrant Public: The Case of the 1925 Syrian Revolt," *Mashriq & Mahjar: Journal of Middle East Migration Studies* 1, no. 1 (2013), 8–29.

40. This estimate comes from a worksheet that al-Khuri prepared on April 30, 1921; however, al-Khuri excluded an estimated 500 Maronites in New Jersey and had not yet visited Vermont. The figures given for New York and Massachusetts (7,500 and 5,977, respectively) are probably accurate and are confirmed by the secondary literature. His curious attribution of 500 for New Jersey, and then scratching out of this group, raises further questions. Bkerke, Huwayyik, folder 096, document 0161, Bishop Shukrallah al-Khuri's calculations of Lebanese Maronites in the northeastern United States.

41. Bkerke, Huwayyik, folder 96, document 163–164, Bishop Shukrallah al-Khuri to French Consul of New York, New York City, May 1, 1921.

42. Georges Labaki explains Bishop al-Khuri could later account for 40,000 Lebanese Maronites in the United States and that his addition of 15,000 more accounted for those not registered or whose registrations were lost. Labaki, *The Maronites in the United States*, 60.

43. Bkerke, Huwayyik, folder 96, document 161, Shukrallah al-Khuri's calculations of Lebanese Maronites in the northeastern United States.

44. Fourteenth Census of the United States, 1920, via Gualtieri, *Between Arab and White*, 49.

45. Fourteenth Census of the United States, 1920, via Gualtieri, *Between Arab and White*, 49.

46. Between 1915 and 1922, the Syrian American Club prepared Declarations of Intent for hundreds of Syrian and Lebanese migrants and assisted them with naturalization. Dozens of these applications are preserved within the Syrian American Club Records, Evelyn Shakir Collection, Box 1, Arab American National Museum, Dearborn, MI.

47. US Department of Labor, *Annual Report of the Commissioner General of Immigration to the Secretary of Labor*, Fiscal Year 1920 (Washington D.C.: Government Printing Office, 1920), 168.

48. Hitti, *The Syrians in America*, 62. Although the figure is unattributed, it is likely that Hitti derived this sum from the US Commissioner General of Immigration Report of 1920, which reported that 89,971 Syrians legally entered the United States between 1899 and 1919.

49. Alixa Naff, *Becoming American: Tthe Early Arab Immigrant Experience* (Carbondale: University of Illinois Press, 1992), 2–3; Labaki, *The Maronites in the United States*, 60–61.

50. For a reflection on the use of statistics in Lebanese migration history, see Kohei Hashimoto, "Lebanese Population Movement 1920–1939: Towards a Study," in *The Lebanese in the World: A Century of Emigration*, ed. Albert Hourani and Nadim Shehadi (London: I.B. Tauris, 1992), 72–79. On problems stemming from return migration, circulation, and statistical inflation see Akram Khater, *Inventing Home: Gender, Emigration, and the Middle Class in Lebanon* (Berkeley: University of California Press, 20012), 112; Sarah Gualtieri, "Gendering the Chain Migration Thesis: Women and Syrian Transatlantic Migration," *Comparative Studies of South Asia, Africa and the Middle East* 24, no. 1 (2004), 67–78.

51. Bkerke, Huwayyik, folder 96, documents 165–166, Bishop Shukrallah al-Khuri to French Consul of New York, New York City, May 1, 1919.

52. Bkerke, Huwayyik, folder 96, document 168, French Ambassador of the United States to Bishop Shukrallah al-Khuri, Washington, D.C., May 21, 1921.

53. M.A.E., SL, 67–70 (June 22, 1921), via Hashimoto, "Lebanese Population Movement," 72.

54. Arrêté 1307, article 26, "De l' électorat et de l'inéligibilité," *Correpondance d'Orient* (Paris), June 15–30, 1922, 366; Sami ʿAbdallah, *al-Jinsiyya al-Lubnaniyya Muqarana bi-l-Jinsiyya al-ʿArabiyya al-Suriyya wa-l-Faransiyya* (Beirut: Maktabat Matabiʿ al-Suhuf al-Haditha, 1986), 29, via Maktabi, "The Lebanese Census of 1932," 225.

55. Arrêté 1304, "Le conseil représentatif du Grand Liban," *Correpondance d'Orient* 285–286, May 15–20, 1922, 283–284.

56. Arrêté 1307, article 26, "De l' électorat et de l'inéligibilité," 366.

57. Ministère des Affaires Étrangères, *Rapport sur la Situation de la Syrie et du Liban, Juillet 1922–Juillet 1923* (Paris: Imprimerie Nationale, 1924), 9.

58. Maktabi, "State Formation and Citizenship in Lebanon," 161

59. M.A.E., *Rapport sur la Situation de la Syrie et du Liban, Juillet 1922–Juillet 1923*, 9–10; Zamir, *Formation of Modern Lebanon*, 98. The same ratio was invoked in the 1932 Census and the 1943 National Pact. In the 1932 Census, a clause was added that to be counted, Lebanese must be able to provide proof of residency for the date of August 31, 1924. However, Lebanese who could document their registration with the 1921 census fulfilled this residency requirement; as a result, they were recounted in 1932 regardless of domicile. Maktabi, "The Lebanese Census of 1932," 225–226.

60. In addition to these two categories, a third emigrant category was created for Lebanese emigrants who had not paid taxes in Lebanon. Totaling 81,243, this third group of emigrants was included on the census but not incorporated into the electoral ratio. "Population du Grand Liban," *Correpondance d'Orient* (Paris), May 15–30, 1922, 270.

61. M.A.E., *Rapport sur la Situation de la Syrie et du Liban, Juillet 1922–Juillet 1923*, 9–10.

62. Arrêté 1307, article 28, "De l' électorat et de l'inéligibilité," 366.

63. Hashimoto, "Lebanese Population Movement," 79.

64. Labaki, *The Maronites in the United States*, 88–90.

65. On Arab settlement in Argentina's interior, see Lily Pearl Balloffet, "From the Pampa to the Mashriq: Arab-Argentine Philanthropic Networks," *Mashriq & Mahjar: Journal of Middle Eastern Migration Studies* 4, no. 1 (2017), 4–28.

66. Melanie S. Tanielian, *The Charity of War: Famine, Humanitarian Aid, and World War I in the Middle East* (Palo Alto: Stanford University Press, 2017); Labaki, *The Maronites in the United States*, 90–91; Graham Auman Pitts, "Fallow Fields: Famine and the Making of Lebanon" (PhD diss., Georgetown University, 2016).

67. Hakim, *Origins of the Lebanese National Idea*, 231–236.

68. Bkerke, Huwayyik, folder 96, document 1A7, Bishop Shukrallah al-Khuri to Patriarch Ilyas Huwayyik, Brooklyn (s.d.).

69. Bkerke, Huwayyik, folder 96, document 1D. Father Jirjis Baʿalani to Bishop Shukrallah al-Khuri, "Ajwaba ʿala asʾila siyada al-Mutran Shukrallah al-Khuri raʾis ʾasaqifa wa-l-zaʾir al-Batrirki fi-l-diyar al-Amrikiyya," (s.d.).

70. Bkerke, Huwayyik, folder 96, document 1D. Father Jirjis Baʿalani to Bishop Shukrallah al-Khuri (s.d.).

71. Theresa Alfaro-Velcamp, *So Far from Allah, So Close to Mexico: Middle Eastern Immigrants in Modern Mexico* (Austin: University of Texas Press, 2007), 65.

72. Bkerke, Huwayyik, folder 96, document 1DF. Petition to Bishop Shukrallah al-Khuri forwarded to Patriarch Ilyas Huwayyik, Mexico City, August 21, 1921.

73. Bkerke, Huwayyik, folder 96, document 1A6-1A7. Bishop Shukrallah al-Khuri to Patriarch Ilyas Huwayyik, Brooklyn (s.d.).

74. Alfaro-Velcamp, *So Far from Allah*, 65.

75. Naff, *Becoming American*, 294–298.

76. In South America, the *Hizb al-Ittihad al-Lubnani* dissented from its Cairene headquarters over the church's role in politics. A faction calling itself the *Hizb al-Tahalluf al-Lubnani* broke away from the anti-clerical leadership of the Buenos Aires *Hizb al-Ittihad al-Lubnani* in 1920, moving instead to support the Maronite Patriarchate's influence in Lebanese politics. Elsewhere in the Latin America, however, the *Hizb al-Ittiad al-Lubnani* deeply opposed the convergence of church and state and took on progressively anticolonial colorings. See "Nazar ʿAm fi-Hawadith Khama Aʿwam," *al-Tahalluf al-Lubnani* (Buenos Aires), January 23, 1920, 17–18. French Mandate dragoman Shukri Abi Saʿab was a founding member of *Hizb al-Tahalluf al-Lubnani*.

77. Bkerke, Huwayyik, folder 96, document 1A7. Shukrallah al-Khuri to Ilyas Huwayyik, Brooklyn (s.d.).

78. Bkerke, Huwayyik, folder 87, document 229. Newspaper clipping of Patriarch Huwayyik's proclamation, "al-Kanisa al-Maruniyya fi ʿAsimat al-Barazil," reprinted in Lebanese press (s.p.), August 14, 1921.

79. Bkerke, Huwayyik, folder 96; Sallum Mukarzil, *Al-Qanun al-Asasi li-Jamʿiyyat al-Ittihad al-Maruni fi-l-Wilayat al-Mutahida* (New York: al-Matbaʾat al-Tijariyya al-Suriyya al-Amerikiyya fi-New York, 1921), 13–16.

80. Bkerke, Huwayyik, folder 88, document 118, United Maronites Society (Jamʿiyyat al-Ittihad al-Maruni) to Ilyas Huwayyik, March 13, 1924. Naʿum Hatem was the uncle and guardian of Albert Hatem, the US Army recruiter who appears in chapter 3.

81. Bkerke, Huwayyik, folder 96, documents 17–18B, Naʿum Mukarzil to Ilyas Huwayyik, New York, June 22, 1920.

82. Bkerke, Huwayyik, folder 88, document 118, United Maronites Society to Ilyas Huwayyik, March 13, 1924.

83. Mukarzil, *Al-Qanun al-Asasi li-Jamʿiyyat al-Ittihad al-Maruni*, 13–16.

84. Mukarzil, *Al-Qanun al-Asasi li-Jamʿiyyat al-Ittihad al-Maruni*, 4.

85. Bkerke, Huwayyik, folder 89, document 368, Butrus Kairuz and United Maronite Society of Argentina to Ilyas Huwayyik, Buenos Aires, November 26, 1928.

86. Mukarzil, *Al-Qanun al-Asasi li-Jamʿiyyat al-Ittihad al-Maruni*, 4.

87. Hourani, *Lebanese in the World*, 5–6.

88. Ministére des Affaires Etrangeres, *Rapport sur la Situation de la Syrie et du Liban, Année 1924* (Paris: Imprimerie Nationale, 1925), 52–53.

89. Andrew Arsan, "Under the Influence? Translation and Transgressions in Late Ottoman Imperial Thought," *Modern Intellectual History* 10, no. 2 (2013), 375–397; Engin Akarli, *The Long Peace: Ottoman Lebanon, 1861–1920* (Berkeley: University of California Press, 1993), 61–63.

90. Regulation 15 did not allow for Lebanese women to pass their nationality on to children; Maktabi, "Lebanese Census of 1932," 25–26.

91. Sarah Gualtieri, *Between Arab and White: Race and Ethnicity in the Early Syrian American Diaspora* (Berkeley: University of California, 2009), 79; Mae M. Ngai, "The Architecture of Race in American Immigration Law: A Reexamination of the Immigration Act of 1924," *Journal of American History* 86, no. 1 (1999), 67–92.

92. Khater, *Inventing Home*, 158–161.

93. M.A.E., *Rapport sur la Situation de la Syrie et du Liban, Année 1924*, 53; Alfaro-Velcamp, *So Far from Allah*, 111–112.

94. Prosecuting shipping companies engaged in passenger traffic was difficult because ships made several Mediterranean stops before crossing the Atlantic, creating problems of jurisdiction. M.A.E., *Rapport sur la Situation de la Syrie et du Liban, Année 1924*, 53–54.

95. The diplomatic interchange between the French consulate of Buenos Aires and local Syrian and Lebanese activists began earlier. Amin Arslan had been regular conversation with the consulate since at least 1915, connections that contributed to his dismissal by the Unionists that year. Similarly, the man named the Consul's premier dragoman in 1924, Shukri Abi Sa'ab, had been working there as a translator since 1920; M.A.E., *Rapport sur la Situation de la Syrie et du Liban, Année 1924*, 54.

96. M.A.E., *Rapport sur la Situation de la Syrie et du Liban, Année 1924*, 54.

97. M.A.E., SL, carton 408, Takieddine to Weygand, New York, September 26, 1924, 30.

98. Emmanuel Taub, *Otredad, Orientalismo e Identidad: Nociones sobre la Construcción de un Otro Oriental en la Revista Caras y Caretas, 1898–1918* (Buenos Aires: Universidad de Belgrano Press, 2008), 115.

99. M.A.E., *Rapport sur la Situation de la Syrie et du Liban, Année 1924*, 50, 52.

100. Firro, *Inventing Lebanon*, 122; Laura Robson, *States of Separation: Transfer, Partition, and the Making of the Modern Middle East* (Berkeley: University of California Press, 2017); Keith David Watenpaugh, *Bread from Stone: The Middle East and the Making of Modern Humanitarianism* (Berkeley: University of California Press, 2015.

101. Maktabi, "Lebanese Census of 1932," 227.

102. Nicola Migliorino, *(Re)Constructing Armenia in Lebanon and Syria: Ethno-Cultural Diversity and the State in the Aftermath of a Refugee Crisis* (New York: Berghahn, 2008), 49.

103. M.A.E., *Rapport sur la Situation de la Syrie et du Liban, Année 1924*, 49–51.

104. M.A.E., *Rapport sur la Situation de la Syrie et du Liban, Année 1924*, 52.

105. Keith David Watenpaugh, *Being Modern in the Middle East: Revolution, Nationalism, Colonialism, and the Arab Middle Class* (Princeton: Princeton University Press, 2012), 288.

106. Bkerke, Huwayyik, folder 89, document 368, Butrus Kairuz to Patriarch Ilyas Huwayyik, *al-Ittihad al-Maruni* appeal attached, November 26, 1928.

Conclusion

1. Ministère des Affaires Etrangères, Paris, *E-Levant 1918–1940, Syrie-Liban* (henceforth MAE, SL), translated letter from Arslan to President Wilson, November 10, 1918. Antoine Hokayem, Daad Bou Malhab 'Atallah, and Jean Charaf, *Documents diplomatiques Français relatifs à l'histoire du Liban et de la Syrie à l'époque du mandat, Vol. 1: Le Démantèlement de l'Empire Ottoman et les préludes du mandat* (Paris: l'Harmattan, 2003), 403–406.

2. Pablo Tornielli, "Hombre de tres mundos: Para una biografía política e intelectual del emir Emín Arslán," *Dirasat Hispanicas: Revista Tunecina de Estudios Hispanicos* 2 (2015), 157–181.

3. Arslan, *La Revolución Siria Contra el Mandato Francés* (Buenos Aires: Imp. Radio Correintes, 1926), 28. For a close discussion of this theme in Arslan's writings, see Maria del Mar Logroño Narbona, "The Development of Nationalist Ideologies in French Syria and Lebanon" (PhD diss., University of California, Santa Barbara, 2007).

4. "Comunicaciones Oficiales de la Legación de Francia," *La Nacion*, October 10, 1918, 10. See also Gildas Brégain, *Syriens et Libanais d'Amérique du Sud, 1918-1945* (Paris: l'Harmattan, 2008), 144.

5. Arslan to President Wilson, November 10, 1918, in *Documents diplomatiques*, 403–406.

6. Amin Arslan joined a delegation of Lebanese Druze leaders to confer with the American Commission in Paris, reminding them that Syrians overwhelmingly appealed for American, not French, assistance in reconstructing Syria. Arslan proposed accomplishing this through a treaty relationship with the Emir Faysal already in Damascus. American Commissioner Wallace and Consul Paul Knabenshue to Secretary of State, Beirut, October 9, 1919 (National Archives Microfilm Publication M367, roll 381), Records of the Department of State, Record Group 59, National Archives and Records Administration (henceforth NARA/RG59/ M367/R-440/763.72119/7232, 1–2; 'Abd al-Wahab Akmir, al-'Arab fi-l-Arjintin: al-Nushu' wa-l-Tatawwur (Beirut: Markaz Dirasat al-Wahda al-'Arabiyya, 2000), 134–135.

7. Emin Arslan, "La Repúbliqueta del Líbano," La Revolución Siria, 118.

8. Michael Provence, The Great Syrian Revolt and the Rise of Arab Nationalism (Austin: University of Texas Press, 2005), 92; Daniel Neep, Occupying Syria under the French Mandate: Insurgency, Space, and State Formation (Cambridge: Cambridge University Press, 2012), 37.

9. Provence, The Great Syrian Revolt, 34–35.

10. On Jurj Sawaya, see Najib Sawaya/Nagib Savoia, Riwaya Safinat al-Wataniyya (São Paulo: Matba'at al-Funun, 1946), preface; on Homad, see Telegram to US Embassy, "War Trade Board, Enemy Trading List," Buenos Aires, June 5, 1918, NARA/RG59/M367/R-246/763.72112a/1347, 1. The intensity of international reproach over the issue of European diplomats injured in Damascus juxtaposed with the League Nations' relative silence on Syrian casualties was a major source of protest among emigrant nationalists, George E. Sawaya, "Ha Llegado un Lier: Quien es M. Emile Vandervelde," al-Islah September 11, 1928, 15.

11. Arslan, La Revolución Siria, 28.

12. Arslan, La Revolución Siria, 24, caps in original. His reference is to the 1916 Sykes-Picot Agreement.

13. By the interwar period, French economic interests in the Levant were already trenchant. In the nineteenth century, French companies provided half of the investment capital employed in the Lebanese silk industry; Roger Owen, The Middle East in the World Economy, 1800– 1914 (New York: I.B. Tauris, 2002), 154–156. During the Mandate, the French discussed agricultural reform and the possibility of introducing a cotton industry to improve the Syrian countryside's profitability; see Philip Shukry Khoury, Syria and the French Mandate: the Politics of Arab Nationalism, 1920–1945 (Princeton: Princeton University Press, 1987), 50–52.

14. Arslan, La Revolución Siria, 46–48.

15. Arslan, La Revolución Siria, 34.

16. M.A.E., Rapport sur la Situation de la Syrie et du Liban, Année 1924, 54; Emmanuel Taub, Otredad, Orientalismo e Identidad: Nociones sobre la Construcción de un Otro Oriental en la Revista Caras y Caretas, 1898–1918 (Buenos Aires: Universidad de Belgrano Press, 2008), 115.

17. Brégain, Syriens et Libanais d'Amérique du Sud, 59.

18. Ignacio Klich, "Criollos and Arabic Speakers in Argentina," Lebanese in the World: a Century of Emigration, ed. Albert Hourani and Nadim Shehadi (London: Centre for Lebanese Studies, 1992), 256.

19. The nationality option appears in articles 34 and 36 of the Lausanne Treaty. See Rania Maktabi, "The Lebanese Census of 1932 Revisited: Who Are the Lebanese?" British Journal of Middle Eastern Studies 26, no. 2 (1999), 227–228; Kohei Hashimoto, "Lebanese Population Movement 1920–1939: Towards a Study," in The Lebanese in the World: A Century of Emigration, ed. Albert Hourani and Nadim Shehadi (London: I.B. Tauris, 1992), 75–76.

20. Denise Ammoun, Histoire du Liban Contemporain I: 1860–1943 (Paris, Fayard, 1997), 290.

21. Kais Firro, Inventing Lebanon: Nationalism and the State Under the Mandate (London: I.B. Tauris, 2003), 122.

22. Elian Fersan, "L'Émigration Libanaise aux États-Unis: d'Après les Archives du Ministére de Affaires Étrangeres de France" (PhD diss., Université Saint-Espirit de Kaslik, 2006), 116.

23. Akmir, al-'Arab fi-l-Arjintin, 136.

24. Narbona, "La Actividad Política Transnacional," 221. Together with Amin Arslan, Jurj Sawaya would found an Arab nationalist party in 1927 called the Hizb al-Istiqlal li-l-Aqtar al-'Arabiyya. The organization also ran al-Islah newspaper in Buenos Aires.

25. Bkerke, Huwayyik, folder 89, document 368, Butrus Kairuz to Patriarch Ilyas Huwayyik, *al-Ittihad al-Maruni* appeal attached, November 26, 1928.

26. Sofia D. Martos, "The Balancing Act: Ethnicity, Commerce, and Politics among Syrian and Lebanese Immigrants in Argentina, 1890–1955" (PhD diss., University of California, Los Angeles, 2007), 242–244.

27. In August 1926, Amin Arslan reported that only 600 Syrians in Buenos Aires had confirmed their new identity with the Mandate (out of around 160,000, a number Arslan insists upon but which historians have argued was closer to 110,000 at the time); Arslan, *La Revolución Siria*, 124. In 1928, Shukri Abi Sa'ab reported to the French Consul in Buenos Aires that despite the problems associated with not having identity documents, 90 percent of Syrians had not opted for new papers from the Mandate; Narbona, *The Development of Nationalist Identities*, 137.

28. Camila Pastor, *The Mexican Mahjar: Transnational Maronites, Jews, and Arabs under the French Mandate* (Austin: University of Texas Press, 2017), 153–176; Isa Blumi, *Ottoman Refugees, 1878–1939: Migration in a Post-Imperial World* (London: Bloomsbury, 2013), 91–115; Andrew Kerim Arsan, "Failing to Stem the Tide: Lebanese Migration to French West Africa and the Competing Prerogatives of the Imperial State," *Comparative Studies in Society and History* 53, no. 3 (2011), 450–478. The British employed similar strategies in Palestine; see Lauren Banko, *The Invention of Palestinian Citizenship, 1918–1947* (Edinburgh, Edinburgh University Press, 2013); Shira Robinson,*Citizen Strangers: Palestinians and the Birth of Israel's Liberal Settler State* (Palo Alto: Stanford University 2013), 87–109.

29. Mai M. Ngai, *Impossible Subjects: Illegal Aliens and the Making of Modern America* (Princeton: Princeton University Press, 2004), 29; Alixa Naff, *Becoming American: The Early Arab Immigrant Experience* (Carbondale: Southern Illinois University Press, 1993), 123.

30. Musa Kuraym, "Man' al-Muhajira al-Suriyya ila-al-Barazil," *al-Barazil wa-l-Sharq: al-Muhadara allati Ilqiyatha fi-l-Majmu' al-'Ilmi al-'Arabi fi-Dimashq wa-fi-Dar al-Rabitah al-Sharqiyya fi-l-Qahira* (s.p. Musa Kuraym: São Paulo, 1928), 25–29.

31. In Argentina, the Syrian Union of Buenos Aires provided this document processing. The club was founded in 1915 by Khalil Sa'adih and was modelled on Mundji Bey's Syrian Ottoman Union Society in New York; Jurj 'Assaf, "Ma 'ala Zuhr al-Jaliyya," *al-Islah* September 4, 1928, 5. See also Martos, "The Balancing Act," 230–238.

32. 'Assaf, "Ma 'ala Zuhr al-Jaliyya," 5–6. On this funding, see Reem Bailony, "Transnationalism and the Syrian Migrant Community: The Case of the 1925 Syrian Revolt," *Mahjar and Mashriq: Journal of Middle East Migration Studies* 1, no. 1 (2013), 8–29.

33. Laura Robson, *States of Separation: Transfer, Partition, and the Making of the Modern Middle East* (Berkeley: University of California Press, 2017); Samuel Dolbee, "The Locust and the Starling: People, Insects, and Disease in the Late Ottoman Jazira and After, 1860–1940" (PhD diss., New York University, 2017). The British employed similar strategies in Palestine; see Lauren Banko, *The Invention of Palestinian Citizenship, 1918–1947* (Edinburgh, Edinburgh University Press, 2013); Shira Robinson, *Citizen Strangers: Palestinians and the Birth of Israel's Liberal Settler State* (Palo Alto: Stanford University Press, 2013), 87–109.

34. Andreas Wimmer and Nina Glick Schiller, "Methodological Nationalism and Beyond: Nation-State Building, Migration and the Social Science," *Global Networks* 2, no. 4 (2002), 301–334; Cyrus Schayegh, "Small Is Beautiful," *International Journal of Middle East Studies* 46, no. 4 (2014), 374.

INDEX

Printed in the USA
CPSIA information can be obtained
at www.ICGtesting.com
LVHW091312120124
768764LV00002B/241